Colloquial
Somali

The Colloquial Series

The following languages are available in the Colloquial series:

* Albanian
* Amharic
* Arabic (Levantine)
* Arabic of Egypt
* Arabic of the Gulf and Saudi Arabia
* Bulgarian
* Cambodian
* Cantonese
* Chinese
* Czech
* Danish
* Dutch
* English
* Estonian
* French
  German
* Greek
* Gujarati
* Hungarian
* Indonesian

* Italian
* Japanese
* Malay
* Norwegian
* Panjabi
* Persian
* Polish
  Portuguese
* Romanian
* Russian
* Serbo-Croat
* Slovene
* Somali
* Spanish
* Spanish of Latin America
* Swedish
* Thai
* Turkish
* Ukranian
* Vietnamese
* Welsh

* Accompanying cassette(s) available

Colloquial
Somali
A Complete Language Course

Martin Orwin

London and New York

First published 1995
by Routledge
11 New Fetter Lane, London EC4P 4EE

Simultaneously published in the USA and Canada
by Routledge
29 West 35th Street, New York, NY 10001

© 1995 Martin Orwin

Typeset in Times Ten by Florencetype Ltd, Stoodleigh, Devon

Printed and bound in England by Clay Ltd, St Ives plc

All rights reserved. No part of this book may be reprinted or reproduced or utilized in any form or by any electronic, mechanical, or other means, now known or hereafter invented, including photocopying and recording, or in any information storage or retrieval system, without permission in writing from the publishers.

British Library Cataloguing in Publication Data
A catalogue record for this book is available from the British Library

Library of Congress Cataloguing in Publication Data
A catalogue record for this book has been requested

ISBN 0–415–10009–7 (book)
ISBN 0–415–10010–0 (cassettes)
ISBN 0–415–10011–9 (book and cassettes course)

Contents

Acknowledgements vii
Introduction 1

1 **Is ka warran!**
  How are you? 11
2 **Subax wanaagsan**
  Good morning 26
3 **Bill iyo Zaynab**
  Bill and Zaynab 38
4 **Bill waa tegayaa geeska Afrika**
  Bill is going to the Horn of Africa 56
5 **Garoonka dayuuradaha**
  The airport 72
6 **Tagsiga**
  The taxi 88
7 **Hudheelka**
  The hotel 105
8 **Bill telefoon buu diraa**
  Bill makes a telephone call 117
9 **Bill lacag buu sariftaa**
  Bill changes some money 131
10 **Safarka baa la bilaabayaa**
  The beginning of the journey 147
11 **Tuulo baa la joogaa**
  Staying in a village 165
12 **Ma xanuunsantahay?**
  Are you ill? 184

13 Jariidadda
The newspaper 203
14 Raydiyowga
The radio 223

Grammatical tables 237
Key to exercises 248
English–Somali glossary 266
Somali–English glossary 279
Index 293

Acknowledgements

I wish to thank the following people for much help I have received during the preparation of this book: Maxmuud Sheekh Axmed Dalmar, Maxamed Rashiid Sheekh Xasan, Zaynab Maxamed Jaamac, Axmed Cabdi Haybe, Aden Nuux Dhuule, Cabdirazaq Caqli, Faisa Loyaan, Maxmuud Xasan, Kate Lorentz, David Appleyard. I also thank the first ever undergraduate students of the course Somali I in the Department of African Languages and Cultures, School of Oriental and African Studies, who were the first to use this material. Finally I wish to thank my wife, Carolein, who has been helpful and patient during a particularly arduous time.

The two folktales in the book are slightly edited versions of tales in *Hikmad Soomaali* by Muuse Haaji Ismaaciil Galaal and B.W. Andrzejewski; I wish to thank B.W. Andrzejewski for allowing me to use these stories here.

Introduction

The Somali language is spoken by the Somali people who live in the eastern part of the Horn of Africa. This area includes the countries of Somalia, Somaliland[1] and parts of Djibouti, Ethiopia and Kenya. During the late 1980s and early 1990s the Horn of Africa has undergone great change. The former regimes of Somalia and Ethiopia were both ousted and in the time since then there has been fighting in various parts of the area as well as the much-publicized intervention by the international community through the United Nations and the United States. There cannot be a Somali family anywhere that has not been in some way or another affected by these tragic events and it is hoped that peace will return to all parts of the Somali areas soon.

The Somali language is a member of the family of Cushitic languages which are spoken mostly in Ethiopia and Kenya. The Cushitic language with the greatest number of speakers is undoubtedly Oromo, spoken in Ethiopia and Kenya. All in all there may be between six and seven million Somali speakers in the world although there are no precise figures. The Somali people, as you will learn in one of the reading passages, are grouped into three main socio-economic groups. Most are nomadic pastoralists herding camels, sheep, goats and, in certain areas, cattle. The camel is the supreme domestic animal for the Somalis, since it is able to survive the most extreme conditions and provides so much nourishment in the form of its milk and meat. Horses are also much prized by the Somalis.

Other Somalis, especially those living along and between the rivers Jubba and Shabeelle, live a sedentary life, cultivating crops and sometimes keeping some livestock. Crops include sorghum, millet, cassava and bananas. The third group is the town dwellers. Over the last few decades more and more people have moved to the main towns and cities such as Mogadishu, Djibouti and Hargeisa.

Since the late 1980s a large number of people have left Somalia as refugees and are living in many different countries. Large numbers of Somalis live in parts of London, Cardiff and Sheffield in the United Kingdom as well as in cities in the Middle East, the United States, Canada, Finland, The Netherlands, Italy, etc.

Somali culture, as with any society, is very much tied in with the way of life of the people. Probably the most important cultural form for the Somalis is poetry. This pervades all aspects of life, from watering camels to political debate. There are many genres of poetry and they follow strict stylistic rules of alliteration and metre, which demand great knowledge and skill of the poet. In recent decades the scope of poetry and the ways in which it is performed have expanded. In the 1940s and 1950s new genres of poetry developed in which a musical accompaniment became common. The instrument most used is the **kaman**, 'lute', although nowadays electrical instruments are also used.

Another important cultural movement was the development of Somali theatre. Theatre became very popular and important in Somali life, and at the core of the plays is poetry, the most important parts of the plays being composed in poetry.

Writing the Somali language and spelling

Somali has had an official orthography since 1972 when the Roman script was introduced by the ruling regime of the time. This script is now used by Somalis wherever they may be, and has proved very successful. There is one major factor, however, which must be borne in mind with regard to the orthography, namely that spelling has not become standardized. This means that the same word may be spelt in different ways. Most .words are spelt in a regular way but there are some common spellings that seem to be optional. Perhaps the most common of these is the past tense ending **-ay** which may also be spelt **-ey**. Somali is essentially written as it is pronounced[2] and so such variations in spelling will not cause any problems. There are no 'odd' spellings in Somali as there are, for example, in English in words such as **bough** and **rough**.

The Somali language

The Somali language is not easy to learn for somebody who knows only English. Despite this, however, it is an extremely satisfying endeavour. The structure of sentences in Somali is different to the structure of sentences in English, and there may at first seem to be a bewildering array of verbal forms. There is, however, a system to all of it and in this book an attempt has been made to convey the basics of the system.

Two main areas of language are dealt with: the structure of words and the way those words are put together into sentences. The structure of words is dealt with from the first lesson and introduced gradually. This includes such things as the plural formation of nouns and the formation of different moods and tenses of verbs, all of which involve patterns aiding the learner. Examples are given in each grammatical section and the vocabulary in the examples is restricted to allow the learner to concentrate on the grammatical point being made.

One important aspect of studying word structure is the way in which certain sound changes take place, for example, when a particular suffix is added to a verb ending in a certain consonant. These sound changes are introduced as necessary in the text but it is important to learn them as they are invariably used in parts of the grammar other than that of immediate concern.

Learning to put words together into sentences in Somali is not a particularly easy task and this book does not provide the most extensive coverage of this matter. Indeed, you will see in the later reading passages that the way in which sentences may be built up is very varied. As with anything, taking a little bit at a time is probably the best way, and building up a knowledge of basic sentence structure will be invaluable for later lessons. The section on relative clauses may prove to be particularly involved but, again, there is a rationale behind it and taking things at a steady pace will be the most successful way.

Pronunciation guide

Learning the correct pronunciation of Somali sounds is only really possible if you have access to the tapes that accompany this course or if you are able to work with a Somali speaker. Pronunciation does vary from speaker to speaker, and as with any language there are different dialects and accents. One of the biggest differences is in the way in which the sound **dh** is pronounced. In this course any instance in which **dh** is found is written as such. Many speakers, however, especially those from the southern regions of Somalia, pronounce **dh** as **r**.

The sounds of Somali

The sounds of the Somali alphabet are each represented by a specific letter. The alphabet does not include all the letters of the English alphabet, and some of the letters used represent sounds not found in English.

The alphabet is as follows:

a b c d dh e f g h i j k kh l m n o q r s sh t u w x y

Note that in the examples you will see accent marks. These are explained in a later section.

Consonants

Each sound is described below:

b This sound is generally pronounced as it is in English, although often at the end of words it may sound more like a **p** sound in English but without aspiration (the puff of air following the sound).

    bád, 'sea'   **dáb**, 'fire'   **dhábar**, 'back'

d This sound is also generally pronounced as it is in English except that the tongue is further forward than in English, touching the teeth.

    dád, 'people'   **badán**, 'many'

dh This sound is made by curling the tongue back on itself so that the bottom part of the tongue is touching the top part of the mouth. When the sound occurs between two vowels and is not a geminate it is softened and is pronounced like a **r**-type sound, but with the tongue still curling back. In speakers from certain areas, for example Mogadishu, this sound is almost always pronounced as **r** and as such is written in this way.

    dhúl, 'earth'   **yidhi**, 'he said'   **bádh**, 'half'

g This sound is made in the same way as it is in English.

    Gál!, 'Enter!'   **agagáar**, 'surroundings'   **adág**, 'hard'

q This sound is technically known as a voiced uvular plosive. This means that it is made right at the back of the mouth where the uvular drops down. The best way of trying to make this sound is by saying **k** and then moving the back of your tongue as far back as possible, right to the back of the mouth.

qaýb, 'part'   **boqol**, 'hundred'   **Báaq!**, 'Announce!'

t This sound is the same as in English except that it is never found at the end of syllables.

Tág!, 'Go!'   **wáy keentay**, 'she brought it'

k This sound is pronounced in the same manner as in English. Like **t** it is never found at the end of syllables.

kalé, 'other'   **nínka**, 'the man'

j This sound may be pronounced like **ch** in the English word **church**, or it can be pronounced as **j** in the English word **jingle**. Either pronunciation is correct.

jíd, 'road'   **Joóji!**, 'Stop!'   **xáj**, 'pilgrimage to Mecca'

f This sound is pronounced in the same way as it is in English.

fúre, 'key'   **áfar**, 'four'   **áf**, 'mouth, language'

s This sound is pronounced in the same way as in English.

Síi!, 'Give!'   **libsó**, 'Buy!'   **gées**, 'horn'

sh This sound is pronounced in the same way as it is in English.

shán, 'five'   **Cashée!**, 'Have dinner!'   **kíish**, 'bag'

kh This sound is made in the same part of the mouth as **q**, but with friction. It is the sound generally used for the Scottish pronunciation of the word **loch**. In Somali it is only found in loanwords from Arabic.

khudrád, 'vegetables'   **Khamiís**, 'Thursday'

x This sound is technically known as a voiceless pharyngeal fricative. It is made in the pharynx, which is the part of the throat between the voice box and the uvula. This part of the throat is contracted when producing the sound. It is highly advisable to work on this sound with a Somali speaker or with the tapes that go with this course. It is also found in Arabic.

Xídh!, 'Close!'   **wúu baxay**, 'he left'   **Báx!**, 'Leave!'

h This sound is the same as in English.

heés, 'song'   **báhal**, 'wild animal'   **báh**, 'children born of the same mother'

c This sound is made in the same part of the throat as the sound **x** but with vibration of the vocal cords. It is also a difficult sound to make, and thus is best learnt with the help of a speaker of Somali or with the tapes. It is the 'ayn of Arabic. It is somewhat similar to the sound you make when a doctor asks you to open your mouth wide and say 'aaaaa'.

Cáb!, 'Drink!'   **jecél**, 'liking'   **mágac**, 'name'

m This sound is the same as the English sound. It does not occur at the end of syllables (except if the following syllable begins with **b** or **m**).

máya, 'no'   **lamadegáan**, 'desert'

n This sound is the same as in English.

nabád, 'peace'   **mindí**, 'knife'   **maánta**, 'today'

r This sound is a rolled **r** like the sound in Italian. In Somali, however, it is often pronounced in quite a breathy manner.

rún, 'truth'   **wáran**, 'spear'   **Bár!**, 'Teach!'

l This sound is essentially the same as in English.

lúg, 'leg'   **kalé**, 'other'   **hál**, 'female camel'

' The apostrophe is a consonant in Somali. It stands for the glottal stop, which is found in some English dialectal pronunciations of words such as **bu'er** for 'butter' or **wa'er** for 'water'.

go'áan, 'decision'   **ló'**, 'cattle'

Gemination

There are a number of consonants in Somali which may be pronounced as doubled consonants. These are called geminate consonants. The following list gives all of the consonants which may generally be found as geminate consonants:

b, d, dh, g, l, m, n, r

The pronunciation of geminate consonants is the same as normal single consonants but they are held for longer and thus are somewhat stronger in their pronunciation. Geminate consonants are written by doubling the letter as shown in the following examples. It is very important to pronounce and write geminate consonants, as they indicate a difference in meaning.

wáran, 'spear'   Wárran!, 'Give news!'
wúu qaaday, 'he took it'   wáy qaadday, 'she took it'

Vowels

The vowel sounds in Somali are given below:

a This vowel is generally pronounced as the vowel **a** in the English word **bat**, although it is more *open* than the general south of England pronunciation of the word and is more akin to the pronunciation found in the north of England.

e This vowel is generally pronounced as in the English word **red**.

i This vowel is generally pronounced as in the English word **bit**.

o This vowel is generally pronounced as in the English word **top**, although in certain words it is pronounced slightly more *fronted*, similar to the French word **noeud** or the German **öl**.

u This vowel is pronounced in the same way as the **u** vowel in the English word **put**. Note that it is not the same as the sound of the southern English pronunciation of the word **butter**, but is like the northern English pronunciation of that word.

The difference between the two pronunciations of the vowel **o** also occurs in other vowels and is an instance of a phenomenon called *fronting*. This is a matter we shall not address in this book, but listen carefully to the recordings or the pronunciations of Somalis and try and imitate as closely as possible the vowel sounds you hear.

Listen again to the examples given above in the consonant section, specifically concentrating on the vowels.

Long and short vowels

All vowels in Somali may be pronounced long and short. Long vowels are written with double letters and are simply pronounced about twice as long, in terms of time, as a single vowel.

The pronunciation of certain vowels changes a little when they occur as long vowels.

ii When **i** is long it is pronounced like a long version of the vowel found in the English word **feet**.

Nadiifi!, 'Clean!'   **nínkií**, 'the man'

uu When **u** is long it is pronounced like a long version of the English word **fool**.

    Dúul!, 'Fly!'   **wúu baxay**, 'he left'

Diphthongs

Diphthongs are vowel sounds in which the vowel changes from one to other such as in the English word **cow**. If you say this word slowly the vowel sound begins like the vowel **a** and ends like the vowel **u**.

The following diphthongs occur in Somali:

    ay aw ey oy ow

Note that the dipthongs **ay** and **ey** are generally interchangeable.

ay ey These are generally pronounced like the diphthong sound in the English word **bay**.

    wáy tegeen, 'they went'   **sháleyto**, 'yesterday'

aw This is pronounced as the diphthong sound in the English word **cow**.

    cáws, 'grass'

ow This is pronounced as the diphthong sound in the English word **show**.

    dhow, 'near'

Stress-tone in Somali

The intonation of Somali words and sentences is determined by the placement of what we shall call stress-tone on certain vowels in words. Another term often used for stress-tone, especially in linguistic contexts, is tonal accent. The placement of stress-tone on vowels in particular words follows rules which you will learn as you work through the course. Here it is essential to learn one important point: that the stress-tone is placed on what we may call vowel units. A short vowel is one vowel unit and long vowels and diphthongs are all made up of two vowel units. So the word **Gál**, 'Enter!' is made up of one vowel unit and the word **Kéen**, 'Bring!' is made up of two vowel units. To make things simpler we shall simply refer to vowel units as vowels.

A vowel with a stress-tone placed on it is pronounced at a slightly higher pitch to other vowels and is stressed a little more.

Stress-tone is marked in this book by an acute accent, as shown in the following words. The first three words have the stress-tone placed on the first vowel in the word and the second group of three words have the stress-tone placed on the second vowel. Remember the vowel unit with the stress-tone is pronounced at a slightly higher pitch and is a little more stressed.

Group 1	ínan	boy
	béer	liver
	éy	dog
Group 2	inán	girl
	beér	garden
	eý	dogs

It is important to get the stress-tone right because, as you can see from this list, a significant difference in meaning can result from the placement of it.

As you can hear from the above examples, long vowels, essentially made up of two vowels, may be pronounced with a stress-tone on the first part, in which case the pitch of the whole long vowel falls. Or, a stress-tone may be placed on the second vowel, in which case the whole long vowel is slightly rising in pitch. In this latter case it may also be that the pitch stays at the same level. Bear this is mind when you hear the dialogues on the tapes or when listening to a Somali speaker.

There are two words you will learn which have what we shall call a see-saw stress-tone pattern. This we shall mark with a circumflex, ^ . The first of these words you will learn in the first lesson: **wâa**; the other is the question word **mâ**. If the following word has a stress-tone, then there is no stress-tone in the word with the see-saw stress tone. If, on the other hand, the following word has no stress-tone, the word with the see-saw stress-tone is pronounced with a stress-tone on the vowel marked with the circumflex.

In this book stress-tones will be marked in the grammar sections and the vocabularies so that the learner may become familiar with the patterns which are invariably predictable from gender, verb form etc. It is important to note, however, that stress-tones are not marked in Somali orthography, thus in the book you will see that in all the reading passages and dialogues, as well as exercise keys, stress-tones are not marked.

Sound changes

There are a number of sound changes in Somali. These will be dealt with in the lessons. However, it is important to bear in mind that some of the Somali sounds are restricted with regard to the position they may occupy in a word. The important ones to remember are that **t** and **k** never occur at the end of syllables. Thus, if a word that incorporates one of these sounds is used and the sound would potentially arise at the end of a syllable then it will change to **d** or **g** respectively. For example, a word for 'to be ill' is **bug**, but in certain verb forms the **g** occurs at the beginning of a syllable and becomes **k**:

wúu bukay   'he was ill'

This is because the sound in **bug** is, strictly speaking a **k**, but, because a **k** cannot occur at the end of a syllable then the **k** changes to a **g**. Another such sound is **m,** which cannot occur at the end of a word and changes to **n**.

Notes

1 Note that the Republic of Somaliland is a self-declared republic which seceded from the rest of Somalia in May 1991. It has not received recognition from the international community but is conceived of as a separate state by the majority of the inhabitants of that area. For further details of the matters surrounding the recent history of Somalia and the surrounding areas see *Understanding Somalia* by Prof. Ioan Lewis, published by Haan Associates, London, 1993.
2 Note an interesting exception to this rule: **dh** when it is geminate or doubled (see below) is always written **dh** and never **dhdh**.

Further reading

Those interested in pursuing further their study of the Somali language will find the following books of particular interest and use:

John Ibrahim Saeed (1993) *Somali Reference Grammar (second revised edition)* Kensington, MD: Dunwoody Press

R. David Zorc and Abdullaahi A. Issa (1990) *Somali Textbook* Kensington, MD: Dunwoody Press

R. David Zorc (1993) *Somali English Dictionary* Kensington, MD: Dunwoody Press

1 Is ka warran!

How are you?

> **By the end of this lesson you should be able to:**
> - use and reply to some simple greetings
> - give commands and instructions using the imperative
> - know about the third person object pronouns (it, him, her, them) in Somali
> - ask some basic questions
> - use the simple past tense (e.g. 'I went')
> - understand the use of the mood classifiers **wâa** and **mâ** with the verbal subject pronouns

Dialogue

A meeting between two friends

The following dialogue is typical of an exchange of greetings between two men

Vocabulary

waryáa	hey!, hi!
subáx	morning
wanaagsán	good
mâ	positive interrogative mood classifier
nabád	peace
báa	a focus marker
wâa	it is; positive declarative mood classifier
is	oneself
ká	about, from
wárran	give news
la	one (impersonal pronoun)

fiicán well, good
yahay he/it (m.) is

Bill is learning Somali in London in preparation for a trip to the Horn of Africa. He meets a Somali friend called Yoonis

YOONIS: Waryaa Bill, subax wanaagsan.
BILL: Waryaa Yoonis, subax wanaagsan, ma nabad baa?
YOONIS: Waa nabad. Is ka warran!
BILL: Waa la fiicanyahay.

YOONIS: Hi, Bill. Good morning.
BILL: Hi, Yoonis! Good morning. Are things well? (lit.: is it peace?)
YOONIS: Things are well. (lit.: it is peace) How are you?
BILL: I am well. (lit.: one is well)

Language in use

Using greetings and replying to them

There are quite a few greetings and responses to greetings in Somali. The ones given above are very commonly used, especially:

Is ká wárran!

We shall learn other greetings during the course.

There is no distinction in Somali between informal and formal address. This means that you greet and address all people in the same way whether they are young or old, prime minister or cleaner.

The word **waryáa** is not used to address women. If you know a woman's name you use that in the vocative (or address) form given below. If you do not know her name you simply use the greetings straight away.

The vocative form in Somali is formed by the addition of:

-áy on female names and nouns
-ów on male names and nouns

Canabáy!	Anab!
Faadumáy!	Faadumo!
Yoonisów!	Yoonis!
Maxamedów!	Mohamed!

As you can see from the **Faadumo** example, if the word ends in a vowel then that vowel is deleted and the vocative ending added straight after the final consonant.

The use of the impersonal pronoun **la** in the greetings context is much more frequent than the use of the first person pronoun which we shall come to later.

Always use these greetings, as well as the other ones you will come to learn, when you meet Somali friends.

Exercises

1 Reply to the following greetings:

1 Ma nabad baa?
2 Is ka warran!

2 Give the vocative forms of the following names:

1 Women: Maryan, Zaynab, Jawaahir.
2 Men: Cartan, Maxmuud, Cabdinuur.

The imperative

Example: **Wárran!** 'Give news!'

The singular imperative (or order form) in Somali is the basic form of the verb. This means that it is the form found in dictionary entries. Also, it is the form we need to know in order to build any other mood or tense of the verb.

We mentioned above the lack of formality distinction in Somali. This is also reflected in the use of the imperative. Whereas in English we might use a form such as 'Would you please . . .?' when speaking to somebody whom we feel we need to address formally, in Somali the imperative is used when speaking to everybody. Thus, to translate the phrase 'Would you please . . .?' into Somali you would use the imperative. This widespread use of the imperative does not imply being blunt or rude. A further point to mention with regard to this is that there is no word for 'please' in Somali. Although some speakers of English, as well as other languages, may feel uncomfortable about not using a word for 'please', you are by no means being rude. It is simply a fact of the Somali language.

The stress-tone pattern of the imperative is stress-tone on the penultimate vowel, or the only vowel, if there is only one.

To form the plural imperative is very easy in Somali: you just add **-a** to the singular imperative. If the the verb ends in **-i** then **y** is inserted. Note that the stress-tone in plural imperatives is also on the penultimate vowel, but on the plural form.

Wárran!	Give news (sg.)!
Warráma!	Give news (pl.)![1]
Kéen!	Bring it (sg.)!
Keéna!	Bring it (pl.)!

Exercise

3 Practise saying the following imperative verbs. Don't forget to pay attention to the stress-tone pattern; convert the singular imperatives into plural imperatives.

1 Keen!   Bring it!
2 Tag!   Go!
3 Cun!   Eat it!
4 Jooji! Stop!
5 Sug!   Wait!

Third person object pronouns

The third person object pronouns in English (it/him/her/them) do not have any overt translation in Somali. This means that there are no actual words which are the Somali equivalents of 'it', 'him', 'her' or 'them'. The English sentences 'Bring it!', 'Bring him!', 'Bring her!' and 'Bring them!' are therefore all translated in the same way in Somali: **Kéen!**. It is important to remember this as, although you do not actually hear the pronouns, they are implied when a verb which takes a direct object is used (i.e. when a transitive verb is used).

It is important to note also that this implication of pronouns applies not just to the imperative but to all forms of verbs, as well as to other types of words such as prepositions, as we shall see later.

You might think that this state of affairs would lead to ambiguity and confusion but it doesn't. The context invariably provides the means to understanding which pronoun is meant or, if an ambiguity is possible, then you may use a certain type of pronoun (the independent pronoun), which we shall come to later in the course.

Exercise

4 Write down all the possible English translations of the following Somali sentences. The meanings of the verbs are given in brackets:

1 Akhri! (read)
2 Cun! (eat)
3 Eeg! (look at)
4 Qor! (write)
5 Fur! (open)

Asking the question 'Is it . . .?'

In the dialogue we learnt the sentence **Ma nabád báa?**, literally 'Is it peace?'. This type of construction may be used to ask any question of the form 'Is it . . .?'.

Ma sháah báa?	Is it tea?
Ma éy báa?	Is it a dog?

To answer a question of this sort we use the word **wâa**. This translates the phrase 'It is . . .'.

Waa sháah.	It is tea.
Waa éy.	It is a dog.

Exercise

5 Fill in the blanks in the following sentences:

1 Ma shaah _____?   Is it tea?
2 _____ shaah.   It is tea.
3 Ma _____ _____?   Is it peace?
4 _____ nabad.   It is peace.
5 _____ sonkor _____?   Is it sugar?
6 _____ _____.   It is sugar.

Dialogue

Some shopping

Vocabulary

dukáanka	the shop	laybreérigase	the library + but
tagtay	you went	laybreériga	the library
háa	yes	-se	but
wâan	positive declarative mood classifier + I	búug	book
		-na	and (joins phrases)
tegey	I went	wáa yahay	right, OK (lit.: it is)
caleén	leaves		
sháah	tea	ímminka	now
ká	from	gúriga	the house
keentay	you brought	tag	to go to[2]
iyo	and (joins noun phrases)	kóob	cup
		áh	which is
caáno	milk	samee	to make
sonkórba	as well as sugar (sonkór + ba)	búuggiína	and the book (lit.: the book + and)
sonkór	sugar	búuggií	the book
-ba	emphasizing suffix	-na	and
wáx	thing	akhri	to read
kalé	other	nabád gelyo	goodbye
máya	no		

Yoonis sees that Bill has some shopping.

YOONIS: Dukaanka ma tagtay?
BILL: Haa, waan tegey.
YOONIS: Caleen shaah ma ka keentay?
BILL: Haa, caleen shaah iyo caano iyo sonkorba waan ka keenay.
YOONIS: Wax kale ma ka keentay?
BILL: Maya; laybreerigase waan tegey buugna waan ka keenay.
YOONIS: Waa yahay. Imminka guriga tag, koob shaah ah samee buuggiina akhri.
BILL: Waa yahay. Nabad gelyo.
YOONIS: Nabad gelyo.

YOONIS: *Did you go to the shop?*
BILL: *Yes, I went to it.*
YOONIS: *Did you bring tea leaves from it?*
BILL: *Yes, I brought tea leaves, milk and sugar from it.*
YOONIS: *Did you bring anything else from it?*
BILL: *No; but I went to the library and I brought a book from there.*
YOONIS: *Right. Now go home, make a cup of tea and read the book.*
BILL: *Right. Goodbye.*
YOONIS: *Goodbye.*

Language in use

The general past tense of conjugation 1

Before going on to look at verb forms let us look at some terms used in describing verbs:

Moods: The mood of a verb indicates the attitude the speaker has about what he or she is saying. The indicative mood is used when the speaker is making general factual statements, the interrogative mood is used for asking questions and the imperative mood is used for making requests and giving orders. We shall meet other moods later in the course.

Tenses: The tense of a verb indicates the time when the action described by the verb takes place.

Conjugation: The conjugation of a verb is the group of verbs to which it belongs. The members of conjugations share certain characteristics, so if you know the pattern of one verb in a particular conjugation, then you will know the forms of other verbs in that conjugation.

There are three conjugations in Somali, of which conjugation 1 is the most basic. Of the two basic tenses in Somali (the general past and the general present) the general past tense tends to be used more often and so we shall look at this one first. The tense is used for actions that have been completed in the past.

The tense is formed by adding the general past tense endings to the imperative form of the verb. Note that the stress-tone of the imperative is deleted when it is used as the base from which to construct another verb form. Each verb tense and mood has its own stress-tone pattern, and the pattern for the general past tense in main clauses is no stress-tone on any of the vowels. The verb forms are given below, using the verb **keen**, meaning 'to bring', as an example. The forms mean, therefore, 'I brought', 'you brought' etc.

	verb stem	ending	verb form
I	keen	ay	**keenay**
you (sg.)	keen	tay	**keentay**
he, it (m.)	keen	ay	**keenay**
she, it (f.)	keen	tay	**keentay**
we	keen	nay	**keennay**
you (pl.)	keen	teen	**keenteen**
they	keen	een	**keeneen**

Another example verb is **dhis** meaning 'to build'; the following forms therefore mean 'I built', 'you built' etc.:

	verb stem	ending	verb form
I	dhis	ay	**dhisay**
you (sg.)	dhis	tay	**dhistay**
he, it (m.)	dhis	ay	**dhisay**
she, it (f.)	dhis	tay	**dhistay**
we	dhis	nay	**dhisnay**
you (pl.)	dhis	teen	**dhisteen**
they	dhis	een	**dhiseen**

There are a number of sound changes which occur in verb forms. Some of these are given below. Others will be given later.

(a) **t** changes to **d** when it follows the following Somali sounds:

- **q**, **kh**, **c**, **x**, **h**, and **'** (i.e. all of the guttural consonants),
- **d**,
- **w**, **y** or any vowel.

Wáad ká baxday.	(from: bax-tay)	You left from there.
Wáy qaadday.	(from: qaad-tay)	She took it.
Wáad akhriday.	(from: akhri-tay)	You read it.[3]

(b) **t** changes to **dh** when it follows **dh**.

    Wáy gaadhay.   (from: gaadh-tay)   She reached there.

Note that although the form is written with one **dh** it is in fact a geminate or doubled consonant.

(c) **n** changes to **l** when it follows **l** and changes to **r** when it follows **r**.

    Wáannu hellay.   (from: hel-nay)   We found it.
    Wáannu dirray.   (from: dir-nay)   We sent it.

Note that this is an optional sound change and thus the forms **helnay** and **dirnay** are also correct.

(d) When **t** follows **l** the **lt** sequence is replaced by **sh**.

    Wáydin gasheen.   (from: gal-teen)   You (pl.) entered.
    Wáad heshay.   (from: hel-tay)   You found it.

(e) When the imperative form ends in **i** and the endings beginning with a vowel are added, the letter **y** is inserted between the **i** and the vowel.

    Wáan akhriyay.   (from: akhri-ay)   I read it.
    Wáy akhriyeen.   (from: akhri-een)   They read it.

(f) When a verb ends in the short vowel **a** plus a guttural consonant, the vowel changes to **e** when the **een** ending is added. This is a case of assimilation across a guttural consonant.

    Wáy bexeen.   (from: bax-een)   They left.

(g) **Tag**: When the endings **-ay** and **-een** are added to this verb the resulting form is often pronounced and written in the following way: **tegey** and **tegeen**.

There are some verbs in which the final consonant of the verb alternates. One such example is **bug**, 'to be ill'. When an ending beginning with a vowel is added, the **g** changes to a **k**.

    Wúu bukay.   (from: bug-ay)   He was ill.
    Wáy bukeen.   (from: bug-een)   They were ill.

but

    Wáy bugtay.   (from: bug-tay)   She was ill.

The reason for this change is given in the pronunciation guide. There are only a few verbs that behave in this way, and they are marked in the glossary.

It is important to know that the final **-ay** ending of the past tense may equally be written **-ey**. Somali spelling is not standardized in the same way as English is, and both these spellings are correct.

Exercise

6 Write out all the forms of the general past tense of the following verbs:

1 diid   refuse
2 baaq   announce
3 go'   cut (intr.)
4 akhri   read
5 dil   kill, hit
6 tag   go

Mood classifiers: the positive declarative classifier
wâa

The verb moods in Somali are marked in the form of the verb. In addition to this, in many cases, words we shall call mood classifiers also show the mood of the verb, in combination with the verb form. We have already met one positive mood: the positive imperative. This is an example of a mood without a classifier. **Tág!**, 'Go!' is a correct sentence which needs no classifiers to make it a correct sentence.

The positive declarative mood is used for making positive declarative statements, for example, the English sentence 'They played football yesterday' is a positive declarative sentence. The classifier for this mood in Somali is **wâa**. This may be replaced by a focus marker, which will be discussed later. The stress-tone pattern for **wâa** is the see-saw pattern.

The use of either the positive declarative mood classifier or a focus marker is obligatory in a positive declarative sentence in Somali. If you say a positive declarative sentence without **wâa** or a focus marker then it is incorrect, so don't forget it!

The verbal subject pronouns

The verbal subject pronouns are very often used if there is no specific subject noun in the sentence. The verbal subject pronouns do not stand on their own in main clauses (a main clause is a clause that may stand on its own as a sentence). You must use them in conjunction with a mood classifier (or a focus marker). The forms of these pronouns are as follows (the hyphens show that they must be attached to a mood classifier or a focus marker):

I	-aan	we (incl.)	-aynu
you (sg.)	-aad	we (excl.)	-aannu
he, it (m.)	-uu	you (pl.)	-aydin
she, it (f.)	-ay	they	-ay

There are two ways of saying 'we' in Somali. The inclusive (incl.) pronoun is used when you are saying 'we' and including the person to whom you are speaking. The exclusive (excl.) pronoun is used when you are saying 'we' but not including the person to whom you are speaking.

To combine these pronoun forms with **wâa** simply add **w-** to the beginning of the pronoun form as listed above. The long vowel **-aa** of **wâa** is deleted. Note that the stress-tone pattern in these combinations is also the see-saw pattern, that is, if the following word does not have stress-tone then stress-tone is placed on the vowel marked in the **wâa** + pronoun word. If the following word has a stress-tone the **wâa** + pronoun word has no stress-tone. The forms are given below:

I	wâa + aan	**wâan**
you (sg.)	wâa + aad	**wâad**
he, it (m.)	wâa + uu	**wûu**
she, it (f.)	wâa + ay	**wây**
we (incl.)	wâa + aynu	**wâynu**
we (excl.)	wâa + aanu	**wâannu**
you (pl.)	wâa + aydin	**wâydin**
they	wâa + ay	**wây**

Note that **wâa** does not have to go with a subject pronoun. It may equally stand on its own in a sentence. In these cases it tends to imply the third person subject pronoun, according to the verb ending. Compare the following sentences which are all correct.

Wáy cuntay.   She ate it.
Wáa cuntay.   She ate it.

Wúu cunay.	He ate it.
Wáa cunay.	He ate it.

Note, however, that the forms with the pronouns are used more often, and thus you are encouraged to use these, especially when there is no explicit subject word.

Exercise

7 Translate the following sentences into Somali; think carefully about the different aspects of grammar you must use to translate these sentences correctly:

1 They found it.
2 She sent them.
3 You (sg.) brought her.
4 You (pl.) took them.
5 He left.
6 We (excl.) entered.

Mood classifiers: the positive interrogative classifier ma

We have already met this word on p. 15. Here is another of its uses.

The mood classifier **mâ** is used in positive yes–no questions. These are questions to which the answer 'yes' or 'no' may be given. It does not include 'wh- questions' (those involving words such as 'which', 'who' or 'what' etc.). For example, the question 'Did you cook it?' can be answered 'Yes' or 'No'. The question 'Who cooked it?', on the other hand, cannot be answered in this way. It requires some specific new information to be given.

Like **wâa**, **mâ** also has the see-saw stress-tone pattern.

Similarly, as with **wâa**, the verbal subject pronouns combine with this positive interrogative classifier. They do this in the following way: the **a** in **mâ** is replaced by **iy** and the verbal subject pronoun added. The stress-tone pattern on these combined forms is assigned to the penultimate vowel. You will see in a later lesson that when this particular form is used it often focuses a noun phrase. It may, however, also be used in the general way as described here.

I	ma + aan	**miyáan**
you (sg.)	ma + aad	**miyáad**
he, it (m.)	ma + uu	**miyúu**
she, it (f.)	ma + ay	**miyáy**
we (incl.)	ma + aynu	**miyáynu**
we (excl.)	ma + aannu	**miyáannu**
you (pl.)	ma + aydin	**miyáydin**
they	ma + ay	**miyáy**

Exercises

8 Reply to the following questions positively:

Example: Dukaanka ma tagtay?   Did you go to the shop?
          Haa, waan tegey.   Yes, I went to it.

1 Buuggii miyaad akhriday?
2 Guriga miyay heshay?
3 Guriga miyaydin ka baxdeen? (**ká** means 'from')
4 Dukaanka miyay heleen?
5 Laybreeriga miyuu galay?

9 Write questions to which the following sentences could be the answers:

Example: Waan baxay.   I left.
          Miyaad baxday?   Did you leave?

1 Way direen.
2 Waannu hellay.
3 Wuu keenay.
4 Way gashay.
5 Waan ka baxay.

10 Think up some questions of your own, write them down and use them the next time you meet a Somali friend.

Reading practice

Read and translate the following, carefully noting the use of the various words and grammatical constructions you have learnt in this lesson.

Vocabulary

halkaás	there	**qoray**	I wrote
ká	from	**nín**	man
búug fiicán	a good book	**aammúsa**	be quiet (pl.)
dabádéedna	and then	**aammus**	to be quiet
warqád	letter	**akhríyayaa**	I am reading

Maryan guriga way ka baxday, laybreerigana way tagtay. Halkaas buug way ka heshay, wayna akhriday. Maxamed laybreeriga wuu galay:

MAXAMED: Maryanay, is ka warran!
MARYAN: Waryaa Maxamed, waa la wanaagsanyahay. Ma nabad baa?
MAXAMED: Waa nabad. Ma buug fiican baa?
MARYAN: Haa, waa buug fiican. Waan akhriyay, dabadeedna warqad waan qoray.
MAXAMED: Waa yahay, Maryan, nabad gelyo.
MARYAN: Nabad gelyo, Maxamed.
NIN KALE: Aammusa! Waan akhriyayaa.

Maryan left the house and went to the library. She took a book and read it. Maxamed entered the library:

MAXAMED: *Maryan, how are you?*
MARYAN: *Hi, Maxamed, I am well. How are you?*
MAXAMED: *I am well. Is it a good book?*
MARYAN: *Yes, it is a good book. I read it then I wrote a letter.*
MAXAMED: *Right. Goodbye, Maryan.*
MARYAN: *Goodbye, Maxamed.*
ANOTHER MAN: *Be quiet! I am reading.*

Notes

1 Note that this verb is one which ends in an **n** which is also an **m**: see the pronunciation guide.
2 Note that when a verb is given in its basic form in vocabularies and the glossary there will be no stress-tone given, since this is added according to the mood and tense of the verb.
3 Note that this is only with the conjugation 1 verbs which rarely end in **-i**. Conjugation 2A verbs also end in **-i** and, as you will see, another sound change occurs with them.

2 Subax wanaagsan
Good morning

> By the end of this lesson you should be able to:
> - use and reply to some more greetings
> - learn some basic facts about nouns
> - use the present progressive (e.g. 'I am going')
> - learn another way of asking 'Is it . . .?'

Dialogue

Zaynab visits Canab at home

Vocabulary

galáb	afternoon
miyáa	question word: 'Is it . . .?'
maxáad	what + you
sheegtay	you told
maxáad sheegtay	how are you (lit.: 'what did you tell?')
wáa la wanaagsányahay	I am well (lit.: 'one is well')
soó	a particle meaning towards the speaker or person referred to
dhowow	to move nearer
soó dhowow	come in
ayáy	focus marker (**ayáa**) + **-ay** 'they'; here the word **gúriga** is focused
galaan	they enter
fadhiiso	to sit down
soó fadhiíso	sit down (this is the phrase used most often)

kóob sháah áh	'a cup of tea' (lit.: 'a cup which is tea'; the word **áh** is needed here)
doónaysaa	you want, you are wanting
ín	part, amount
yár	small
ká dib	after
kán	this
waa kán	here it is (lit.: it is this)
mahadsánid	thank you

CANAB: Zaynabay, galab wanaagsan. Nabad miyaa?
ZAYNAB: Waa nabad. Maxaad sheegtay?
CANAB: Waa la wanaagsanyahay.
ZAYNAB: Soo dhowow.

Guriga ayay galaan.

ZAYNAB: Soo fadhiiso. Koob shaah ah ma doonaysaa.
CANAB: Haa.
ZAYNAB: (In yar ka dib) Waa kan.
CANAB: Mahadsanid.

CANAB: *Zaynab, good afternoon. Are things well?*
ZAYNAB: *Things are well. How are you?*
CANAB: *I am well.* (lit.: *one is well*)
ZAYNAB: *Come in.*

They enter the house.

ZAYNAB: *Sit down. Would you like a cup of tea?*
CANAB: *Yes.*
ZAYNAB: (After a short while) *Here it is.*
CANAB: *Thank you.*

Language in use

Greetings for particular times of the day

subáx wanaagsán	good morning
galáb wanaagsán	good afternoon
habéen wanaagsán	good evening
maalín wanaagsán	good day
nabád kú bári	good night (lit.: 'break the day in peace')
nabád ma kú bariday	good morning (lit.: 'did you break the day in peace?')

All of these greetings are used when meeting someone. **Habéen wanaagsán** may also be used when you are leaving somebody in the evening.

Using miyáa

In the dialogue Zaynab says **Nabád miyáa**. The use of **miyáa** is equivalent to the use of **mâ ... báa**.

| **Shimbír miyáa?** | Is it a bird? |
| **Kúrsi miyáa?** | Is it a chair? |

To answer a question of this sort we use **wâa**.

| **Waa shimbír.** | It is a bird. |
| **Waa kúrsi.** | It is a chair. |

Exercises

1 Fill in the blanks in the following sentences:

1 Shandad _____? Is it a suitcase?
2 Haa, _____ _____. Yes, it is a suitcase.
3 Kubbad _____? Is it a ball?
4 _____, _____ _____. Yes, it is a ball.

2 Arrange the following groups of words to form questions in Somali, then write answers to the questions:

1 koob   baa   ma
2 miyaa   warqad
3 guri   miyaa
4 baa   dukaan   ma

The present progressive of conjugation 1

Of the two present tenses, the present progressive is probably used more in general conversation than the general present, so we shall look at this tense first. The present progressive tense is used for actions that are currently in progress. In English this is rendered by the verb form, for example, 'I am running'. This tense may also be used for an action that is to happen in the near future, for example the sentence **Waan cúnayaa** may mean 'I am eating it' or 'I will eat it (very soon)', i.e. 'I am about to eat it'.

The form of the present progressive in conjugation 1 is made up of the basic form of the verb plus the progressive marker **-ay-** followed by the present tense endings. These present tense endings are also used in the general present tense.

	verb stem	progressive marker	present tense ending	verb form
I	keen	ay	aa	**keénayaa**
you (sg.)	keen	ay	taa	**keénaysaa**
he, it (m.)	keen	ay	aa	**keénayaa**
she, it (f.)	keen	ay	taa	**keénaysaa**
we	keen	ay	naa	**keénaynaa**
you (pl.)	keen	ay	taan	**keénaysaan**
they	keen	ay	aan	**keénayaan**

As you can see from the table the stress-tone in the present progressive is placed on the vowel that immediately precedes the progressive marker. This means that with the verb **keen** the long vowel **ee** is pronounced steady or slightly rising (see pronunciation guide).

You can also see from the table that when a present tense ending beginning with **-t-** follows the progressive marker **-ay-**, the **-t-** changes to **-s-**. See how this works with **dhis**, 'to build', also.

	verb stem	progressive marker	present tense ending	verb form
I	dhis	ay	aa	**dhísayaa**
you (sg.)	dhis	ay	taa	**dhísaysaa**
he, it (m.)	dhis	ay	aa	**dhísayaa**
she, it (f.)	dhis	ay	taa	**dhísaysaa**
we	dhis	ay	naa	**dhísaynaa**
you (pl.)	dhis	ay	taan	**dhísaysaan**
they	dhis	ay	aan	**dhísayaan**

When the progressive ending is added to a verb ending in **-i** the sound **y** is inserted between **i** and **a**.

Waan akhríyayaa.   I am reading.

Here are some more examples of present progressive verb forms:

Way ká báxaysaa. She is leaving./She is going to leave.
Way gálayaan. They are entering./They are going to enter.
Waynu akhríyaynaa. We (incl.) are reading./We (incl.) are going to read.

From now on in the course we shall not give two separate translations for the present progressive; instead we shall give the present meaning unless the context demands the future meaning. Do not forget, though, these two aspects of this verb form.

Exercises

3 Write out all the forms of the present progressive tense of the following verbs:

1 xidh   to close
2 dhig   to put down, teach
3 bar   to teach
4 doon   to want, wish (also used as the auxiliary verb for the future tense, as explained later)
5 gaadh   to arrive, reach, catch up with
6 akhri   to read

4 Reply positively to the following questions:

Example: Hilib ma cunaysaa?   Are you eating meat?
               Haa, hilib waan cunayaa.   Yes, I am eating meat.

1 Guriga miyay ka baxayaan?
2 Landhan miyaydin tegaysaan?
3 Buug miyay akhriyaysaa?
4 Shandadda miyaad furaysaa?
5 Warqad miyuu qorayaa?

5 Translate the following sentences into Somali:

1 Maxamed is eating.
2 Ruqiya is entering the house.
3 Cali is reading it.
4 They reached the library.
5 Did he take the chair?
6 They are building the house.

Reading practice

Vocabulary

maánta	today	wada	together
isniín	Monday	quraacdeen	they had breakfast
jaamacád	university	kibís	bread
jaamacádda	the university	súbag	butter
árdey	student	súbagléh	with butter (lit.: 'owning butter')
saaxíibkíisa	his friend		
saaxíibkíisuna	and his friend (subject case)	sháleyto	yesterday
		subáxdií	in the morning
mágaciisu	his name (subject case)	galábtií	in the afternoon
		waláalkaý	my brother
búu	focus marker báa + he	báan	focus marker + 'I' focusing waláalkaý
raácayaa	is accompanying	booqday	I visited

Maanta waa isniin. Maxamed waa tagayaa jaamacadda. Maxamed waa ardey saaxiibkiisuna waa ardey. Magaciisu waa Yoonis. Maxamed buu raacayaa. Maanta way wada quraacdeen. Shaah way cabbeen, kibis subaglehna way cuneen.

MAXAMED: Shaleyto jaamacadda miyaad tagtay?
YOONIS: Haa subaxdii waan tagay. Galabtiina walaalkay baan booqday.

Today is Monday. Maxamed is going to the university. Maxamed is a student and his friend is a student. His name is Yoonis. He is accompanying Maxamed. Today they had breakfast together. They drank tea and ate bread with butter.

MAXAMED: *Did you go to the university yesterday?*
YOONIS: *Yes, I went in the morning. In the afternoon I visited my brother.*

Language in use

Nouns in Somali

Gender: There are two genders for nouns in Somali: masculine and feminine. For some words the gender is obvious, e.g. **naág**, 'woman', is feminine, whereas **nín**, 'man', is masculine. In other cases, the gender must be learnt with the noun. Note that in the plural the gender of a noun is often different to that of the singular, thus for example the word **naág**, 'woman', is feminine in the singular but the plural, **naago**, is grammatically masculine. Equally **ínan**, 'boy', is masculine in the singular but the plural, **inammo**, is grammatically feminine.

Declensions: Nouns are classified into groups, called declensions. The members of a particular declension share certain characteristics, specifically: the way in which the plural is formed, the gender of plural nouns and the stress-tone pattern. In some declensions the nouns all share the same gender in the singular whereas in others most nouns are of the same gender but not all. In the tables in this and following lessons we shall give the following characteristics which are shared by nouns in a particular declension:

- stress-tone pattern in singular and plural
- gender in singular and plural
- word shape in the singular
- plural formation

Declensions 1, 2 and 3

These three declensions are taken together here because they form the plural in roughly the same way, although there are, as we shall see, some differences. All three declensions share the following stress-tone patterns:

singular	masculine	*stress-tone on the penultimate vowel*
	feminine	*stress-tone on the final vowel*
plural		*no stress-tone on any vowel*

Declension 1

gender	singular	*mostly feminine*
	plural	*always masculine*
word shape in singular		*do not end in -o*
plural formation		*add -o*

Examples of declension 1 nouns:

warqád, 'letter' **warqado**, 'letters'
saacád, 'hour, clock, watch' **saacado**, 'hours, clocks, watches'
naág, 'woman' **naago**, 'women'
shimbír, 'bird' **shimbiro**, 'birds'

Sound change: if the singular ends in **-i** then add **-yo** in the plural.

mindí, 'knife' **mindiyo**, 'knives'
gúri, 'house' **guriyo**, 'houses' (sometimes spelt **guryo**)[1]

Exercises

6 Give the plural form of the following nouns, all of which are from declension 1:

1 beer   garden, farm
2 sabab   reason
3 daar   stone building
4 kab   shoe
5 qayb   part, share
6 saaxiibad   female friend

7 Give the singular form of the following plural nouns, all from declension 1:

1 saacado   hours, clocks
2 jidho   bodies
3 dayuurado   aeroplanes
4 su'aalo   questions
5 dhakhtarado   female doctors
6 bilo   months

Declension 2

gender	singular	**mostly masculine**
	plural	**always feminine**
word shape		**mostly more than one syllable, do not end in -e**
plural formation		**add -o (see sound changes below)**

There are sound changes which must be learnt in this declension.

(a) If the singular ends in **-i** then add **-yo**.

 tágsi, 'taxi'   **tagsiyo**, 'taxis'

(b) If a singular noun ends in a guttural consonant, **j** or **s** then add **-yo**.

 sác, 'cow'   **sacyo**, 'cows'
 nácas, 'fool'   **nacasyo**, 'fools'
 daríiq, 'road'   **dariiqyo**, 'roads'

(c) If a singular noun ends in **b**, **d**, **dh**, **r**, **l**, or **n** then the consonant is doubled in the plural.

 albáab, 'door'   **albaabbo**, 'doors'
 baabúur, 'lorry'   **baabuurro**, 'lorries'
 sánad, 'year'   **sanaddo**, 'years'

(d) If a singular noun ends in **n** it may be one of those that changes to **m** (see pronunciation guide): note that the **m** is geminated.

 ínan, 'boy'   **inammo**, 'boys'

Exercises

8 Give the plural forms of the following nouns, all of which are from declension 2:

1 gidaar wall
2 barnaamij programme
3 madax head
4 bangi bank
5 subax morning
6 laybreeri library

9 Give the singular form of the following plural nouns, all from declension 2:

1 dukaammo shops
2 kursiyo chairs
3 casharro lessons
4 dhakhtarro doctors
5 baabuurro cars, lorries
6 laabbisyo pencils

Declension 3

gender	singular plural	*masculine or feminine* *always masculine*	
word shape		$(C)V(V)CVC^2$	$C = consonant$ $V = vowel$
plural formation		*add -o and delete the final vowel of the singular*	

There are some sound changes which need to be learnt with this declension.

(a) Sometimes the singular noun's final consonant changes because the sound of the basic form is not one that can occur at the end of a syllable (see pronunciation guide). When the plural is formed the consonant changes, as shown in the following examples:

ílig, 'tooth'   **ilko**, 'teeth'
qálin, 'pen'   **qalmo**, 'pens'

Further examples of declension 3 nouns:

galáb, 'afternoon'   **galbo**, 'afternoons'
maalín, 'day'   **maalmo**, 'days'
hílib, 'meat'   **hilbo**, 'meats'
xádhig, 'rope'   **xadhko**, 'ropes'

Exercises

10 Change the singular nouns to plurals and the plural nouns to singular; all nouns are from declension 3:

1 gabadh   girl
2 gacmo   hands
3 garab   shoulder
4 jilib   knee
5 kibis   bread
6 warmo   spears

11 Translate the following sentences from English into Somali:

1 They built roads.
2 Today they are going to markets.
3 They took chairs.

4 She brought pencils.
5 Will you bring shoes?

Saying 'and'

We have met two words meaning 'and' in Somali: **-na** and **iyo**.

-na This is a word which, as we have seen, is attached to other words. It is used to join two *positive declarative* or *imperative* sentences together and is added to the first grammatical unit of the second sentence. We shall see during the course that this does not necessarily coincide with the first word in the sentence; look back to the last sentence in the reading passage on p. 31 above and see how the first grammatical unit is **kibís súbagléh**.

Gúriga wúu tegey wúuna galay. He went to the house and entered it.

iyo This word is used to join nouns or noun phrases together.

nabád iyo caáno peace and milk

When there is a list of more than two nouns, the word **iyo** is generally placed between the final two members of the list only, as in English.

Maxámed, Idríis iyo Maxmuud wáy sugeen. Maxamed, Idriis and Maxmuud waited.

We shall learn other words meaning 'and' which join other types of phrase later in the course.

Exercise

12 Join together the following words or sentences in the correct manner and translate the sentences or phrases:

1 buug qalin
2 Guriga waan galay. Shaah waan cabbay.
3 Hargeysa Muqdishu Baydhaba Harar (all names of towns and cities in the Horn of Africa)
4 Guriga waydin ka baxdeen. Albaabka waydin xidheen.
5 Buug waan akhriyay. Warqad waan qoray.
6 kibis subag shaah sonkor

Reading practice

Read and translate the following dialogue:

Shamis sees Idil

Vocabulary

fiicánahay	I am well	maxáad sameýnaysaa?	what are you doing?
Ilaáhi	God, Allah	nínkaý	my husband
maháddi	to thank	carruúrtaý	my children
qóyska	the family	xeébta	the coast
maxáad	what + you		
sameýnaysaa	you are doing		

SHAMIS: Idilay! Is ka warran.
IDIL: Waa la wanaagsanyahay. Ma nabad baa?
SHAMIS: Waan fiicanahay, Illaah mahaddi.
IDIL: Qoyska ka warran.
SHAMIS: Way fiicanyihiin.
IDIL: Maxaad sameynaysaa?
SHAMIS: Ninkay iyo caruurtay baan sugayaa. Xeebta bay tegeen.

SHAMIS: *Idil! How are you?*
IDIL: *I am well. How are things?*
SHAMIS: *I am well, thanks be to God.*
IDIL: *How is the family?*
SHAMIS: *They are well.*
IDIL: *What are you doing?*
SHAMIS: *I am waiting for my husband and my children. They went to the coast.*

Notes

1 As you can see from the stress-tone pattern, this is an example of a masculine noun in declension 1.
2 Note that the last two consonants must be different. Compare **sabab** given above in declension 1. The parentheses indicate options.

3 Bill iyo Zaynab

Bill and Zaynab

By the end of this lesson you should:
- know about and use the definite article in Somali
- know about and use the cases of Somali nouns
- have learnt declensions 4 and 5
- have learnt conjugation 2A
- have learnt to say 'what is it?'
- have learnt the days of the week

Dialogue

Vocabulary: Note that from now on when a noun is given in a vocabulary list, the following information will be given: the gender of the noun in the singular and the declension to which the noun belongs. Look in the glossary for nouns already met. Note: collec. stands for *collective*, and mass refers to a type of noun which may not be counted. Details of the use of such nouns will be given in a later lesson. Some nouns do not have a plural form. In these cases they do not necessarily belong to any particular declension; such nouns will be provided simply with their gender.

Vocabulary

boósto (f. d6)	post office
boostáda	the post office
xaggée	where (lit.: 'which direction')
báad	focus marker **báa** and the pronoun **-aad**, 'you'
adígu	you (independent pronoun, used here for emphasis)
súuq (m. d2)	market

báan	focus marker **báa** and the pronoun **-aan**, 'I'
ku	you
raac	to accompany
maxáad soó iibsánaysaa	what will you buy?
hílib (m. d3)	meat
baríis (m. d2 mass)	rice
khudrád (f. d1 collec.)	vegetables
waa tán	here is (f.) (lit.: 'it is this')
saaxíibkáyga	my friend
ú	to
dir	send

Bill is going to the post office and meets Zaynab

ZAYNAB: Waryaa, Bill.
BILL: Zaynabay, is ka warran.
ZAYNAB: Waa la wanaagsanyahay. Xaggee baad tagaysaa?
BILL: Boosta baan tagayaa. Xaggee baad tagaysaa, adigu?
ZAYNAB: Suuqa baan tagayaa.
BILL: Waa yahay. Waan ku raacayaa. Maxaad soo iibsanaysaa?
ZAYNAB: Hilib, bariis, sonkor iyo khudradba waan soo iibsanayaa.
BILL: Waa yahay. Waa tan boostadu. Warqad baan saaxiibkayga u dirayaa. Nabad gelyo, Zaynab.
ZAYNAB: Nabad gelyo, Bill.

ZAYNAB: *Hi, Bill.*
BILL: *Hi, Zaynab, how are you?*
ZAYNAB: *I am well. Where are you going?*
BILL: *I am going to the post office. Where are you going?*
ZAYNAB: *I am going to the market.*
BILL: *Right. I'll accompany you. What are you going to buy?*
ZAYNAB: *I'm going to buy meat, rice, sugar and vegetables.*
BILL: *Right, here's the post office. I am sending a letter to my friend. Goodbye, Zaynab.*
ZAYNAB: *Goodbye, Bill.*

Language in use

Case in Somali nouns

The case of a noun depends on the role it plays in a sentence. In Somali a noun often has different forms, depending on whether or not it is the subject of a sentence. There are four cases in Somali: the absolutive case, the subject case, the genitive case and the vocative case. We have already met the vocative case: see Lesson 1. In this section we shall look at the use and form of the absolutive and subject cases.

The absolutive case

Use: The easiest way of describing the use of this case is to say that it is used in all instances other than when any one of the other cases is used. Thus, for example, the citation form, the form used when you just say a word on its own, is in the absolutive case. Also, the direct and indirect objects of sentences are in the absolutive case. Nouns associated with prepositions are also in this case.

Form: The absolutive case is as the citation form. Thus for nouns of declensions 1, 2 and 3 we already know the absolutive form.

mindí	knife
naág	woman
baabúur	car

The subject case

Use: As its name implies, this case is used when the noun is the subject of a sentence. There are two particular cases when subjects are not marked for this case, which we shall meet later.

Form: When a noun is on its own, without any definite article or other suffix or adjective or genitive noun after it, the form of the subject case is marked by no stress-tone on any vowels in the word. Also, on feminine nouns ending in a consonant you must also add **-i**; this also includes women's names, although with these it is optional.

mindi	knife (subject)
naagi	woman (subject)
baabuur	car (subject)

The premodifier form

Use: This noun form is not a case in that it is not used for a particular grammatical purpose. It is the form a noun takes when it is part of a noun phrase in which something comes after it. This may be a grammatical suffix or another noun or an adjective. For most nouns the premodifier form is the same as the absolutive form, but for some it is marked by a particular stress-tone pattern according to the rules given on p. 43.

Exercises

1 Change the following nouns to the subject case:

1 báre
2 áf
3 Soomaalí
4 naág
5 sháah
6 gabádh

2 Change the following nouns from subject case to absolutive case; put in the stress-tone marks for this exercise:

1 habeen
2 bariis
3 magac
4 qalmo
5 hilib
6 warqadi

Word order in Somali

The basic order of words in Somali is as follows:

SUBJECT   OBJECT   VERB

However, you must not forget to use a mood classifier or one of the focus constructions which we shall meet soon.

Nin	**wáa**	**tegey**		A man went.
subject	mood cl.	verb		
a man	mood cl.	went		
Nin	**sháah**	**wúu**	**cabbay**	A man drank tea.
subject	object	mood cl. + pronoun	verb	
a man	tea	mood cl. + he	drank	

As you can see, the positive declarative mood classifier generally comes after the subject and object. The rule of thumb for this mood classifier is that it comes as close to the verb as possible.

As you will see in the dialogues and reading passages, it is also possible to put objects and nouns associated with preverbal prepositions after the verb.

This word order also holds for imperative sentences.

Kóob	kéen!		Bring a cup.
object	verb (the subject is implied in the verb)		
a cup	bring!		

Adverbial words such as time adverbials come generally at the beginning of the sentence, although they may also come at the end of a sentence.

Sháleyto	baríis	wáan	cunay	Yesterday I ate rice.
adverb	direct object	mood cl. + I	verb	
yesterday	rice	mood cl. + I	ate	

Exercise

3 Unjumble the lists of words to form correct Somali sentences:

1	dhán	caáno		
2	tágayaa	gúriga	waan	
3	qortay	Canabi	warqád	wáy
4	tág	dúgsiga		
5	furay	Maxamed	albáabka	wáa
6	kéen	kibís		
7	cuntay	naagi	hílib	wáy
8	Maxamed	gaádhayaa	wúu	dukáanka
9	búug	wáy	dhakhtaradi	akhriday
10	wáa	warqád	shimbiri	qaadday

The definite article in Somali

In English the definite article is the word 'the'. In Somali, this is expressed by a suffix which begins with **k-** for masculine nouns and **t-** for feminine nouns. The vowel that follows the consonant depends on the context and case of the word. The different possibilities are shown in the following table:

	absolutive	*subject*
masculine	**-ka**	**-ku**
feminine	**-ta**	**-tu**
masculine	**-kií**	**-kii**
feminine	**-tií**	**-tii**

Note that the difference between absolutive and subject case with the **-kií/-tií** definite article is the same as the difference between nouns, namely no stress-tone on the subject case.

A rough guide for when to use **-ka** and when to use **-kií** is given below.

-kií/-tií/-kii/-tii: This article is used when the noun has previously been referred to in the conversation or if the noun is referred to in the past. It may sometimes be more appropriately translated into English with the demonstrative 'that' or 'those'.

> **Búuggií wáan akhriyay.**   I read the book. (**-kií** is used here because 'the book' is referred to in the past; it is presumably a book which is known to the speaker and hearer)

-ka/-ta/-ku/-tu: This article is used more generally: specifically, when a noun is referred to for the first time in a conversation or if the noun is not known to the speaker. It is also generally used when referring to nouns in the future or in the present.

> **Dukáanka waan tágayaa.**   I am going to the shop. (**-ka** is used here because the shop is generally being referred in the present/near future. If it was a particular shop which was the topic of conversation then **-kií** would probably be used)

This is intended as a guide only to the use of **-kií/-tií** and **-ka/-ta**. This is an area of Somali usage that will become clearer as you become more experienced with Somali.

On pp. 40–1 we mentioned the premodifier form. The definite article is one instance when the premodifier form is used in a noun. Of the declensions we have already met, 1, 2 and 3, the premodifier is the same as the absolutive form except for the plural of each declension. In the premodifier form of the plural of all of these declensions *the final vowel of the plural form takes stress-tone.*

So we can now give some examples of nouns with the definite article:

dukáan	a shop	**dukáanka**	the shop
kóob	a cup	**kóobka**	the cup
galáb	an afternoon	**galábta**	the afternoon
naago	women	**naagáha**	the women
baabuurro	lorries	**baabuurráha**	the lorries

There are various sound changes that occur when the definite article is added to nouns ending in vowels and certain consonants. The changes that occur with the feminine article are identical to the sound changes which occur when a verb ending beginning with -t- is added to certain verbs; see pp. 18–19. We shall not repeat these changes here so go back to that section now and review the changes. Examples are given below of these sound changes with nouns.

One sound change particular to nouns is if a noun ends in **o** and the definite article is added, not only does the **t** change to **d** but the **o** also changes to **a**. Example: **casharro**, 'lessons', gives **casharráda** with the definite article. Notice in these examples also the stress-tone pattern of the premodifier form.

nabád	+ ta	**nabádda**	the peace
gabádh	+ tií	**gabádhií**	the girl[1]
mindí	+ ta	**mindída**	the knife
hál	+ tií	**háshií**	the female camel
subáx	+ ta	**subáxda**	the morning
inammo	+ ta	**inammáda**	the boys

The sound changes that occur with the masculine nouns are as follows:

(a) **k** disappears when it follows the following sounds: **q, kh, c, x, h,** and **'** (i.e. all the guttural consonants). Also, if the final vowel of the noun is short **a** and the final consonant is a guttural consonant, the vowel **a** changes to the same vowel as the definite article.

mádax	+ ka	**mádaxa**	the head
súuq	+ kií	**súuqií**	the market
ráh	+ ku	**rúhu**	the frog
mágac	+ kií	**mágicií**	the name

(b) **k** changes to **h** when it follows any vowel except **i** and the final vowel changes to the same vowel as that of the definite article, but always short.

| báre | + ka | **baráha** | the teacher[2] |
| gacmo | + kií | **gacmíhií** | the hands |

(c) **k** changes to **g** when it follows **g**, **i**, **w** or **y**.

gúri	+ kií	**gúrigií**	the house
éy	+ ka	**éyga**	the dog
cádow	+ kií	**cádowgií**	the enemy

Exercises

4 Combine the nouns and articles:

1 magac   ka
2 shimbir tii
3 shaah   ku
4 kubbad   ta
5 subax   tu
6 kursi   kii

5 Translate the following sentences from English into Somali:

1 The boys took the female camel.
2 Is the teacher going to teach the student?
3 You (pl.) built the wall.
4 Go to the shop!
5 The girl found the shoes.
6 The women ate the bread and drank the tea.

Dialogue

Vocabulary

khamiís (f.)	Thursday	**búu**	focus marker **báa**
soó mar	to pass along		+ **uu**, 'he'
jíd (m. d4)	street	**arkaa**	he sees
bartáme (m. d7)	centre	**mágacíisu**	his name (subject)
magaálo (f. d6)	town	**má la**	are you well?
kú yaál	which is in	**wanaagsányahay**	
háwo (f. d6)	air, weather	**bal**	and as to...
kuláyl (m.)	heat, hot	**adíga**	you (emphatic)

booqánayaa	I am visiting (present progressive of **booqo**, a conjugation 3B verb)
booqo	to visit
meél (f. d1)	place
dhoẃ	near
deggéntahay	she lives
sów má aha?	is it not, isn't it?
áad iyo áad	very much so
waan harraadsánahay	I am thirsty

Maanta waa khamiis. Cali waa soo marayaa jidka bartamaha magaalada ku yaal. Hawadu waa kulayl. Cali saaxiibkiisa buu arkaa. Jidka wuu soo marayaa. Magaciisu waa Rooble.

CALI: Waryaa, Rooble.
ROOBLE: Waryaa, Cali. Is ka warran. Ma la wanaagsanyahay?
CALI: Waan fiicanahay. Bal is ka warran adigu.
ROOBLE: Waa la wanaagsanyahay.
CALI: Xaggee baad tagaysaa?
ROOBLE: Waxaan booqanayaa walaashay.
CALI: Xaggee bay deggentahay?
ROOBLE: Meel dhow bay deggentahay.
CALI: Maanta waa kulayl, sow ma aha?
ROOBLE: Haa, aad iyo aad. Waan harraadsanahay.
CALI: Waa yahay, nabad gelyo.
ROOBLE: Nabad gelyo.

Today is Thursday. Cali is going along the street in the centre of the town. The weather is hot. Cali sees his friend. He is going along the street. His name is Rooble.

CALI: *Hi, Rooble.*
ROOBLE: *Hi, Cali. How are you? Are you well?*
CALI: *I am well. And how are you?*
ROOBLE: *I am well.*
CALI: *Where are you going?*
ROOBLE: *I am visiting my sister.*
CALI: *Where does she live?*
ROOBLE: *She lives nearby [in a near place].*
CALI: *Today it is hot, isn't it?*
ROOBLE: *Yes, very. I am thirsty.*
CALI: *Right, goodbye.*
ROOBLE: *Goodbye.*

Language in use

Declension 4

stress-tone pattern	singular	*on the penultimate or only vowel*
	plural	*no stress-tone*
gender	singular	*always masculine*
	plural	*always masculine*
word shape in singular		*one syllable ending in a consonant*
plural formation		*add -a and a copy of the final consonant*
premodifier form	singular	*as absolutive*
	plural	*stress-tone on final vowel*

Note that there is one exception to the plural gender. The noun **wíil**, 'boy, son', becomes **wiilal** in the plural but is feminine in gender, thus with the definite article becomes **wiilásha**.

Examples of declension 4 nouns:

míis	table	**miisas**	tables
áf	mouth, language	**afaf**	mouths, languages
qóys	family	**qoysas**	families

The only sound change to be aware of in this declension is the change between **n** and **m**, for example: **nín**, 'man'; **niman**, 'men', (see pronunciation guide).

Exercise

6 Make the singular nouns plural and the plural nouns singular; all are declension 4 nouns:

1 dab   fire
2 buugag   books
3 koob   cup
4 roobab   rains
5 dal   country
6 sanan   noses

Declension 5

stress-tone pattern	singular	on the penultimate vowel
	plural	on the final vowel
gender	singular	always masculine
	plural	always feminine
word shape in singular		1–3 syllables but never 1 syllable with 1 short vowel
plural formation		change the gender and stress-tone pattern according to what is given above
premodifier form		as absolutive in both singular and plural

Note that the only difference between these nouns in the singular and the plural is in the gender and stress-tone pattern. In writing therefore there is no difference in the way the words look. In practice this does not often lead to ambiguities because the definite article (or other noun suffix) and/or verbal agreement shows the gender of the noun and therefore the number.

Examples of declension 5 nouns:

éy	dog	eý	dogs
Soomaáli	a Somali	**Soomaalí**	Somalis
mádax	head	**madáx**	heads

You will remember that 'head' is also a declension 2 noun and thus also has the plural form **madaxyo**.[3] This is an example of a noun that has two possibilities. There are a few of these in Somali, and they will be indicated as such in the vocabularies and the glossary. Another example is **cáday**, given below.

If the noun ends in a diphthong with no following consonant, then the diphthong counts as one vowel.

| **árdey** | student | **ardéy** | students |
| **cáday** | tooth-brushing stick | **cadáy** or **cadayo** | tooth-brushing sticks |

There are no sound changes particular to this declension, but don't forget the general sound changes when you add the definite article.

Exercises

7 Make the singular nouns plural and the plural nouns singular. In this exercise put in the stress-tone marks. All the nouns are from declension 5.

1. madáx — heads
2. éy — dog
3. áwr — burden camel[4]
4. haád — large birds (especially birds of prey)
5. Caráb — Arabs
6. dibí — bulls

8 Translate the following sentences from English into Somali:

1. Read the books.
2. He brought the cups.
3. The students entered the university.
4. They reached the country.
5. The birds of prey are waiting.
6. The female doctor refused the letter.

Conjugation 2

In Somali there are additions that may be made to basic verb forms in order to alter the meaning of the basic verb in some predictable way. Two of these affixes when added to basic verbs form verbs of conjugation 2. Although very similar, the affixes do differ a little in the verb patterns, and so they are divided into conjugations 2A and 2B.

Conjugation 2A

This conjugation is formed by adding the suffix **-i** to the basic verb form. When the **-i** is added it makes the verb into a causative form. For example, the verb **toos** means 'to get up'. When **-i** is added, **toosi**, the verb means 'to cause to get up, wake up (trans.)'.

Nínku wáa toosay.	The man got up.
Nínku wáa toosiyay.	The man caused him to get up.[5]

Along with this idea of forming a causative, the **-i** suffix also forms transitive verbs from intransitive verbs, for example **kar** means 'to boil (intr.)' whereas when **-i** is added the verb becomes 'to boil (trans.)'.

Baríisku wáa karay.	The rice boiled/cooked.
Baríiska wúu kariyay.	He boiled/cooked the rice.
Míisku wáa jabay.	The table broke.
Míiska wáy jabiyeen.	They broke the table.

There are some sound changes when **-i** is added to a basic form verb:

(a) If the suffix is added to a verb ending in **g** or **q** then that consonant changes to **j**.

daaq	to graze	**daaji**	to cause to graze, pasture
hagaag	to be straight	**hagaaji**	to straighten, mend

(b) If the **-i** suffix is added to a verb that ends in the vowel **a** plus a guttural consonant then the **a** changes to **i** (this is vowel assimilation across a guttural consonant again).

bax	to leave	**bixi**	to cause to leave, extract, pay (money)
ba'	to be destroyed	**bi'i**	to destroy

We shall now look at the verb forms of conjugation 2A. We shall give here an example pattern of conjugation 2A in the tenses we have already met.

Plural imperative

You will remember from Lesson 1 that to form the plural imperative of verbs ending in **-i** you add **-ya**.

Bixíya!	Pay (pl.)!
Karíya!	Cook (pl.) it!

General past

	verb stem	ending	verb form
I	kari	ay	**kariyay**
you (sg.)	kari	tay	**karisay**
he, it (m.)	kari	ay	**kariyay**
she, it (f.)	kari	tay	**karisay**
we	kari	nay	**karinnay**
you (pl.)	kari	teen	**kariseen**
they	kari	een	**kariyeen**

You can see from this table that when the past tense endings are added to a conjugation 2A verb there are some sound changes.

- **t** changes to **s**;
- **y** is inserted between **i** and **a**;
- the **n** of the first person plural ending is geminated.

Note that the verb **akhri** which we have already met is a conjugation 1 verb, even though it ends in **i**. You may hear it used as a conjugation 2 verb sometimes.

Present progressive

For the present progressive form of conjugation 2 the base form of the verb is not the imperative, as with the conjugation 1 verbs, but the infinitive. To form the infinitive of conjugation 2A verbs just add **n** to the base form and put a stress-tone on the **i**.

bi'i   **bi'ín** (infinitive)
toosi   **toosín** (infinitive)

	verb stem	progressive marker	ending	verb form
I	karin	ay	aa	**karínayaa**
you (sg.)	karin	ay	taa	**karínaysaa**
he, it (m.)	karin	ay	aa	**karínayaa**
she, it (f.)	karin	ay	taa	**karínaysaa**
we	karin	ay	naa	**karínaynaa**
you (pl.)	karin	ay	taan	**karínaysaan**
they	karin	ay	aan	**karínayaan**

Note that the same sound change, **t** changing to **s**, occurs as with the conjugation 1 verbs and that the stress-tone pattern is the same as that of the conjugation 1 verbs.

Exercises

9 Write out in full the forms of the following verbs in the general past and the present progressive:

1 bixi   to cause to leave, extract, pay
2 jooji   to stop
3 dhoofi   to export

10 Translate into Somali:

1 The woman woke the boy.
2 The man is pasturing the burden camels.
3 Maxamed broke the table.
4 Canab paid.
5 A woman cooked the meat.
6 The enemy destroyed the farm.

11 Put in the correct endings to the nouns and verbs in the following sentences:

1 Waad keen _____. 'You brought it.'
2 Mindi _____ waa jab _____. 'The knife broke.'
3 Maanta inamm _____ magaal _____ way teg _____. 'Today the boys went to the town.'
4 Maxamed awr_____ wuu daaji_____. 'Maxamed grazed the burden camels.'
5 Niman_____ way ka bex_____. 'The men left.'

Asking 'What is it?'

The way to ask 'What is it?' in Somali is **Wáa maxay?**
The reply to this question you know already: **Waa . . ..**

Wáa maxay? Waa qálin.   What is it? It is a pen.

Practise using this expression whenever you have the opportunity.

Vocabulary building

Days of the week

The days of the week in Somali are as follows; they are taken from the Arabic names of the days:

Sunday	**axád**	axádda
Monday	**isniín**	isniínta
Tuesday	**salaasá**	salaasáda (sometimes: **talaadá**)
Wednesday	**arbacá**	arbacáda
Thursday	**khamiís**	khamiísta
Friday	**jímce**	jimcáha
Saturday	**sábti**	sábtida

Note that the names of the days are given here also with the definite article. When you refer to a particular day you must use the definite article. If you are referring to a day in the past, last week, for example, then you must use the **-kií/-tií** article but if you are referring to a day in the future or the present you must use the **-ka/-ta** article.

Jimcáha waan tágayaa. I am going on Friday.
Khamiístií wáan helay. I found it on Thursday.

Exercise

12 Translate the following sentences into English; note where the day of the week comes in the word order:

1 Sabtidii awrta way daajiyeen.
2 Khamiistii guriga waan ka baxay.
3 Arbacadii wuu bukay.
4 Isniintii way hagaajisay.
5 Salaasada waan akhriyayaa.

Reading practice

Now that we have met conjugation 2, in all the vocabularies the conjugation to which a particular verb belongs will be given with the verb. This is also given in the glossary. The conjugation is simply given as a number in parentheses following the verb.

Vocabulary

subáx (f. d2)	morning
subaxnímo (f. d6)	in the morning (lit.: 'morningness')
qól (m. d4)	room
carruúr (f. collec.)	children
masaájid (m. d2)	mosque
ayúu	focus marker **ayáa** + **uu**, 'he'
wada	together (this word always comes just before the verb)
quraacánayaa	is having breakfast
quraác (f. d2)	breakfast
ká dib	after
dúgsi (m. d2)	school

joogaan	general present tense of **joog**, 'they are at'
joog (1)	to be in a place (only used for people or animals)
salaan (1) (**salaamaa**)	to greet
fiicántihiin	you (pl.) are well
fiicánnahay	we are well
heés (f. d1)	song
báynu	focus marker **báa** + **-aynu** 'we' (incl.)
qaad (1)	to take; when used with **hées**, 'sing'

Waa isniin, subaxnimo. Canabi waa toostay. Shaaha way sameynaysaa. Qol kale way galaysaa. Caruurta way toosinaysaa. Ninkeedu masaajidka ayuu tagay, imminkana guriga wuu galayaa. Dabadeedna qoysku waa wada quraacanayaa. Shaah way cabbayaan kibis subaglehna way cunayaan. Quraacda ka dib caruurtu dugsiga way tagayaan.

Imminka dugsiga way joogaan, macallinkana way salaamayaan:

CARUURTA: Subax wanaagsan, macallin.
MACALLINKA: Subax wanaagsan. Ma fiicantihiin?
CARUURTA: Waannu fiicannahay. Maanta maxaannu samaynaynaa?
MACALLINKA: Maanta hees baynnu qaadaynaa.

It is Monday morning. Canab has got up. She is making tea. She goes into another room. She is waking the children. Her husband went to the mosque, and now he is entering the house. Then the family is having breakfast together. They are drinking tea and eating bread with butter. After breakfast the children will go to school.

Now they are at school and are greeting the teacher:

THE CHILDREN: *Good morning, teacher.*
THE TEACHER: *Good morning. Are you well?*
THE CHILDREN: *We are well. Today what are we doing?*
THE TEACHER: *Today we are going to sing a song.*

Notes

1 Although written with a single **dh** this is in fact a geminate. See pronunciation guide for further details.
2 This noun is from declension 7, which will be dealt with later.
3 Note that the plural form **madáx** refers to heads of countries, governments etc.

4 A camel that is used for carrying household goods, tents and so on will be referred to in this book as a 'burden camel'.
5 Remember that this sentence could also be translated as 'the man caused her/it/them to get up'.

4 Bill waa tegayaa geeska Afrika

Bill is going to the Horn of Africa

By the end of this lesson you should:
- know declensions 6 and 7
- know conjugation 2B
- know something of the use of adjectives
- know about the genitive case
- be able to use numbers

Dialogue

Bill plans to go to the Horn of Africa

Vocabulary

búu	focus marker **báa** + **uu**, 'he'
tégi doonaa	he will go to
doon	to want, also auxiliary verb for the future tense
gées (m. d1)	horn
macállin (m. d2)	teacher
dhig (1)	to teach
áf (m. d4)	language
ingriísi (m.)	English
áf ingriísiga	the English language
ímminka	now
-se	but
bartaa	he learns (from **baro**, 'to learn', conj. 3B)
wáayo	because
lába	two
bíl (f. d1)	month

biloód	genitive form of 'months'
labá biloód ká díb	in two months
ká dhígi doonaa	he will teach at
dúgsi (m. d2)	school
magaálo (f. d6)	town
waqoóyi (m.)	north
dál (m. d4)	country
kú taal	which is in (f.)
carruúr (f. d1 collec.)	children
waxbari (2A)	to teach
macállinkíisu	his teacher (subj.)
la yidhaahdó	called (lit.: which one says)
saaxíibkíisa	his friend
jéer (m. d4)	time, occasion
todobáadkiíba	each week
toddobáad (m. d2)	week
ayúu	focus marker **ayáa** + **uu**, 'he'
lá kulmaa	he meets with (general present tense of the verb **kulan**)
kulan (1, kulmaa)	to meet; **lá**: with
hádal (1, hadlaa)	to speak; **lá**: with; **kú**: in
wúxuu yidhaahdaa	he says (a type of focus construction)
adág (adj.)	difficult
wúxuu kú celiyaa	he replies (general present of **kú celi**)
kú celi	to reply
máya	no
waláal (m. d1)	brother; used here to address Bill; the word may be used generally to address anyone. **walaál** (f. d1) 'sister', is used when addressing women
fudúd (adj.)	easy
qoslaan	they laugh (general present of the verb **qosol**)
qosol (1, qoslaa)	to laugh

Bill geeska Afrika wuu tegi doonaa.

Bill waa macallin. Af ingiriisiga wuu dhigaa. Imminkase af soomaaliga buu bartaa, waayo geeska Afrika ayuu tegi doonaa laba bilood ka dib. Af ingiriisiga buu ka dhigi doonaa dugsi ku yaal magaalada Burco. Burco waa magaalo waqooyiga dalka Soomaaliya/ dalka Somaliland ku taal. Wuxuu waxbari doonaa carruurta magaalada Burco. Macallinkiisa af Soomaaligu waa nin Yoonis la yidhaahdo. Yoonis waa saaxiibkiisa. Laba jeer toddobaadkiiba ayuu Yoonis la kulmaa. Wayna ku wada hadlaan af Soomaaliga. Bill wuxuu yidhaahdaa:

'Af Soomaaligu waa af adag!'

Yoonisna wuxuu ku celiyaa:

'Maya walaal af Soomaaligu waa af fudud. Af ingiriisiguse waa af adag!'

Wayna wada qoslaan.

Bill is going to go to the Horn of Africa.

Bill is a teacher. He teaches the English language. But now he is learning the Somali language because he is going to go to the Horn of Africa in two months. He will teach the English language at a school in the town of Burco. Burco is a town in the north of Somalia/ Somaliland. He will teach the children of the town of Burco. His Somali teacher is a man called Yoonis. Yoonis is his friend. Twice a week he meets with Yoonis. They speak in Somali. Bill says:

'Somali is a difficult language!'

And Yoonis replies:

'No, brother, Somali is an easy language. But English is a difficult language!'

And they laugh together.

Language in use

Declension 6

stress-tone pattern	singular	*on the penultimate vowel*
	plural	*on the penultimate vowel*
gender	singular	*always feminine*
	plural	*always masculine*
word shape in singular		*ends in -o*
plural formation		*add -oyin*
premodifier form	singular	*stress-tone moves to the final vowel*
	plural	*as absolutive*

Examples of declension 6 nouns:

hoóyo	mother	**hoyoóyin**	mothers
wáddo	road	**waddoóyin**	roads
waddáda	the road	**waddoóyinka**	the roads

Exercise

1 Make the singular nouns plural and the plural nouns singular; all nouns are declension 6 nouns:

1 sheekooyin   tales, stories
2 dawo   medicine
3 magaalooyin   towns
4 shaneemo   film
5 kiilooyin   kilos
6 ayeeyo   grandmother

Declension 7

stress-tone pattern	singular	on the penultimate vowel
	plural	no stress-tone
gender	singular	always masculine
	plural	always feminine
word shape in singular		ends in *-e*
plural formation		delete *-e* and add *-ayaal*
premodifier form		stress-tone on final vowel in both singular and plural

Examples of declension 7 nouns:

aábbe   father   **aabbayaal**   fathers
báre   teacher   **barayaal**   teachers
baráha the teacher   **barayaásha**   the teachers

Note that there are two words that do not end in *-e* but which are declension 7 nouns:

óday   old man, elder   **odayaal**   old men, elders
bíyo   water   **biyayaal**   waters
biyáha the water   **biyayaásha**   the waters

Exercise

2 Make the singular nouns plural and the plural nouns singular; all nouns are declension 7 nouns:

1 fure   key
2 danjirayaal   ambassadors
3 xoghaye   secretary

4 golayaal   committees
5 waraabayaal hyenas
6 madaxweyne   president

Conjugation 2B

This conjugation is made up of verbs that are formed by adding the suffix **-ee** to nouns and adjectives. With adjectives the meaning is 'to make like the adjective', for example: **cas** means 'red' and **casee** means 'to make red, redden'.

With nouns the meaning is not always quite so clear and it is best to learn the individual verbs themselves. Verb meanings can also be extended from their literal meaning, for example, **cad** means 'white, clear' and **caddee** means 'to make white, make clear' and also, by extension, 'to explain'. Examples of conjugation 2B verbs are the following:

samee	to do, make
safee	to clean
cashee	to eat dinner

The verb forms of conjugation 2B are similar to the forms of conjugation 2A. We shall give here an example pattern of conjugation 2B in the tenses we have already met.

Plural imperative

The plural imperative is formed as with conjugation 2A, that is to say **-ya** is added.

Sameéya!	Make it (pl.)!
Casheéya!	Have dinner (pl.)!

General past

	verb stem	ending	verb form
I	samee	ay	**sameeyay**
you (sg.)	samee	tay	**sameysay**
he, it (m.)	samee	ay	**sameeyay**
she, it (f.)	samee	tay	**sameysay**
we	samee	nay	**sameynay**
you (pl.)	samee	teen	**sameyseen**
they	samee	een	**sameeyeen**

As you can see there are some sound changes when the past tense endings are added to this conjugation:
(a) when an ending beginning with a consonant is added the final -ee changes to -ey;
(b) t changes to s when it follows y;
(c) y is inserted between e and a.

Present progressive

As with the conjugation 2A verbs the present progressive base form is the infinitive. To form the infinitive of conjugation 2B verbs, the ee changes to ey and n is added. Stress-tone is placed on the y.

samee   **sameýn** (infinitive)
cashee   **casheýn** (infinitive)

Thus the form of the present progressive is as follows:

	verb stem	progressive marker	ending	verb form
I	sameyn	ay	aa	**sameýnayaa**
you (sg.)	sameyn	ay	taa	**sameýnaysaa**
he, it (m.)	sameyn	ay	aa	**sameýnayaa**
she, it (f.)	sameyn	ay	taa	**sameýnaysaa**
we	sameyn	ay	naa	**sameýnaynaa**
you (pl.)	sameyn	ay	taan	**sameýnaysaan**
they	sameyn	ay	aan	**sameýnayaan**

Note that the same sound change occurs with **t** as with the present progressive in the other conjugations.

Exercises

3 Write out in full the forms of the following verbs in the general past and the present progressive:

1 malee   to suppose
2 caddee   to explain, make white, make clear
3 cawee   to spend the evening

4 Translate into Somali; the appropriate verb is given in brackets:

1 He is driving the burden camels.   (kexee 2B)
2 The children are cleaning the tables.   (safee 2B)
3 She is explaining the book.   (caddee 2B)
4 They finished the house yesterday.   (dhammee 2B)
5 Will you eat lunch today?   (qadee 2B)

Using ká wárran

We have already seen what **ká wárran** means in the phrase **Is ká wárran**, 'Give news about oneself'. The phrase may be used to ask about other things as well, for example **Shaqáda ká wárran**, 'give news about the work' or 'How is your work?'. You can also ask about somebody's family:

Qóyska ká wárran.	How is the family?
Carruúrta ká wárran.	How are the children?

Adjectives

The use of adjectives in Somali is not a topic we can deal with just in this one section. More will be said in later sections. There are two main types of adjective in Somali: basic adjectives and derived adjectives. The basic adjectives are those that stand on their own and are not formed from any other word; there are about 45 such adjectives. Some of the more common basic adjectives are:

fóg	far
dhoẃ	near
fudúd	light, easy
culús	heavy
adág	difficult, strong

Other adjectives are formed by adding various endings to nouns and verbs. The two most common endings are given below.

-an This is added to verbs and nouns and means 'being in the state described by the verb or noun'. This should be made clear by studying the following examples:

xidh	to close	**xidhán**	closed
fur	to open	**furán**	open
gub	to burn	**gubán**	burnt

| **balláadh** | broadness | **ballaadhán** | broad |
| **gáab** | shortness | **gaabán** | short |

-san This ending also forms adjectives from nouns and verbs, and implies being in the state described by the noun or verb.

farax	to be happy	**faraxsán**	happy
dhereg	to be satisfied, full	**dheregsán**	satisfied, full
qurúx	beauty	**quruxsán**	beautiful
cádho	anger	**cadhosán**	angry

Despite the fact that many adjectives are derived from nouns or verbs, as shown above, in the rest of the course we shall simply take adjectives on their own. If you wish to find out from which word a particular adjective is derived look in the glossary at the back or in a good dictionary. Note that some adjectives which have the ending **-án** or **-sán** have no particular base word from which they may be seen to be derived.

Note that adjectives, whether derived or basic, almost always have a stress-tone on the final vowel.

In Somali the adjective follows the noun it describes.[1]

gúri cusúb	a new house
shimbír yár	a small bird
albáab cás	a red door

If the definite article is used with the noun + adjective phrase, then it is attached only to the noun.

gúriga cusúb	the new house
shimbírtii yár	the small bird
albáabka cás	the red door

Subject case

Adjectives mark the subject case by lack of stress-tone, as we have seen in nouns. They also add **-i**. In Lesson 13 we shall see the reason for this.

If the noun + adjective phrase is the subject of a sentence then the subject marking goes on the final part of the phrase. Compare carefully the subject marking in the following two sentences:

Nínku wáa tagay.	The man went.
Nínka dheeri wáa tagay.	The tall man went.
(**dhéer** means 'tall')	

Gabádhu wáa tagtay. The girl went.
Gabádha yari wáa toostay. The small girl got up.
(**yár** means 'small')

Note that in the examples without adjectives the definite article is in the subject case form because it is the final part of the subject noun phrase. In the examples with adjectives, on the other hand, the definite article shows the absolutive case because the definite article on the noun is not the last part of the noun phrase, the adjective is, and so that is marked for the subject case by no stress-tone and **-i**.

Exercise

5 Translate the following sentences into Somali:

1 The tall man ate the meat.
2 The beautiful girl drank the milk. (For 'drink' use the verb **dhan** (1, **dhamaa**), which is used when drinking milk.)
3 They are reading the easy book.
4 You are taking the heavy suitcase.
5 They broke the new door.
6 She wrote the good book.

The plural form of adjectives

The plural form of an adjective is used when the adjective is describing a plural noun. It is formed by taking the largest possible syllable from the beginning of the adjective and adding this to the beginning of the singular form. So, for the adjective **cusúb**, 'new', the largest possible syllable from the beginning of the word is **cus-**. This is then added to the singular form, giving **cuscusúb**. If an adjective is made up of only one syllable the syllable is simply repeated. For example, the plural form of **yár** is **yaryár**.

quruxsán	beautiful (sg.)	**qurquruxsán**	beautiful (pl.)
fudúd	easy, light (sg.)	**fudfudúd**	easy, light (pl.)
adág	difficult, hard (sg.)	**ad'adág**	difficult, hard (pl.)[2]

There are some adjectives that repeat the first syllable but without any consonant at the end of the syllable. When this syllable is then added to the singular form the consonant immediately following the copied syllable is geminated or doubled. Adjectives whose first largest syllable ends in **b** tend to behave in this way.

gaabán	short (sg.)	**gaaggaabán**	short (pl.)
laabán	folded (sg.)	**laallaabán**	folded (pl.)

Note: **jabán**, 'broken' (sg.), **jajabán**, 'broken' (pl.) (since **j** may not be doubled this form is as shown).

There are two irregular plural forms:

dhéer	long, tall (sg.)	**dhaadhéer**	long, tall (pl.)
wéyn	big (sg.)	**waawéyn**	big (pl.)

Plural forms are marked for the subject case in the same way as the singular forms.

Plural forms are not always used when an adjective is describing a plural noun. There are no hard and fast rules to say when a plural form should be used. As a rule of thumb you could say that the plural forms of short adjectives tend to be used more often than those of long adjectives.

Exercise

6 Translate the following sentences into Somali:

1 The tall men went to the town.
2 Look at the large birds.
3 Are you (pl.) going to the far towns?
4 He found the broken cups.
5 I am bringing the heavy suitcases.
6 The girls are reading good books.

The genitive case

The genitive case in Somali is the case used to indicate possession. It is the possessor in such a phrase that is in the genitive case. So, for example, the phrase 'Maxamed's book' would be translated into Somali with 'Maxamed' in the genitive case in Somali.

The form of the genitive case differs from the absolutive primarily in the stress-tone pattern, and the rule for stress-tone marking is very simple.

The stress-tone pattern for the genitive case: **stress-tone on the final or only vowel.**

So the example given above, 'Maxamed's book', is translated as follows:

búuggií Maxaméd	Maxamed's book

There are some nouns that have an extra part in the genitive.

(a) Nouns that are feminine in the singular and do not end in **-o** often add **-eéd** (which becomes **-yeéd** following **i**).

xanúun lugeéd	foot pain
pain foot (genitive)	
áf shimbireéd	a mouth of a bird, beak

Note: the use of this suffix tends to imply that the genitive is less specific: for example: **dhár naageéd** can mean 'women's clothes' in general, whereas **dhár naág** means 'a woman's clothes', meaning some particular woman. The use of the **-eéd** ending in this context may be found with some other nouns.

(b) Nouns that are feminine in the singular and form the plural in **-o** add **-od** when the plural is in the genitive case.

mídabka shimbiroód	the colour of birds

Nouns for domestic animals which would fall into these two categories end in **-aád** instead of **-eéd** or **-oód**.

hárag lo'aád	cow's hide	**ló'**(f. sg.), 'cattle'
caanó riyaád	goats' milk	**riyo**, 'goats'
		rí (f. d1), 'goat'

There is another way of expressing possession, which we shall look at later.

Note that when the definite article is added to a noun the noun itself must be in the premodifier form and the article in the absolutive or subject case, according to its role in the sentence. There is no specific genitive form for the definite article. Thus, the genitive form is only used with nouns that have no suffix added to them.

qálinka árdeyga	the student's pen
Barayaásha dúgsigu wáy tegeen.	The teachers of the school went.

When you use adjectives with nouns in genitive constructions you need to be a little careful. If the adjective is describing the possessor then the phrase is straightforward:

qálinka macállinka cusúb	the pen of the new teacher

If, however, you are using an adjective to describe the possessed noun, then you must use the word **ee** as follows:

qálinka cusúb ee macállinka   the new pen of the teacher

Exercises

7 Translate the following pairs of nouns and make them into genitive constructions:

1	door	the house
2	the Horn of Africa	the coast
3	the week	the day
4	Cali	pen
5	meat	cow
6	language	Arabs

8 Translate the following sentences into Somali:

1 Cali broke Jawaahir's pen.
2 She explained Samatar's good book.
3 They cleaned the elder's shoes.
4 The ambassador's new secretary is going to the capital city of the country.
5 You (pl.) went to the centre of the city.

Numbers

The important point to remember about numbers in Somali is that they are all nouns and share all the characteristics of nouns which we have met and will meet. The gender of the numbers is easy to remember; all numbers up to and including eight are feminine and all the rest are masculine. The numbers one to ten are given below:

1	ków	6	líx
2	lába	7	toddobá
3	sáddex	8	siddéed
4	áfar	9	sagaal
5	shán	10	toban

Since numbers are nouns when a number is used with another word, as in 'three books', the number is in the premodifier form and the noun being counted is in the genitive case. Note that the appropriate genitive form is used according to the rules given above in the section dealing with the genitive. There is an important rule to remember, however: nouns occuring with numbers are in the genitive *singular* form unless the noun is from declension 1, 2 or 3, in which case it is in the genitive plural form (except, of course, with the number one).

áfar dál	four countries
labá kaboód	two shoes

The stress-tone pattern on the numbers in the premodifier form is as the absolutive form given above except for the numbers with no stress-tone in the absolutive which then take a stress-tone on the final vowel. **Note: lába** also does this, giving **labá**.

sáddex buúg	three books
toddobá nín	seven men
sagaál riyaád	nine goats
labá naagoód	two women

When the definite article is used with a noun and number combination, the definite article is added to the number.

sáddexda buúg	the three books
toddobáda nín	the seven men

The number one

There are various ways of saying 'one' in Somali, depending on how the word is used.

In counting the word **ków** is used, as in the list of numbers above.

When the number one is used to count a noun, as in the phrase 'one book', the word used is **hál**.

hál buúg	one book
hál naág	one woman[3]

When you are referring to one on its own, as in the sentence 'They ate one', you use the word **míd**.

Míd	**báy**	**cuneen.**	They ate one.
one	focus + they	ate	

Exercises

9 Take a number from the left-hand list and use it with a noun from the right-hand list:

1	hal	guri
2	sagaal	bil
3	shan	baabuur
4	saddex	koob
5	toban	kab

10 Translate the following sentences into Somali:

1 Take two shoes!
2 How are the three schools?
3 They built seven houses.
4 The teacher teaches eight students.
5 He brought five donkeys.
6 Cali is pasturing nine burden camels.

Dialogue

Maxamed and Axmed decide to have something to eat

Vocabulary

dukáan (m. d2 **dukaammo**)	shop
wáddo (f. d6)	street, road
waan fiicánahay	I am well
sháqo (f. d6)	work
subáxdií	in the morning (lit.: the morning)
tágsigáyga	my taxi
tágsi (m. d2)	taxi
báan	focus marker **báa** + **-aan**, 'I'
watay	I drove
iíbis (m. d2)	trade
wáx (m., **waxyaabo** (m.))	thing; used here as a sort of empty direct object roughly meaning 'something'
soó iibsadeen	they bought (from the verb **iibso**)
iibso (3A)	to buy

maánta	today
dád badán ayáa yimí	many people came
badán (adj.)	many
qasacád (f. d1)	tin
khudrád (f. d1 collec.)	vegetables
iibi (2A)	to sell
wéli	yet
wáa yahay	right (lit.: 'it is')
ma qadeýn doontaa?	do you want to have lunch?
qadee (2B)	to have lunch
waan gaajeysánahay	I am hungry
xidh (1)	to close
makhaayád (f. d1)	restaurant

Maxamed wuu ka baxayaa dukaanka. Axmedna waddada buu soo marayaa.

MAXAMED: Waryaa, Axmed. Iska warran.
AXMED: Waryaa, Maxamed. Waa la wanaagsanyahay. Iska warran adigu.
MAXAMED: Waan fiicanahay. Shaqadan ka warran. Maxaad sameysey subaxdan?
AXMED: Tagsigayga baan watay. Iibiska ka warran, dad badan wax miyay soo iibsadeen?
MAXAMED: Haa maanta dad badan ayaa yimi, waxyaabo badanna way soo iibsadeen. Qasacado iyo khudrad badan baan iibiyay.
AXMED: Waa yahay. Weli ma qadeysay?
MAXAMED: Maya.
AXMED: Imminka ma qadeyn doontaa?
MAXAMED: Haa waan gaajeysanahay. Dukaanka waan xidhayaa makhaayadana waynu tagaynaa.
AXMED: Waa yahay.

Maxamed comes out of the shop. And Axmed is passing along the street.

MAXAMED: *Hi, Axmed. How are you?*
AXMED: *Hi, Maxamed. I am well. How are you?*
MAXAMED: *I am well. How is work? What did you do this morning?*
AXMED: *I drove my taxi. How is trade? Did many people buy something?*
MAXAMED: *Yes, today many people came and they bought many things. I sold tins and many vegetables.*

AXMED: *Right. Have you had lunch yet?*
MAXAMED: *No.*
AXMED: *Do you want to have lunch now?*
MAXAMED: *Yes, I am hungry. I will close the shop and we will go to the restaurant.*
AXMED: *Right.*

Notes

1 We shall see later that adjectives in Somali always go with part of the verb 'to be'. In this case the verb part is deleted for reasons that will be made clear later.
2 Note in this case the introduction of a glottal stop after the additional prefix, because the singular begins with a vowel.
3 Note the use of the singular here. The singular is used with the number one for obvious reasons.

5 Garoonka dayuuradaha

The airport

By the end of this lesson you should:

- know about verbs that lose a vowel
- know about irregular plural forms
- know the present general tense
- know how to use 'prepositions' and prepositional expressions
- know and be able to use the object pronouns
- know conjugation 3A

Dialogue

Bill arrives at Djibouti airport

Vocabulary

ú	to
raac (1)	to accompany, go with
dayuurád (f. d1)	aeroplane
wéyntahay	it is big
dád (m. collec.)	people
badán	many
ayáana	focus marker **ayáa** + **na**, 'and'
raacaý	general past form of **raac**, used when the subject of the sentence is focused (see Lesson 6)
soó deg (1)	to land
dhísmo (f. d6)	building (the singular of this noun may also be masculine)
garóonka dayuuradáha	the airport

dhismáha garóonka dayuuradáha	the airport building
garóon (m. d2)	ground, field
hálkaás	there
shandadíhíisií	his suitcases
sarkáal (m. saraakiil (f.))	official
baadhís (f.)	inspection
waraáq (f. d1)	paper
Illaáh maháddi	thanks be to God
magacáa	what is your name?
xaggeé	where (lit.: which direction)?
ká	from
timi	you came
imi	I came
baasabóor (m. d2)	passport
i	me
tus (1)	to show
fiíse (m. d7)	visa
ká qaado (3B)	to get, take from
ká qaatay	I got from
Baariis	Paris
intéed	how long + you (from: inteé + báa + aad)
toddobáad (m. d2)	week
ká dib	afterwards, after
rajee (2B)	to hope
ínaad	that you
ká hel	to like
dál (m.d4)	country

Bill wuxuu yimi Djibouti. Wuxuu u raacay dayuurad. Dayuuraddu waa weyntahay. Dad badan ayaa raacay.
   Dayuuraddu way soo degtay.
   Bill wuxuu tagaa dhismaha garoonka dayuuradaha. Halkaas ayuu ka helaa shandadihiisii dabadeedna wuxuu tagaa meesha baadhista waraaqaha.

NINKA: Soo dhowow.
BILL: Mahadsanid. Is ka warran.
NINKA: Waa la wanaagsanyahay. Iska warran adigu.
BILL: Waa la fiicanyahay, Illaah mahaddi.
NINKA: Magacaa?
BILL: Magacaygu waa Bill.
NINKA: Xaggee baad ka timi?

BILL: Landhan ayaan ka imi.
NINKA: Baasaboorkaaga i tus. Fiisaha xaggee baad ka qaadatay?
BILL: Baariis baan ka qaatay.

Bill basaboorkiisa wuu tusaa.

NINKA: Waa wanaagsanyahay. Inteed joogaysaa Djibouti?
BILL: Toddobaad ayaan joogayaa. Ka dibna magaalada Burco ayaan tagayaa.
NINKA: Waa yahay, mahadsanid walaal.
BILL: Mahadsanid.
NINKA: Waxaan rajeynayaa inaad dalka Djibouti ka helaysaa.
BILL: Mahadsanid, nabad gelyo.
NINKA: Nabad gelyo.

Bill has come to Djibouti. He came by aeroplane. The aeroplane is large. Many people travelled on it.
   The plane has landed.
   Bill goes to the airport building. There he finds his suitcases, then he goes to the passport control (lit.: papers inspection place).

THE MAN: *Welcome.*
BILL: *Thank you. How are you?*
THE MAN: *I am well. How are you?*
BILL: *I am well, thanks be to God.*
THE MAN: *What is your name?*
BILL: *My name is Bill.*
THE MAN: *Where have you come from?*
BILL: *I have come from London.*
THE MAN: *Show me your passport. Where did you get the visa?*
BILL: *I got it in Paris.*

Bill shows his passport.

THE MAN: *Good. How long are you staying in Djibouti?*
BILL: *I am staying a week. Afterwards I am going to the town of Burco.*
THE MAN: *Right, thank you, brother.*
BILL: *Thank you.*
THE MAN: *I hope that you will like Djibouti.*
BILL: *Thank you, goodbye.*
THE MAN: *Goodbye.*

Language in use

Verbs that lose a vowel

In Lesson 2 we looked at declension 3, in which nouns of the same pattern as **gabádh** lose the final vowel when the plural marker is added. There are some verbs that behave in the same way. All are conjugation 1 verbs, and they pattern like the example verb **maqal**, 'to hear', given below:

	verb stem	ending	verb form
I	maqal	ay	**maqlay**
you (sg.)	maqal	tay	**maqashay**
he, it (m.)	maqal	ay	**maqlay**
she, it (f.)	maqal	tay	**maqashay**
we	maqal	nay	**maqallay**
you (pl.)	maqal	teen	**maqasheen**
they	maqal	een	**maqleen**

As you can see, when any ending beginning with a vowel is added to the verb stem, then the final vowel is deleted. Look back to the declension 3 nouns and compare this with them. Note that these verbs are not a separate conjugation but are simply a group of conjugation 1 verbs which behave in a manner different to most.

Note that there are a few verbs which, although they are the right shape, do not delete the vowel. This is the case, for example, if the middle consonant is **k** or **t**.

| **feker** | to think |
| **Waan ká fekeray.** | I thought about it. |

Verbs that behave in this way are marked in the glossary and future vocabularies by giving the third person masculine general present tense form in parentheses.

There are a number of sound changes that occur with these verbs. All the sound changes we have met above relating to verbs apply, as you can see with the **maqal** example above. In addition, the final consonant of the verb may change according to whether the ending following the stem begins with a vowel or a consonant. This is similar to the verb **bug**, 'to be ill', mentioned in Lesson 1. Look at the example verb **arag**, 'to see', given below:

	verb stem	ending	verb form
I	arag	ay	**arkay**
you (sg.)	arag	tay	**aragtay**
he, it (m.)	arag	ay	**arkay**
she, it (f.)	arag	tay	**aragtay**
we	arag	nay	**aragnay**
you (pl.)	arag	teen	**aragteen**
they	arag	een	**arkeen**

Verbs that have these changing consonants are given as such in vocabularies and the glossary.

Note that the vowel is deleted also when the vowel of the progressive marker follows the stem, as indeed it is deleted when any suffix is added to the verb which begins with a vowel.

Way maqlayaan.   They are hearing.

Exercise

1 Translate the following sentences into Somali; the relevant verbs are given in parentheses with the two forms of the verb stem:

1 The girl saw the car.   (**arag** arag-, ark-)
2 Cali is speaking.   (**hadal** hadal-, hadl-)
3 The boys heard the burden camels.   (**maqal** maqal-, maql-)
4 Canab, Maxamed and the teacher are laughing.   (**qosol** qosol-, qosl-)
5 The men are running.   (**orod** orod-, ord-)
6 The family slept.   (**hurud** hurud-, hurd-)

Irregular plurals

We have dealt with all the regular declensions of nouns in the previous chapters, and in this section we shall look at nouns that do not fit into any of these declensions. Most such nouns are Arabic loanwords which form the plural in the same way as they do in Arabic.

jariidád (f.)	newspaper	**jaraá'id** (m.)	newspapers
márkab (m.)	ship	**maraakiíb** (f.)	ships
maxbúus (m.)	prisoner	**maxaabiís** (f.)	prisoners

Alongside the use of the Arabic plurals, these nouns may also be given Somali plurals and treated as nouns of a particular Somali declension. An example of such a noun is:

kúrsi chair **kuraasi** or **kursiyo** chairs

This noun may take the Arabic plural or behave like a noun of declension 2.

A few other words in Somali form irregular plurals. Some common ones are the following:

dhágax (m.)	stone	**dhagxán** (f.)	stones
úgax (m. and f.)	egg	**ugxán** (f.)	eggs[1]
wáx (m.)	thing	**waxyaabo** (m.)	things
íl (f.)	eye	**indho** (m.)	eyes

Note that most of these irregular nouns reverse their gender in the plural. The only way to learn these irregular plurals is to learn the singular and the plural together.

Exercise

2 Translate the following sentences into Somali:

1 I found eggs.
2 They took the stones.
3 He made three chairs.
4 He taught the easy lessons.
5 Today many people are reading the newspapers.
6 The ships left.

The general present tense

In Lesson 2 we met the present progressive tense which you should be using now. In this section we shall look at the general present tense. This tense is used for actions that happen 'generally', habitually or repeatedly. In form it is similar to the general past tense, except that it uses the present tense endings which are familiar to you from the present progressive. Below is the general present tense of conjugation 1, the example verb being **keen**, 'to bring'. The forms mean therefore 'I bring', 'you bring' etc.

	verb stem	ending	verb form
I	keen	aa	**keenaa**
you (sg.)	keen	taa	**keentaa**
he, it (m.)	keen	aa	**keenaa**
she, it (f.)	keen	taa	**keentaa**
we	keen	naa	**keennaa**
you (pl.)	keen	taan	**keentaan**
they	keen	aan	**keenaan**

The general present for conjugation 2 is as follows.

The general present of conjugation 2A is shown in example verb **kari**, 'to cook':

	verb stem	ending	verb form
I	kari	aa	**kariyaa**
you (sg.)	kari	taa	**karisaa**
he, it (m.)	kari	aa	**kariyaa**
she, it (f.)	kari	taa	**karisaa**
we	kari	naa	**karinnaa**
you (pl.)	kari	taan	**karisaan**
they	kari	aan	**kariyaan**

The general present of conjugation 2B, example verb **samee**, 'to make, do' is as follows:

	verb stem	ending	verb form
I	samee	aa	**sameeyaa**
you (sg.)	samee	taa	**sameysaa**
he, it (m.)	samee	aa	**sameeyaa**
she, it (f.)	samee	taa	**sameysaa**
we	samee	naa	**sameynaa**
you (pl.)	samee	taan	**sameysaan**
they	samee	aan	**sameeyaan**

Note that all the sound changes relating to the general past are relevant for the general present. This means that when an ending beginning with **t** follows a guttural consonant it changes to **d** etc. Look back to Lesson 1 to review these sound changes. Note the first person plural geminate pronunciation of the **n** in conjugation 2A. The stress-tone pattern of this tense is as in the general past: no stress-tone on any vowel.

Exercise

3 Write the general present forms of the following verbs:
1 tag
2 casee
3 bixi

Prepositions

Prepositions in English are words such as 'in, at, with' etc. Prepositions in Somali are not used in the same way. There are two main ways in which prepositions may be expressed in Somali: first with preverbal prepositions, and second with words of place. In this chapter we shall begin looking at preverbal prepositions.

Preverbal prepositions

Preverbal prepositions are short words which come before the verb (hence 'preverbal') and which refer back to a noun or noun phrase in the sentence.

    Gabádhu laybreériga way   The girl writes in the library.
    kú qortaa.

This may be broken down as follows:

Gabádhu	**laybreériga**	**way**	**kú**	**qortaa**
The girl (subj.)	the library	mood classifier + she	in	she writes

In this sentence the preverbal preposition **kú** refers back to the noun **laybreériga**, 'the library'. It is important to remember that in Somali these preverbal prepositions always come immediately before the verb and never before the noun they refer to.

There are four preverbal prepositions, given here with their basic meanings:

ú	to, for
kú	at, in, by means of
ká	from, about
lá	with

There is always a stress-tone on these preverbal prepositions. Note that these may occur in clusters, which induces certain changes which we shall deal with later.

Example sentences with preverbal prepositions are shown below.

Vocabulary

géed (m. d1)   tree
duul (1)   to fly
shub (1)   to pour

Maánta Maxámed waan lá joogay.	Today I was with Maxamed.
Shimbírtu géedka way ká duushay.	The bird flew from the tree.
Maxmúud waan ú sheégayaa.	I will tell Maxmuud.
Caáno kóobka kú shúb.	Pour milk in the cup.

Note that as a rule of thumb the word order for the noun phrases referred to by a preverbal preposition is for the noun phrase to be as close to the preverbal preposition as possible within the overall word order you have learnt and will learn in future chapters.

Exercise

4 Translate the following sentences into Somali:

1 She spoke with Cali.
2 Bring meat from the shop!
3 The children are playing in the room. (to play: **ciyaar** (1))
4 He is taking it by car.
5 Rooble sliced the bread with a knife. (to slice: **jadh** (1))
6 Yesterday you waited in the house. (yesterday: **sháleyto**)

Verbal object pronouns

We have already seen in Lesson 1 that there are no actual words in Somali for the third person object pronouns. All other persons do, however, have object pronouns in Somali, which we shall look at here. The verbal object pronouns are those forms that, like the verbal subject pronouns, do not occur independently of a verb. That is to say, you must always use these verbal object pronouns with a verb. The position of the object verbal pronoun is just before the verb in a sentence but before any preverbal prepositions. Thus the order of preverbal words you have met so far is as follows:

OBJECT PRONOUNS – PREVERBAL PREPOSITIONS – DEICTICS

The deictics are the words **sií**, **soó**, **wada** ('together') and **kala** ('apart')

The forms of the verbal object pronouns are given below:

i	me	**na**	us (excl.)
ku	you	**ina**	us (incl.)
		idin	you (pl.)

Wáy idin bartay. She taught you (pl.).
Wáy ina booqdeen. They visited us (incl.).
Wáad i tustay. You showed me it.

Note that there is no stress-tone on any of the object verbal pronouns.

Exercise

5 Translate the following sentences into Somali:

1 I heard you.
2 Canab showed me the town.
3 They eat it.
4 Today the new teacher will teach you (pl.).
5 They greet us (excl.).
6 He met with them yesterday.

Conjugation 3

This conjugation is made up of verbs that end in **-o**. As with conjugation 2 the **-o** ending provides some extra meaning to a root form verb. The most common meaning for the **-o** ending is 'doing the action for one's own benefit'; for this reason this ending is often called the *autobenefactive* ending.

qaad	to take	**qaado**	to take for oneself
fur	to open	**furo**	to open for oneself
wad	to drive	**wado**	to drive for oneself

Another function the ending has is to make a transitive verb intransitive. (This is the opposite of the **-i** ending making intransitive verbs transitive.)

gub	to burn (trans.)	**gubo**	to burn (intrans.)
waal	to drive mad (trans.)	**waalo**	to go mad (intrans.)

Note that although there is this 'extra' meaning, in this course we shall simply give the meanings of the verbs as they stand and not link them with verbs from which they might be derived.

Sometimes, instead of just **-o** the ending might be **-so**.

joogso	to stop (intrans.)
buuxso	to fill for oneself
baxso	to escape

As to the form of this conjugation there are two slightly different forms which we shall call conjugations 3A and 3B.

The imperative

Remember that the imperative stress-tone pattern on verbs we have met until now has been on the penultimate vowel. In conjugation 3 verbs, however, the stress-tone is on the final vowel. This is the same for 3A and 3B.

Joogsó!	Stop!
Buuxsó!	Fill for yourself!

Conjugation 3A

The plural imperative

To form the plural imperative of conjugation 3A verbs you add **-da** and change the final **-o** of the stem to **a**. Note that the stress-tone in the plural is on the penultimate vowel.

| buuxso | **Buuxsáda!** | Fill for yourselves (pl.)! |
| joogso | **Joogsáda!** | Stop (pl.)! |

The general past of conjugation 3A is given below using the example verb **joogso**, 'to stop (intrans.)':

	verb stem	ending	verb form
I	joogso	ay	**joogsaday**
you (sg.)	joogso	tay	**joogsatay**
he, it (m.)	joogso	ay	**joogsaday**
she, it (f.)	joogso	tay	**joogsatay**
we	joogso	nay	**joogsannay**
you (pl.)	joogso	teen	**joogsateen**
they	joogso	een	**joogsadeen**

You can see from the table that the form is not as straightforward as might be expected. The **o** ending changes to **a** all the way through and when an ending beginning with a vowel is added, a **d** is inserted before the ending. The other point to note is that the **-n-** in the first person plural is geminated as in conjugation 2A.

The general present

The general present is formed in the same way, except for the present tense endings which are as given in the section on the general present.

The present progressive

To form the other tense we have met, the present progressive, you add the present progressive endings to the infinitive form of the verb. The infinitive of all conjugation 3 verbs is formed by taking away the **-o** ending and adding **-an** to what remains. Note that the stress-tone, as in the conjugation 2 verbs, is on the final vowel.

joogso → joogsán

The present progressive of the verb **joogso** is therefore as follows, with the stress-tone again on the vowel immediately before the progressive marker:

	verb stem	progressive marker	ending	verb form
I	joogsan	ay	aa	**joogsánayaa**
you (sg.)	joogsan	ay	taa	**joogsánaysaa**
he, it (m.)	joogsan	ay	aa	**joogsánayaa**
she, it (f.)	joogsan	ay	taa	**joogsánaysaa**
we	joogsan	ay	naa	**joogsánaynaa**
you (pl.)	joogsan	ay	taan	**joogsánaysaan**
they	joogsan	ay	aan	**joogsánayaan**

Exercise

6 Write out in full the general present and the present progressive tense of the following verbs:

1 baxso (to escape)
2 iibso (to buy)
3 guurso (to get married)

The ordinal numbers

The ordinal numbers are those such as 'first, second, third' etc. In Somali the ordinal numbers are formed by adding **-aád** to the cardinal number. Note that the sound change in which certain verbs lose a vowel discussed above also occurs when the **-aád** ending is added to certain numbers. The following list gives all the ordinal numbers from 1 to 10. Compare them with the cardinal numbers you now know:

kowaád	first	**lixaád**	sixth
labaád	second	**toddobaád**	seventh
saddexaád	third	**siddeedaád**	eighth
afraád	fourth	**sagaalaád**	ninth
shanaád	fifth	**tobnaád**	tenth

It is possible to use the number itself and **aad** to write the ordinal numbers.

| 2aad | 2nd |
| 9aad | 9th |

Dialogue 🎧

Maxamed and Axmed go to the restaurant

Vocabulary

aynu gállo	let us enter (a form of the verb called the optative; the verb is **gal** (1))
jirá	this is the general present of **jir** but has a short vowel because the subject is focused (this is dealt with later)
kú	'to' used with the prefixing verb **yidhi**
yidhaahdaan	they say
assalaámu calaýkum	an Islamic greeting which is used by Somalis; the words are Arabic, meaning 'Peace be with you'
jawaab (1)	to answer, reply
calaýkum assaláam	reply to **assalaámu calaýkum**, again Arabic meaning 'with you peace'
ká shaqeeyá	works for
ká shaqee (2B)	to work for
yimaaddá	he comes
soó dhowaáda	plural imperative of **soó dhowow**
qadee (2B)	to have lunch
qadeýn rabnaa	we wish to have lunch
waa hagáag	fine, OK
hagáag (m. d2)	straightness
soó fadhiísta	plural imperative of **soó fadhiíso**, 'to sit down (pl.)'
maxáan	what + 'I'
idiín	**idin** + **ú** 'for you (pl.)'
maxáa	what
jir (1)	to be, exist
kallúun (m. d2, also collec., **kalluummo**)	fish
baríis (m. mass)	rice

baásto (f. d6, mass)	pasta
doon (1)	to want
ií	**i** + **ú**, 'for me'
máraq (m. mass)	soup
iilá	**i** + **ú** + **lá**, 'for me with'
waan ká xúmahay	'I am sorry'
xún (adj.)	bad
má jiró	is not
basbáas (m. d2)	hot chilli pepper
-leh	owning, with
basbáas leh (adj.)	hot, spicy
bismillaah	Arabic, meaning 'In the name of God'; this is uttered just before starting to eat, in a manner similar to the Christian grace

MAXAMED: Waa tan makhaayaddu.
AXMED: Haa aynu gallo.

Makhaayadda ayay galaan. Dad badan ayaa makhaayadda ku jira. Maxamed iyo Axmed waxay dadka ku yidhaahdaan: 'Assalamu calaykum'. Dadkuna way jawaabaan: 'Calaykum assalaam'.

Nin makhaayadda ka shaqeeya ayaa yimaada. Magaciisu waa Yuusuf.

YUUSUF: Soo dhowaada. Iska warrama.
AXMED: Waa la wanaagsanyahay. Iska warran adigu.
YUUSUF: Waan ladanahay.
MAXAMED: Halkan waynu qadeyn rabnaa.
YUUSUF: Waa hagaag. Soo fadhiista. Maxaan idiin keenaa?
AXMED: Maxaa jira?[2]
YUUSUF: Waxa jira hilib adhi, kalluun, bariis, baasto.
AXMED: Hilib adhi iyo bariis ii keen.
YUUSUF: Maraqna ma doonaysaa?
AXMED: Haa maraq iila keen.
YUUSUF: Adigana; maxaad doonaysaa?
MAXAMED: Hilib lo'aad ma jiraa?
YUUSUF: Waan ka xumahay walaal. Hilib lo'aad ma jiro maanta.
MAXAMED: Waa yahay. Kalluun iyo baasto ii keen.
YUUSUF: Waa yahay.
MAXAMED: Maraqna ii keen. Ma maraq basbaas leh baa?
YUUSUF: Haa, basbaas leh.

Yuusuf cuntada wuu keenaa. Maxamed iyo Axmed waxay yidhaadaan: 'Mahadsanid'. Dabadeedna waxay yidhaadaan: 'Bismillaah'. Dabadeedna way cunaan.

MAXAMED: *Here is the restaurant.*
AXMED: *Yes, let's go in.*

They enter the restaurant. Many people are in the restaurant. Maxamed and Axmed say to the people: 'Assalaamu calaykum'. *And the people reply:* 'Calaykum assalaam'.
A man working for the restaurant comes up. His name is Yuusuf.

YUUSUF: *Welcome. How are you?*
AXMED: *I am well. How are you?*
YUUSUF: *I am well.*
MAXAMED: *We wish to have lunch here.*
YUUSUF: *Fine. Sit down. What shall I bring for you?*
AXMED: *What is there?*
YUUSUF: *There is mutton, fish, rice and pasta.*
AXMED: *Bring mutton and rice for me.*
YUUSUF: *And would you like soup?*
AXMED: *Yes, bring soup for me with it.*
YUUSUF: *And you; what would you like?*
MAXAMED: *Is there any beef?*
YUUSUF: *I'm sorry, brother. There is no beef today.*
MAXAMED: *Right. Bring me fish and pasta.*
YUUSUF: *OK.*
MAXAMED: *And bring soup for me. Is it spicy soup?*
YUUSUF: *Yes, it is spicy.*

Yuusuf brings the food. Maxamed and Axmed say: 'Thank you'. *Then they say:* 'Bismillaah'. *Then they eat.*

Note

1 This word means eggs other than those of a chicken.
2 This verb form is used because **maxaa** includes a focus marker focusing the subject **max-**. See Lesson 6.

6 Tagsiga
The taxi

> **By the end of this lesson you should:**
> - have learnt how to say 'What. . .?'
> - have learnt something about focus constructions
> - have learnt conjugation 3B
> - have learnt the rest of the numbers
> - have learnt expressions related to the date

Dialogue

Bill finds a taxi

baxayá	he leaves (this form is used because the subject is focused; see later)
doondoon (1)	to look for
tágsi (m. d2)	taxi
hórtíisa	in front of (lit.: its front)
ú yeedh	to call for
tagsíle (m. d7)	taxi owner
háyye	'Hi'; an interjection (this word is used a lot in Somali)
tégi rabtaa	you want to go
rab (1)	to want, desire (used as an auxiliary verb with the infinitive to express 'to want to do something')
hudhéel (m. d2)	hotel
gee (2B)	to take someone/something (in the sense such as here, in a taxi)
má taqaan	do you know it?
wallaáh	an exclamation used when someone is rather surprised at something (from **wa** and **Allaah**, Arabic meaning 'and God')

sí (f)	way
xaggeé	where (lit.: which place)?
baratay	you learnt (from baro)
Lándhan	London
saaxíibkáyga	my friend
la yidhaahdó	called (lit.: 'one says')
kú hádli kartaa	you can speak in
kalé	other
lagú	la + kú (one + in (in the languages))
Cafár	Afar (a Cushitic language spoken in Djibouti, as well as in Eritrea and Ethiopia)
Faransíis	French
ín (f.)	amount
yár	small
fiicántahay	you are well
wáayo	because
hálkán lagú hadló	that are spoken here (lit.: that one speaks in here)
háwo (f. d6)	air, weather
ká hel (1)	to like, enjoy
kuláyl (m.)	heat (this expression is always used for the weather)
áad iyo áad	very very much

Bill ayaa garoonka dayuuradaha ka baxaya. Tagsi ayuu doondoonayaa. Tagsiyo badan ayaa jira garoonka dayuuradaha hortiisa. Bill tagsi wuu u yeedhayaa.

TAGSILAHA: Hayye. Soo dhowow.
BILL: Hayye, is ka warran.
TAGSILAHA: Waa la wanaagsanyahay. Ma nabad baa?
BILL: Waa nabad.
TAGSILAHA: Xaggee baad tegi rabtaa?
BILL: Hudheel Djibouti i gee. Ma taqaan?
TAGSILAHA: Haa waan aqaan. Halkaas miyaad joogaysaa?
BILL: Haa halkaas ayaan joogayaa.
TAGSILAHA: Wallaah af soomaaliga si wanaagsan ayaad ugu hadlaysaa. Xaggee baad ku baratay.
BILL: Landhan ayaan ku bartay.
TAGSILAHA: Landhan!
BILL: Haa. Saaxiibkayga ayaa i baray. Waa nin Yoonis la yidhaahdo.
TAGSILAHA: Waa yahay. Halkan af soomaaliga baad ku hadli kartaa. Afaf kale ayaana dalka Djibouti lagu hadlaa.

	Waxa lagu hadlaa af Soomaaliga, af Cafarta, af Carabeedka iyo af Faransiiska. Afafkan ma taqaan?
BILL:	Af Faransiiska in yar ayaan ka aqaan.
TAGSILAHA:	Waa yahay. Halkan baad ku fiicantahay waayo laba af oo halkan lagu hadlo baad taqaan. Hawada Djibouti ma ka heshaa?
BILL:	Wallaah waa kulayl. Aad iyo aad.

Tagsilaha ayaa qoslaya.

Bill leaves the airport. He is looking for a taxi. There are many taxis in front of the airport. Bill calls a taxi.

THE TAXI OWNER:	Hi, welcome.
BILL:	Hi. How are you?
THE TAXI OWNER:	I am well. How are you?
BILL:	I am well.
THE TAXI OWNER:	Where do you want to go?
BILL:	Take me to the Djibouti Hotel. Do you know it?
THE TAXI OWNER:	Yes, I know it. Are you going to stay there?
BILL:	Yes, I am going to stay there.
THE TAXI OWNER:	My goodness, you speak Somali well. Where did you learn it?
BILL:	I learnt it in London.
THE TAXI OWNER:	London!
BILL:	Yes. My friend taught me. He is a man called Yoonis.
THE TAXI OWNER:	Well. Here you can speak in Somali. And other languages are spoken in Djibouti. Somali, Afar, Arabic and French are spoken. Do you know these languages?
BILL:	I know French a little.
THE TAXI OWNER:	Right. It is good for you here because you know two languages that are spoken here. Do you like the Djibouti weather?
BILL:	My goodness, it is hot. Very very much.

The driver laughs.

Language in use

Asking 'What . . .?'

To ask 'What . . .?' in Somali requires us to use the special question word **max-**. The subject pronouns are then added to **max-** as, for example, in:

Maxáad sameysay? What did you do?
Maxáy dhisayaan? What are they building?

The full set of pronouns with **max-** is as follows:

I	max + aan	**maxáan**
you (sg.)	max + aad	**maxáad**
he, it (m.)	max + uu	**muxúu**
she, it (f.)	max + ay	**maxáy**
we (incl.)	max + aynu	**maxáynu**
we (excl.)	max + aannu	**maxáannu**
you (pl.)	max + aydin	**maxáydin**
they	max + ay	**maxáy**

Note where the stress-tone falls and the sound change in the form **muxúu**.

Note that the form without any subject pronoun **maxáa** is used when a general non-defined subject is implied, or when the impersonal third person pronoun **la** is used.

Maxáa dhacaý? What happened?
Maxáa lagá sameeyay? What did one make it out of?' (**lagá: la + ká**)

Exercise

1 Complete the following sentences using **max-** with a pronoun and translate them:

1 _____ maqasheen?
2 _____ sameynaynaa?
3 _____ jabisay?
4 Cali _____ u sheegay?

5 Dukaanka _____ ka keentay?
6 Makhaayadda _____ ku cuneen?

Using focus markers

When you ask the question 'What did they build?' you are asking for some specific new information. When the question is answered in Somali this new information is *focused* in the answer.

In Lesson 1 we looked at the use of the mood classifier **wâa**; we also mentioned that a positive declarative sentence in Somali must have a mood classifier or a focus marker for it to be correct. We shall look at the use of the focus markers **báa** and **ayáa** in this section. There is a further way of focusing a noun phrase, using the **wáxa** construction, which is dealt with in Lesson 10.

The first thing to be said about **báa** and **ayáa** is that they are interchangeable. They are used in exactly the same way with no difference in meaning, and what is said of one is true of the other.

The role of the focus marker is to emphasize or highlight a particular noun or noun phrase in the sentence. In English this is generally done by intonation. Compare, for example, the following different ways of saying the sentence 'The girl ate the rice'. Say this sentence out loud, emphasizing the parts in italics. Note that we shall use italics to mark any noun phrase that is focused.

1. *The girl* ate the rice.   (and not someone else)
2. The girl ate *the rice*.   (and not something else)
3. The girl *ate* the rice.   (and did not do anything else with it)

Ask yourself the following questions and match each question with one of the sentences above. Say everything out loud and notice the difference in meaning.

A What did the girl do to the rice?
B Who ate the rice?
C What did the girl eat?

Question A matches up with answer 3.
Question B matches up with answer 1.
Question C matches up with answer 2.

In sentences 1 and 2 above we shall call the italicized noun phrases *focused* noun phrases. Note that the use of the mood classifier **wâa** does not, strictly speaking, imply particular emphasis of the verb, but you may find this a useful concept to work with.

Understanding focus through the use of questions and answers is important because it is important to focus the correct part of an answer to a question. In Somali if a question is asking for a particular new piece of information then that information is focused in the answer. If this is not done then the answer may be grammatically correct but it would sound odd.

Focusing any noun phrase other than the subject

To focus a noun phrase the focus marker **báa** or **ayáa** is used immediately following the noun phrase it is focusing. As with the mood classifier **wâa** the verbal subject pronoun may be attached to the focus marker.

I	báa/ayáa	+ aan	**báan**	**ayáan**
you (sg.)	báa/ayáa	+ aad	**báad**	**ayáad**
he, it (m.)	báa/ayáa	+ uu	**búu**	**ayúu**
she, it (f.)	báa/ayáa	+ ay	**báy**	**ayáy**
we (incl.)	báa/ayáa	+ aynu	**báynu**	**ayáynu**
we (excl.)	báa/ayáa	+ aannu	**báannu**	**ayáannu**
you (pl.)	báa/ayáa	+ aydin	**báydin**	**ayáydin**
they	báa/ayáa	+ ay	**báy**	**ayáy**

So the Somali translation of 'The girl ate *the rice*' is

gabádhu	**baríiska**	**ayáy**	**cuntay**
the girl-subject	the rice	focus + she	ate

or

gabádhu	**baríiska**	**báy**	**cuntay**
the girl-subject	the rice	focus + she	ate

As with **wâa**, if the subject is overtly given, as in the example above, then the verbal subject pronoun need not necessarily be given with the focus marker. Thus the following is also correct:

Gabádhu baríiska báa cuntay.

Other example sentences with focus markers are the following:

Ínanku kóobka búu jabiyay.   The boy broke *the cup*.
Nimánku gúriga báy ká bexeen.   The men left *the house*.

Exercises

2 Translate the following sentences, focusing the noun phrases in italics:

1 The bird flew from *the tree*.
2 The large man eats *a lot of rice*.
3 They brought *the new cups*.
4 She will go to the market with *Canab*.
5 She will go to *the market* with Canab.
6 They saw Maxamed *yesterday*.

3 Answer the following questions in Somali, paying careful attention to focusing the noun phrases where appropriate or to using the mood classifier **wâa**:

1 Guriga miyaydin tagaysaan?
2 Maxaad cabbaysaa?
3 Habeenka maxay keenaysaa?
4 Xaggee baydin tagteen?
5 Dukaanka maxay ku aragtay?
6 Guri miyay sameeyeen?

Focusing the subject

When the subject is focused, some aspects of the sentence are different from the way they are in sentences in which something other than the subject is focused. These differences may be summed up as follows:
When the subject is focused:

- the subject is in the absolutive case;
- the subject verbal pronoun is not used with the focus marker;
- the reduced verb paradigm is used.[1]

All these aspects are exemplified in the following sentences, which are similar to the examples given above so that you may compare them:

Gabádha báa baríiska cuntaý.	*The girl* ate the rice.
Ínanka báa kóobka jabiyaý.	*The boy* broke the cup.
Nimánka báa gúriga ká baxaý.	*The men* left the house.

You can see from these examples that the subjects are in the absolutive case, that is to say **gabádha** is used, as opposed to **gabádhu** etc. You can also see that the focus marker is present on its own, without the verbal subject pronouns. Futhermore, you can see that the stress-tone on the verb is different and in the final example, the plural subject seems to go with a singular verb. This is because we need to use the reduced verb paradigm in these cases.

The reduced verb forms

This verb paradigm is not a separate tense or mood but is used when the subject of a sentence is focused and also in some instances in relative clauses, which you will learn in Lesson 12.

General past tense

	verb stem	*ending*	*verb form*
I	keen	aý	**keenaý**
you (sg.)	keen	aý	**keenaý**
he, it (m.)	keen	aý	**keenaý**
she, it (f.)	keen	taý	**keentaý**
we	keen	naý	**keennaý**
you (pl.)	keen	aý	**keenaý**
they	keen	aý	**keenaý**

General present tense

	verb stem	*ending*	*verb form*
I	keen	á	**keená**
you (sg.)	keen	á	**keená**
he, it (m.)	keen	á	**keená**
she, it (f.)	keen	tá	**keentá**
we	keen	ná	**keenná**
you (pl.)	keen	á	**keená**
they	keen	á	**keená**

Present progressive tense

	verb stem	progressive marker	present tense ending	verb form
I	keen	ay	á	**keénayá**
you (sg.)	keen	ay	á	**keénayá**
he, it (m.)	keen	ay	á	**keénayá**
she, it (f.)	keen	ay	tá	**keénaysá**
we	keen	ay	ná	**keénayná**
you (pl.)	keen	ay	á	**keénayá**
they	keen	ay	á	**keénayá**

We can see from these tables that the reduced paradigm is the same as the full forms except for the following points:

- in the general present and the present progressive the long final **aa** vowel is changed to a short **a** vowel;
- there is a stress-tone on the final vowel in all forms;
- all persons have the same ending except for the third person feminine singular and the first person plural (hence the name reduced paradigm, because there are a reduced number of person and number distinctions).

All the conjugations behave in the same way and thus you will be able to work out the forms of all the verb conjugations we have met.

Contractions of báa

When a noun phrase ends in a short vowel, particularly the short vowel of the definite article, it is possible for **báa** to become part of the noun it is focusing. When this happens, the **b** is deleted and all that remains is the vowel.

    Nínkáa tagaý.   *The man* went.

This is from: **Nínka báa tagaý.**

This contraction may also be made when there is a subject verbal pronoun with the focus marker.

    Nínkúu arkay.   He saw *the man*.

Exercise

4 Translate the following question and answer pairs into Somali; pay attention to the parts of the sentence that require focus:

1. What did you break?   I broke the pencils.
2. What did they eat yesterday?   They ate bread yesterday.
3. What did they see?   They saw many camels.
4. What did they build in the town?   They built a large mosque in the town.
5. What did the children enjoy?   They enjoyed the new programmes.
6. What is Canab looking for?   She is looking for a taxi.

Conjugation 3B

The forms of conjugation 3B differ from those in 3A only in certain tenses.

The general past of conjugation 3B is given below, using the verb **furo**, 'to open for oneself', as an example:

	verb stem	ending	verb form
I	furo	ay	**furtay**
you (sg.)	furo	tay	**furatay**
he, it (m.)	furo	ay	**furtay**
she, it (f.)	furo	tay	**furatay**
we	furo	nay	**furannay**
you (pl.)	furo	teen	**furateen**
they	furo	een	**furteen**

You can see from the table that with the endings beginning with a vowel a **-t-** is added before the vowel and the **-o** of the stem is lost. With the endings beginning with **t-** the **-o** of the stem changes to **-a-**. The other point to note is that the **-n-** in the first person plural is geminated, as in conjugation 3A.

The general present is formed in the same way, except, of course, that the present tense endings are used.

Note that there is a sound change which you must be aware of with this conjugation: when the ending **-tay** is added directly to a guttural consonant[2] then the **t** changes to **d**.

booqo	**Wáan booqday.**	I visited.

Also if the verb ends in **-do**, such as **wado**, 'to drive', then the **d** is deleted when the endings beginning with a vowel are added.

watay (from **wado** + **ay**)	I drove
wateen (from **wado** + **een**)	they drove
wadatay (from **wado** + **tay**)	you drove

The plural imperative

To form the plural imperative the ending **-ta** replaces the **-o** of the stem.

wado	**Wáta!**	Drive it (pl.)!
furo	**Fúrta!**	Open it for yourselves!

The present progressive

To form the other tense we have met, the present progressive, you add the present progressive endings to the infinitive form of the verb, as with conjugation 3A.

The infinitive of conjugation 3B is formed in the same way as the infinitive of 3A, so the present progressive of the verb **furo** is as follows:

	verb stem	progressive marker	ending	verb form
I	furan	ay	aa	**furánayaa**
you (sg.)	furan	ay	taa	**furánaysaa**
he, it (m.)	furan	ay	aa	**furánayaa**
she, it (f.)	furan	ay	taa	**furánaysaa**
we	furan	ay	naa	**furánaynaa**
you (pl.)	furan	ay	taan	**furánaysaan**
they	furan	ay	aan	**furánayaan**

Exercise

5 Write out in full the general present and present progressive tense of the following verbs, all of which are conjugation 3B verbs:

1 dhegeyso   to listen
2 baro   to learn
3 qaado   to take for oneself

Numbers above ten

labaátan	20	boqol	100
sóddon	30	kún	1,000
afártan	40	malyúun	1,000,000
kónton	50		
líxdan	60		
toddobaátan	70		
siddeétan	80		
sagaáshan	90		

All these numbers are masculine nouns.

The combination of these in numbers such as 34, 57 etc. is according to the following pattern, which is also the pattern for the 'teen' numbers. Note that sometimes when the number one **ków** is used in a combination before a vowel it may become **koób**. Note also that any number followed by another number in a combination must be used in the premodifier form.

ków/koób iyo toban	11	líx iyo sóddon	36
		toddobá iyo sóddon	37
labá iyo toban	12	siddeéd iyo afártan	48
sáddex iyo toban	13	sagaál iyo kónton	59
áfar iyo toban	14	labá iyo líxdan	62
ków iyo labaátan	21	sáddex iyo toddobaátan	73
labá iyo labaátan	22	áfar iyo siddeétan	84
shán iyo labaátan	25	shán iyo sagaáshan	95

To count hundreds, thousands and millions the genitive construction is used.

sáddex boqól	300
labá kún	2,000
siddeéd malyuún	8,000,000

These are then joined by **iyo** with the combinations for the numbers up to 99 as well as with each other.

sáddex boqól iyo labá iyo líxdan	362
labá kún iyo shán boqól iyo labá iyo siddeetan	2582
kún iyo sagaál boqól iyo sáddex iyo sagaáshan	1993
sáddex kún iyo shán boqól iyo toddobá iyo labaátan	3527

Exercise

6 Write out the following numbers in Somali:

74; 29; 52; 628; 893; 1920; 4864

The time

To ask what the time is use the phrase:

Saacáddu waa ímmisa?	What is the time?
Waa ímmisádií?	What is the time?

To give the time is very straightforward. You use the number of the hour with the definite article.

Waa kówda.	It is one o'clock.
Waa shánta.	It is five o'clock.

Remember the above times are in the future, shown by the use of the **-ka/-ta** definite article. If you wish to refer to a time in the past then use the **-kií/-tií** definite article.

Tobánkií.	Ten o'clock (in the past).
Labá iyo tobánkií.	Twelve o'clock (in the past).

The following words are also used in the time:

rúbuc (m. d2)	quarter
bádh (m. d4)	half
Waa afárta iyo bádhka.	It is half past four.
Waa labáda iyo rúbuca.	It is quarter past two.
Waa koób iyo tobánka oo rúbuc lá'.	It is quarter to eleven (lit.: 'eleven less a quarter').

The date

The names of the months in Somali are borrowed from Europe. They vary a little, since they have been borrowed from both English and Italian.

Janaáyo	January
Febraáyo	February
Maárso	March
Abriíl	April
Maájo	May
Juún	June
Luúlyo	July
Agoósto	August
Sebtember	September
Oktoóbar	October
Noofémbar	November
Disémbar	December

All of the months are feminine nouns.

To give the date with the month, the number for the date is used with the definite article followed by the name of the month.

    shán iyo labaátanka Juún   25 June
    sáddex iyo tobánka Disémbar   13 December

Think about the usage of the different types of the definite article; if the date you are referring to is in the past then the **-kií** type article must be used.

    sáddex iyo labaátankií Abriíl   23 April (in the past)

Exercises

7 Translate the following dates into Somali:

1 12 March 1942
2 25 August 1984
3 16 April 1993
4 20 December 1954
5 19 September 1999

8 Translate the following times into Somali:

1 seven o'clock
2 twelve o'clock (in the past)
3 quarter past five
4 quarter to eight (in the past)
5 half past nine
6 half past seven

Dialogue

Maxamed and Axmed finish their meal

qadee (2B)	to have lunch
dhamee (2B)	to finish
macaán (adj.)	sweet, good tasting
ahaa	it was
fiicnaa	it was good (from **fiicán** + **ahaa**)
yimmaadá	comes (reduced paradigm of **yimi**)
cánab (m. d2)	grapes
ií	**i** + **ú**, 'for me'
múus (m. d4)	banana
macaányihiin	they are sweet
lagú	**la** + **kú**, 'one + in'
beer (1)	to cultivate, grow
walaál (f. d2)	sister
mar (1)	to pass along
heédheh	this is an interjection which is often used to call somebody
ímminkáannu	from **ímminka** + **báannu** '*now* we have ...', 'we have just ...'
mídho (m. collec.)	fruit
má doonayó	I do not want it
sáddex koób oo sháah áh	three cups of tea (**oo** is used here because there is a number with **kóob**)
waa hagáag	right (lit.: it is straightness)

Maxamed iyo Axmed makhaayadda way ku qadeynayaan. Imminkana cuntada way dhammeeyeen.

MAXAMED: Cuntadu ma macaanayd?
AXMED: Haa, aad bay u fiicnayd.

Yuusuf ayaa yimmaada.

Yuusuf:	Wax kale ma doonaysaan?
Maxamed:	Haa. Canab ii keen.
Axmed:	Muus ii keen.
Yuusuf:	Waa yahay. Canabku waa macaanyahay. Dalka Yaman ayaa lagu beeray.

Maxamed walaashiis ayaa maraysa waddada. Magaceedu waa Sacdiya. Maxamed wuu arkaa.

Maxamed:	Sacdiyay, heedheh.
Sacdiya:	War, Maxamed. Hayye.
Maxamed:	Is ka warran. Ma la wanaagsanyahay?
Sacdiya:	Waa la fiicanyahay. Bal adiga, is ka warran.
Maxamed:	Aad iyo aad baan u fiicanahay. Illaah mahaddi. Soo dhowow. Soo fadhiiso. Imminkaannu qadeynay.
Sacdiya:	Mahadsanid.
Maxamed:	Axmed, waa tan walaashay Sacdiya.
Axmed:	Barasho wanaagsan.
Sacdiya:	Barasho wanaagsan. Iska warran.
Axmed:	Waan fiicanahay.

Yuusuf ayaa keena midhaha.

Maxamed:	Sacdiya, canab ma doonaysaa?
Sacdiya:	Maya ma doonayo. Shaahse ayaan idinla cabbayaa.
Maxamed:	Waa yahay. Yuusuf. Saddex koob oo shaah ah noo keen.
Yuusuf:	Waa hagaag.

Maxamed and Axmed are having lunch in the restaurant; and now they have finished their food.

Maxamed:	*Was the food tasty?*
Axmed:	*Yes, it was very good.*

Yuusuf comes.

Yuusuf:	*Would you like something else?*
Maxamed:	*Yes. Bring me grapes.*
Axmed:	*Bring me a banana.*
Yuusuf:	*Right. The grapes are sweet. They were grown in Yemen.*

Maxamed's sister is passing along the street. Her name is Sacdiya. Maxamed sees her.

MAXAMED: *Sacdiya, hey.*
SACDIYA: *Hey, Maxamed. Hi there.*
MAXAMED: *How are you? Are you well?*
SACDIYA: *I am well. How are you?*
MAXAMED: *I am very well. Thanks to God. Welcome. Sit down. We have just had lunch.*
SACDIYA: *Thank you.*
MAXAMED: *Axmed, this is my sister Sacdiya.*
AXMED: *Pleased to meet you.*
SACDIYA: *Pleased to meet you. How are you?*
AXMED: *I am well.*

Yuusuf brings the fruit.

MAXAMED: *Sacdiya, would you like some grapes?*
SACDIYA: *No, I would not like any. But I will drink some tea with you.*
MAXAMED: *Right. Yuusuf. Bring us three cups of tea.*
YUUSUF: *OK.*

Notes

1   A paradigm is a pattern which a verb may follow. For example, the set of forms of the general past of conjugation 2A verbs is called the paradigm for 2A verbs in the general past. 'Paradigm' is simply a useful word with which to refer to the set of forms for a particular type of verb in a particular mood or tense.
2   See p. 18 for a list of the guttural consonants.

7 Hudheelka

The hotel

> **By the end of this lesson you should:**
> - know about the infinitive
> - be able to form the future tense, e.g. 'I will go'
> - be able to form the habitual past tense, e.g. 'I used to go'
> - be able to give negative commands, e.g. 'Do not go'
> - know how to form the negative of the general past
> - know something about Somali names

Dialogue

Vocabulary

gaadh (1)	to reach	**jéeb** (m. d4)	pocket
hudhéel gúdihíisa	inside the hotel	**wáxbá**	with a negative verb 'nothing'
yidhaahdaa	says		
ma joógi rabtaa	do you want to stay?	**waan lá'ahay**	I am without it
		igá	**i** + **ká**, 'from me'
qól (m. d4)	room	**waa ínaad heshó**	you must find it
ká timi	you came from	**márkaás**	at that time
immisáad	from **ímmisa** + **báad** 'how long + you'	**dhéxdíisa**	it's inside
		tágsiga dhéxdíisa	inside the taxi
		sów má ahá	is it not?
hayso (3B)	to have	**áad iyo áad báad ú**	very very much
toddobáad (m. d2)	week		
rúntií	lit.: the truth; of course	**mahadsán** (adj.)	thanked
		mahadsántahay	you are thanked
rún (f.)	truth	**muhíim** (m. d2)	importance
hay (2A)	to have	**muhíim áh**	which is important

waa rúntaá	you are right	furán (adj.)	open
musqúl (f. d1)	bathroom	furántahay	it is open
musqúlléh	with a bathroom	telefóon (m. d2)	telephone
námbar (m. d2)	number	telefóon dir (1)	to telephone, ú:
námbarkíisu	its number		someone
wéli maý	not yet	ágtéeda	by, at the side of

Bill Hudheel Djibouti buu gaadhaa. Hudheelka wuu galaa. Hudheelka gudihiisa naag baa joogta. Bill wuxuu yidhaahdaa:

BILL: Assalaamu calaykum.
NAAGTA: Calaykum assalaam. Halkan ma joogi rabtaa?
BILL: Haa. Qol baan doonayaa.
NAAGTA: Waa hagaag. Magacaa?
BILL: Magacaygu waa Bill. Magacaa adiga?
NAAGTA: Khadija baa la yidhaahdaa. Xaggee baad ka timi?
BILL: Landhan baan ka imi.
KHADIIJA: Immisaad joogaysaa Djibouti?
BILL: Toddobaad keliya baan joogi doonaa.
KHADIIJA: Waa yahay. Basaboorkaaga ma haysataa?
BILL: Runtii, waan hayaa. Jeebkayga buu ku jiraa.

Bill basaboorkiisa jeebkiisa buu ka doondoonaa. Waxbase ka ma helo.

BILL: Wallaah basaboorkayga baa iga lumay! Waan la'ahay.
KHADIIJA: Waase inaad hesho, Bill.

Markaas baa tagsiluhu hudheelka galaa.

TAGSILAHA: Waryaa. Wax baan tagsiga dhexdiisa ka helay. Waa basaboorkaaga sow ma aha?
BILL: Haa. Illaah mahaddi. Aad iyo aad baad u mahadsantahay walaal. Basaboorkaygu waa wax muhiim ah.
TAGSILAHA: Waa runtaa.

Bill basaboorkiisa wuu tusaa.

KHADIIJA: Waa yahay. Qol musqulleh ma rabtaa?
BILL: Haa, mid musqulleh baan rabaa.
KHADIIJA: Waa yahay. Qolkaaga nambarkiisu waa siddeed iyo toban. Ma qadeysay?
BILL: Weli may.
KHADIIJA: Waa yahay. Imminka waad qadeyn kartaa. Makhaayaddu waa furantahay.

BILL: Mahadsanid. Telefoon halkan miyaan ka diri karaa?
KHADIIJA: Maya, laakiin telefoon boostada agteeda baa jira.
BILL: Mahadsanid.

Bill makhaayadda wuu galaa, wuuna cunaa.

Bill reaches the Hotel Djibouti. He enters the hotel. There is a woman inside the hotel. Bill says:

BILL: Peace be with you.
THE WOMAN: And peace be with you. Do you want to stay here?
BILL: Yes, I would like a room.
THE WOMAN: Right. What is your name?
BILL: My name is Bill. What is your name?
THE WOMAN: I am called Khadiija. Where have you come from?
BILL: I have come from London.
KHADIIJA: How long are you staying in Djibouti?
BILL: I will stay only one week.
KHADIIJA: Right. Do you have your passport?
BILL: Of course I have it. It is in my pocket.

Bill looks for his passport in his pocket. But he does not find anything.

BILL: My goodness, I have lost my passport! I cannot find it.
KHADIIJA: But you must find it, Bill.

At that point the taxi owner enters the hotel.

THE TAXI DRIVER: Hey, I found something in the taxi. It is your passport, isn't it?
BILL: Yes. Thanks to God. Thank you very very much, brother. My passport is important.
THE TAXI DRIVER: You're right.

Bill shows his passport.

KHADIIJA: Right. Do you want a room with a bathroom?
BILL: Yes, I want one with a bathroom.
KHADIIJA: Right. The number of your room is eighteen. Have you had lunch?
BILL: Not yet.
KHADIIJA: Right. You can have lunch now. The restaurant is open.
BILL: Thank you. Can I telephone from here?
KHADIIJA: No, but there is a telephone by the post office.
BILL: Thank you.

Bill enters the restaurant and eats.

The infinitive

We have already met the infinitive forms of conjugations 2 and 3. The infinitive of conjugation 1 verbs is formed in the following way: add **-i** to the base form.

The stress-tone in the infinitive of these verbs is on the penultimate vowel.

diid	**diídi**	to refuse
dir	**díri**	to send
baaq	**baáqi**	to announce

There are some sound changes when the infinitive ending is added.

(a) If the verb is a single syllable with the vowel **a** then the vowel will change to **e** in the infinitive (except for the cases in (b) immediately below).

| **tag** | **tégi** | to go |
| **gal** | **géli** | to enter |

(b) If the verb is a single syllable with the vowel **a** and the final consonant is a guttural consonant then the **a** changes to **i**.

| **bax** | **bíxi** | to leave |
| **kac** | **kíci** | to rise |

(c) Another sound change is the one that was discussed on pp. 75–76 in Lesson 5.

| **maqal** | **máqli** | to hear |

The infinitive is a verb form that never stands on its own in Somali. It is used as a part of certain tenses and moods and with certain auxiliary verbs.

Exercise

1 Form the infinitive from the following verbs:

1 safee
2 xidh
3 qabo
4 hadal
5 sii
6 qosol

The future

The future tense may be expressed in two ways in Somali. The first, the future meaning of the present progressive, we have already met. The other way is to use the verb **doon**. On its own **doon** means 'to want'. However, when it is used with the infinitive of another verb it conveys the future tense. When used in this way the verb **doon** is always in the general present tense and is preceded by the infinitive of the verb you are using. Note that **doon** in this context is always in the general present tense and no other.

Waan héli doonaa.	I will find it.
Waydin karín doontaan.	You (pl.) will cook it.

The full pattern of the future tense of the verb **dhis**, 'to build', is given below. You can easily work out the future of any other verb. Just use the infinitive of the verb with the appropriate form of **doon**.

	infinitive of the verb	*appropriate form of* **doon**
I	dhisi	**doonaa**
you (sg.)	dhisi	**doontaa**
he, it (m.)	dhisi	**doonaa**
she, it (f.)	dhisi	**doontaa**
we	dhisi	**doonnaa**
you (pl.)	dhisi	**doontaan**
they	dhisi	**doonaan**

Exercise

2 Translate the following sentences into Somali, using the construction with **doon** to express the future:

1 He will have lunch tomorrow.
2 I will teach them the lesson in March.
3 They will send many letters to the ambassador.
4 Will you read this book for the students tomorrow?
5 She will leave the new house.
6 After many months he will visit the brother.

The habitual past

The habitual past is the tense which in English is expressed by 'used to'. This is expressed in Somali by using the verb **jir**. When used on its own this means 'to be in a place'. The verb **jir** is used with the infinitive of the verb you want to use, and the tense of **jir** is the general past, no other.

Waan barán jiray.	I used to learn it.
Waydin karín jirteen.	You (pl.) used to cook it.
Wuu tégi jiray.	He used to go.

Exercise

3 Translate the following sentences into Somali:

1 They used to graze the burden camels here.
2 I used to drink a lot of tea.
3 Did you [used to] learn easy languages?
4 Cabdullaahi used to read good books.
5 She used to bring rice and meat.
6 What did you [used to] make?

The negative imperative

The negative imperative is used when you want to tell somebody not to do something.

It is formed by using the negative imperative form of the verb preceded by the negative imperative word **ha**. The negative imperative form of conjugation 2 and conjugation 3 verbs is the same as the infinitive. For example:

kari	**Ha karín!**	Do not cook!
qadee	**Ha qadeýn!**	Do not have lunch!
joogso	**Ha joogsán!**	Do not stop!
qabo	**Ha qabán!**	Do not catch it!

There is an additional ending to these two conjugations, namely **-nín**. This is used optionally in the singular, but must be used in the plural as described below. Thus we have the following forms:

| **Ha karinín!** | Do not cook! |
| **Ha qadeynín!** | Do not have lunch! |

Ha joogsanín!	Do not stop!
Ha qabanín!	Do not catch it!

With conjugation 1 verbs the negative imperative is formed by adding **-n** to the infinitive of the verb. Note that the stress-tone is on the penultimate vowel in these forms.

keen	Ha keénin!	Do not bring it!
tag	Ha tégin!	Do not go!

Ha comes before any prepositions, object pronouns or deictics in the sentence.

Ha na siín!	Do not give it to us!
Baríiska ha soó iibsán!	Do not buy the rice!
Maxámed ha ú sameýn!	Do not do it for Maxamed!

The plural of the negative imperative is formed by adding **-a** to the negative forms. For verbs of conjugations 2 and 3 you must add the **-a** to the longer form with the **-nin** ending (see above). Note that in all negative imperative plural forms the stress-tone is on the penultimate vowel.

keen	Ha keenína!	Do not bring (pl.) it!
tag	Ha tegína!	Do not go (pl.)!
kari	Ha karinína!	Do not cook (pl.) it!

Exercise

4 Change these positive imperatives into negative imperatives and translate into English:

1 Keen!
2 Suga!
3 Caddee!
4 Inammada toosi!
5 Baraha dhegeyso!
6 Warqadda i tusa!

The negative of the general past

The negative form of the general past tense is easy to learn in Somali because there is only one form for all persons and numbers. For all the conjugations the form of the verb is the same as the short version of the negative imperative verb form. This is used with the negative **má**, which is placed before the verb.

Note in conjugation 1 the only difference in the negative imperative is the stress-tone. There is a stress-tone on the final vowel in the negative general past.

Má cunín. I/you/he/she/we/you(pl.)/they did not eat it.
Má qabán. I/you/he/she/we/you(pl.)/they did not catch it.

When **má** occurs in a sentence it comes after preverbal prepositions and object pronouns but before deictic words.

Ku má arkín. I/you/he/she/we/you(pl.)/they did not see you.

Baríiska má soó iibsán. I/you/he/she/we/you(pl.)/they did not buy the rice.

Ú má keenín. I/you/he/she/we/you(pl.)/they did not bring it for him.[1]

As you can see from these examples some confusion could arise from the lack of distinction in the verb form. Ambiguity can be prevented by the use of the subject verbal pronouns with the **má** negative word. The combined forms are as follows:

I	má + aan	**má'aan**
you (sg.)	má + aad	**má'aad**
he, it (m.)	má + uu	**mú'uu**
she, it (f.)	má + ay	**má'ay**
we (incl.)	má + aynu	**má'aynu**
we (excl.)	má + aannu	**má'aannu**
you (pl.)	má + aydin	**má'aydin**
they	má + ay	**má'ay**

These forms are more often pronounced and written without the glottal stop, giving the following forms:

I	má + aan	**máan**
you (sg.)	má + aad	**máad**
he, it (m.)	má + uu	**múu**
she, it (f.)	má + ay	**máy**
we (incl.)	má + aynu	**máynu**
we (excl.)	má + aannu	**máannu**
you (pl.)	má + aydin	**máydin**
they	má + ay	**máy**

So the sentences above may be as follows with explicit pronoun subjects:

Máan cunín.	I did not eat it.
Máy qabán.	She/they did not catch it.
Ku máannu arkín.	We did not see you.
Baríiska mú'uu soó iibsán.	He did not buy the rice.
Ú máan keenín.	I did not bring it for them (or her or him).

Note that **má** plus the verbal pronoun is ordered in the sentence as we mentioned above.

Despite the fact that these subject pronouns may be used, the most common way of expressing the negative general past seems to be with **má** on its own. In most cases context will provide the means of deciding what the subject is as well as the use of independent pronouns, which we shall meet later.

Exercise

5 Convert the following sentences into negative sentences and translate into English:

1 Dugsiga waan tagay.
2 Bill basaboorkii wuu helay.
3 Caano way dhami jireen.
4 Hudheelka waannu gallay.
5 Shaleyto barnaamijka waan dhegeystay.
6 Wax baan arkay.

Names

A Somali name is made up of the name of the individual person and that person's father. Often the name of the grandfather is also commonly used.

Jawaahir Maxamed Muuse

This would be the name of a woman whose father's name is Maxamed and grandfather's name is Muuse. Most Somalis will be able to take the patrilineal lineage much further back than the names used in everyday situations.

A woman does not take on any names from the man she marries; when a woman marries, her name remains exactly the same.

Reading practice

The seasons

Vocabulary

xílli (m. d2)	season
Jiiláal (m.)	December to March (hot, dry season)
Gú' (f.)	April to June (main wet season)
Xagáa (m.)	July to August (mainly a dry season)
Daýr (f.)	September to November (a lesser wet season)
ugú kulúl	the hottest
yihiin	they are
abaár (f. d1)	drought
róob (m. d4)	rain
má do'ó	does not fall
da'	to fall (of rain), rain
dabaýl (f. d1)	wind
waqoóyi (m.)	north
bári (m.)	east
ilaa	until, up to (in time and also in space)
dhúl (m. d4)	earth, land
barwaáqo (f. d6)	verdant land and the accompanying plentiful milk and food etc.
géel (m. collec.)	camels (the form **géela** means 'the camels'; it is an irregular definite article)

ádhi (m. collec.)	sheep and goats
ló' (f. collec.)	cattle
sí fiicán . . . ú	well
dád (m. collec.)	people
faraxsán	happy
faraxsányihiin	they are happy
soco (3B)	to proceed, continue
dhínac (m. d2)	side; with **ká**: from the direction of
koonfúr (f.)	south
galbéed (m.)	west
xágga	lit.: the direction; in the area of

Xilliyada[2]

Xilliyadu waa afar: Jiilaal, Gu', Xagaa iyo Dayr. Jiilaalku waa xilliga ugu kulul. Bilaha Jiilaalku waxay yihiin: Disembar, Janaayo, Febraayo iyo Maarso. Hawada Jiilaal waa kulayl iyo abaar. Roobku ma do'o dabaysha ayaana waqooyiga bari ka timaadda. Abriil ilaa Juun waa xilliga Gu'. Gu'da roob baa da'a dhulkuna waa barwaaqo. Geela, adhiga iyo lo'du si fiican bay u daaqaan xilliga Gu' ah. Dadkuna way faraxsanyihiin. Gu'da ka dib waa xilliga Xagaa. Luuliyo ilaa Agoosto buu socdaa. Dabaysha ayaa ka timaadda dhinaca koonfurta galbeed roob ayaana da'a xagga xeebta koonfureed. Xilliga Xagaa ka dib waa xilliga Dayr. Sebtembar ilaa Noofembar buu socdaa. Xilligan roob yar baa da'a.

The seasons

There are four seasons (lit.: the seasons are four): *Jiilaal, Gu', Xagaa and Dayr.*[3] *Jiilaal is the hottest season. The months of Jiilaal are: December, January, February and March. The weather of Jiilaal is hot and dry* (lit.: drought). *The rain does not fall and the wind comes from the north-east. April to June is the season Gu'. In Gu' the rain falls and the land is verdant. Camels, sheep and goats and cattle graze well in Gu'. And the people are happy. After Gu' is the season Xagaa. It continues from July to August. The wind comes from the direction of the south-west and rain falls on the south coast. After the season Xagaa is the season Dayr. It continues from September until November. In this season a little rain falls.*

Notes

1. Or her or them!
2. This passage is a slightly edited version of a portion of *Af Soomaali Fasalka Labaad*, a book published for schools in 1976 in Mogadishu by the then Ministry of Education and Training.
3. We shall not translate these seasons into English since, although in terms of time they correspond roughly to winter, spring, summer and autumn respectively, the weather is so different that the English word would provide a different sense of what the season implies.

8 Bill telefoon buu diraa

Bill makes a telephone call

> **By the end of this lesson you should be able to:**
> - use the past progressive, e.g. 'I was going'
> - use the negative of the general present
> - say 'that', 'this', etc.
> - use the auxiliary verbs 'to be able to', 'to want to' and 'to fail to'
> - use the impersonal pronoun **la** and translate the passive of English

Dialogue

Bill wants to telephone his friend Yoonis

Vocabulary

telefóon ú dir (1)	to telephone someone
wáx	used here to mean 'something' (this word is often used in this way)
weydii (2A)	to ask someone something
jídka marayá	passing along the street
raálli ahów	excuse me (lit.: be tolerant, agreeable)
ií	i + ú, 'to me'
sheeg (1)	to tell; with **ú**, to tell someone
agagáar (m.)	surroundings, neighbourhood
agagáarkán	this area
jídkaás dhínacíisa kalé	the other side of that road (lit.: that road, its other side)
míd (m.)	one

eeg (1)	to look
adáa mudán	you're welcome
gudub (1, gudbaa)	to cross
garaac (1)	to knock, dial (on a number-pad telephone)
jawáab (1)	to answer
mágacéedu	her name (subject)
ín yár	a little
ú kaadi (2A)	to wait, delay
ú yeedh (1)	to call someone
degdeg (1)	to hurry
lá hadal (1)	to speak with
kaagá	ku + ú + ká 'you + to + from', 'to you from'
sáfar (m.)	journey
dhówr saacadoód	a few hours
dhówr	few (use this word in the same way as you would a number)
hurud (1, hurdaa)	to sleep
dhaxán (f.)	cold(ness)
dhaxán báy ahayd	it was cold
búste (m. d7)	blanket
hurdo (f.)	sleep
oo	and (among other uses, this word is used to join two declarative clauses as here)
yaab (1)	to be astonished
wébi (m. d2)	river
dégmo (f. d6)	settlement, community
dhinacyádíisa	its sides
kú wareegsán	surrounded by
lamaddegáan (m.)	desert
Eritareya	Eritrea
bád (f. d1)	sea
cás (adj.)	red
Danaákil	Danakil
ú dhoẃ	near to
búur (m. d1)	mountain
tóg (m. d4)	dry valley, ravine, river bed
wareeg (1)	to revolve, go around, tour around

Bill wuxuu joogaa Djibouti. Qol buu helay, wuuna qadeeyay. Imminka telefoon buu saaxiibkiisa Yoonis u diri rabaa. Bill wuxuu ka baxaa hudheelka wuxuuna wax weydiinayaa nin jidka maraya.

BILL:	Raalli ahow. Waxaan doondoonayaa telefoon. Ii sheeg, telefoon ma jiraa agagaarkan?
NINKA:	Haa jidka dhinaciisa kale mid baa jira. Eeg. Boostada agteeda. Ma aragtaa?
BILL:	Haa waan arkaa. Waa yahay. Aad baad u mahadsantahay.
NINKA:	Adaa mudan.

Bill telefoonka buu jidka u gudbaa. Nambarka wuu garaacaa. Yoonis xaaskiisa baa jawaabta. Magaceedu waa Idil.

IDIL:	Hayye.
BILL:	Idilay, waa Bill. Is ka warran.
IDIL:	Bill, waa la wanaagsanyahay. Is ka warran adiga.
BILL:	Waan fiicanahay. Yoonis ma joogaa?
IDIL:	Haa, wuu joogaa. In yar u kaadi waan u yeedhayaa. Yoonis, kaalay, degdeg. Bill la hadal, Djibouti buu kaaga soo dirayaa.
YOONIS:	Waryaa, Bill. Is ka warran.
BILL:	Waryaa, Yoonis, waa la wanaagsanyahay. Is ka warran adigu.
YOONIS:	Waa la fiicanyahay. Safarka ka warran.
BILL:	Safarku aad buu u fiicnaa. Dhowr saacadood baan hurday dayuuradduna dhaxan bay ahayd. Bustese baa la i siiyay. Hurdoda ka dib waan toosay oo yaabay. Webiga Nayl baan arkay. Degmooyinka webiga Nayl dhinacyadiisa baan arkay, webigana waxa ku wareegsanaa lamadegaan. Dabadeedna dayuuraddu xeebta Eritareya bay raacday. Badda cas baan arkay iyo lamaddegaanka Danaakil. Dabadeedna waxaannu gaadhnay Djibouti. Dalka Djibouti agagaarkiisa waxaan ku arkay buuro iyo togag badan.
YOONIS:	Waa yahay. Djibouti ma ka heshaa?
BILL:	Haa. Hudheel baan helay. Imminka in yar magaalada baan wareegi doonaa.
YOONIS:	Waa yahay. Nabad gelyo, Bill.
BILL:	Nabad gelyo, Yoonis.

Bill is in Djibouti. He has found a room and has had lunch. Now he wants to telephone his friend Yoonis. Bill leaves the hotel and asks something of a man passing down the street.

BILL:	*Excuse me. I am looking for a telephone. Tell me, is there a telephone in this area?*
THE MAN:	*Yes, there is one on the other side of the road. Look. By the post office. Do you see it?*

BILL: Yes, I see it. Right. Thank you very much.
THE MAN: You're welcome.

Bill crosses the street to the telephone. He dials the number. Yoonis's wife answers. Her name is Idil.

IDIL: Hello.
BILL: Idil, it's Bill. How are you?
IDIL: Bill, I'm well. How are you?
BILL: I am well. Is Yoonis there?
IDIL: Yes, he's here. Wait a moment, I'll call him. Yoonis, come, hurry. Speak with Bill, he is phoning you from Djibouti.
YOONIS: Hi, Bill. How are you?
BILL: Hi, Yoonis, I am well. How are you?
YOONIS: I am well. How was the journey?
BILL: The journey was very good. I slept for a few hours, and it was cold in the plane. But I was given a blanket. After the sleep I woke up and I was astonished. I saw the river Nile. I saw the settlements on the sides of the Nile and around the river was desert. Then the aeroplane followed the coast of Eritrea. I saw the Red Sea and the Danakil desert. Then we reached Djibouti. In the country of Djibouti I saw many mountains and ravines.
YOONIS: Right. Do you like Djibouti?
BILL: Yes. I found a hotel. Now I am going to tour around the town a little.
YOONIS: Right. Goodbye, Bill.
BILL: Goodbye, Yoonis.

The past progressive

The past progressive tense is used for actions that were in progress at some time in the past, and thus it translates the English 'I was going', 'they were talking', etc. The formation of the tense is easy, as it is formed in the same way as the present progressive except that the past tense endings are used instead of the present tense endings.

Waan cúnayay.   I was eating it.
Waan karínayay.   I was cooking it.

The following table gives the form for conjugation 1 using the example **keen**, 'to bring':

	verb stem	progressive marker	ending	verb form
I	keen	ay	ay	**keénayay**
you (sg.)	keen	ay	tay	**keénaysay**
he, it (m.)	keen	ay	ay	**keénayay**
she, it (f.)	keen	ay	tay	**keénaysay**
we	keen	ay	nay	**keénaynay**
you (pl.)	keen	ay	teen	**keénayseen**
they	keen	ay	een	**keénayeen**

Remember that for conjugations 2 and 3 the form of the verb to which the endings are added is the infinitive. The following tables give examples of the past progressive for these two conjugations:

	verb stem	progressive marker	ending	verb form
I	karin	ay	ay	**karínayay**
you (sg.)	karin	ay	tay	**karínaysay**
he, it (m.)	karin	ay	ay	**karínayay**
she, it (f.)	karin	ay	tay	**karínaysay**
we	karin	ay	nay	**karínaynay**
you (pl.)	karin	ay	teen	**karínayseen**
they	karin	ay	een	**karínayeen**

	verb stem	progressive marker	ending	verb form
I	sameyn	ay	ay	**sameýnayay**
you (sg.)	sameyn	ay	tay	**sameýnaysay**
he, it (m.)	sameyn	ay	ay	**sameýnayay**
she, it (f.)	sameyn	ay	tay	**sameýnaysay**
we	sameyn	ay	nay	**sameýnaynay**
you (pl.)	sameyn	ay	teen	**sameýnayseen**
they	sameyn	ay	een	**sameýnayeen**

	verb stem	progressive marker	ending	verb form
I	joogsan	ay	ay	**joogsánayay**
you (sg.)	joogsan	ay	tay	**joogsánaysay**
he, it (m.)	joogsan	ay	ay	**joogsánayay**
she, it (f.)	joogsan	ay	tay	**joogsánaysay**
we	joogsan	ay	nay	**joogsánaynay**
you (pl.)	joogsan	ay	teen	**joogsánayseen**
they	joogsan	ay	een	**joogsánayeen**

There are no new sound changes to learn with this tense, but remember the change from **t** to **s** following the progressive marker.

Exercise

1 Translate the following sentences into Somali:

1 They were taking the shoes.
2 You were reading it for Cali.
3 Was he having dinner?
4 Yesterday you were passing along the street.
5 It was raining.
6 Were you bringing it for her?

The negative of the general present

The negative of the general present is formed by using the negative word **má** we met in the last lesson and the negative general present form of the verb. The form of the verb is given below in the table. The difference between the negative and the positive is only in the final vowel; note that any sound changes that occur in the positive also occur in the negative, for example:

| **wáad heshaa** | you find |
| **má heshó** | you do not find |

Tables are given for conjugations 1, 2A and 3A; conjugations 2B and 3B are formed in an analogous way to 2A and 3A.

To form the negative you change the **-aa** ending to **-ó**, except for the second and third person plural forms which simply change the stress-tone pattern as shown.

	verb stem	ending	verb form
I	keen	ó	**keenó**
you (sg.)	keen	tó	**keentó**
he, it (m.)	keen	ó	**keenó**
she, it (f.)	keen	tó	**keentó**
we	keen	nó	**keennó**
you (pl.)	keen	táan	**keentáan**
they	keen	áan	**keenáan**

	verb stem	ending	verb form
I	kari	ó	**kariyó**
you (sg.)	kari	tó	**karisó**
he, it (m.)	kari	ó	**kariyó**
she, it (f.)	kari	tó	**karisó**
we	kari	nó	**karinnó**
you (pl.)	kari	táan	**karisáan**
they	kari	áan	**kariyáan**

	verb stem	ending	verb form
I	joogso	ó	**joogsadó**
you (sg.)	joogso	tó	**joogsató**
he, it (m.)	joogso	ó	**joogsadó**
she, it (f.)	joogso	tó	**joogsató**
we	joogso	nó	**joogsannó**
you (pl.)	joogso	táan	**joogsatáan**
they	joogso	áan	**joogsadáan**

There is another optional form for the second person singular; it means exactly the same as the form given in the tables.

má keentíd   you do not bring
má qabatíd   you do not catch

Note that **má** in this tense is used in the same way as for the negative of the general past tense. That is to say, the subject verbal pronouns may be used with **má**, for example:

máynu tagnó   we do not go
máad dhegeysató   you do not listen to it

You will remember that the auxiliary verb **doon** in the future tense was in the general present tense form. To make this into the negative the auxiliary verb **doon** is simply put into the negative general present.

| **má cúni doonáan** | they will not eat it |
| **máydin safeýn doontáan** | you (pl.) will not clean it |

Exercise

2 Change the following sentences from the positive into the negative:

1 Afaf badan way dhigaan.
2 Cadowgu waxyaabo badan waa bi'iyaa.
3 Waqooyiga dalka wuu tagaa.
4 Albaabbada way furaan.
5 Shimbiraha quruxsan waad aragtaa.
6 Koobab badan baan jebiyaa.

Demonstrative suffixes

The demonstrative suffixes are the equivalent of the English 'this' and 'that'. We shall look at four demonstratives here. They are given in the absolutive form and in the subject form:

	absolutive	*subject*
'this'	**-kán/-tán**	**-kani/-tani -kanu/-tanu**
'that'	**-kaás/-taás**	**-kaasi/-taasi -kaasu/taasu**
'that (quite far away)'	**-keér/-teér**	**-keeri/-teeri**
'that (very far away)'	**-koó/-toó**	**-kooyi/tooyi**

The suffixes beginning with **k** are added to masculine nouns and those beginning with **t** are added to feminine nouns. All the sound changes we looked at when the definite article suffixes are added also occur when these suffixes are added:

gabádh + tán	**gabádhán**	this girl
gúri + kaás	**gúrigaás**	that house
magaálo + teér	**magaaládeér**	that far-away town

When these suffixes are added to nouns which are the subject of a sentence then the subject forms as given in the table are used:

Nínkani wáa tagay.	This man went.
Nínkanu wáa tagay.	This man went.
Magaaládeeri waa magaalomádax.	That far-away town is a capital city.

There is no difference in meaning between the subject markers **-i** and **-u**.

These demonstratives, aside from being attached to nouns, may also be used on their own. They are as follows:

	absolutive	*subject*
'this one'	**kán/tán**	**kani/kanu/tani/tanu**
'that one'	**kaás/taás**	**kaasi/kaasu/taasi/taasu**
'that far-away one'	**keér/teér**	**keeri/keeru/teeri/teeru**
'that very far-away one'	**koó/toó**	**kooyi/tooyi**

There are plural forms of the demonstratives standing on their own. These are the following:

kúwán	**kúwanu/kúwani**	these ones
kúwaás	**kúwaasu/kúwaasi**	those ones
kúweér	**kúweeri**	those quite far-away ones
kúwoó	**kúwooyi**	those very far-away ones

Exercises

3 Translate the following sentences into Somali:

1 Did you hear that man?
2 Don't open that door!
3 They didn't go to that (far-away) country.
4 He didn't see that house.
5 She brought that food from the shop and cooked it.
6 He poured this milk into that cup.

4 Translate the following sentences into English:

1 Ninkan baa bari jiray.
2 Siddeed iyo afartan buug baan laybreeriga ka keenay.

3 Koonfurta geeska Afrika miyaydin tegi doontaan?
4 Maanta laybreeriga ku maan qori doono.
5 Qalinkii cusub ee Canab ha jebin!
6 Guriga way ka baxday saaxiibadna way booqatay.

The auxiliary verbs rab, 'to want to', kar, 'to be able to', and waa, 'to fail to'

All of these verbs may be used on their own or may be used as auxiliary verbs, in which case they are used with the infinitive of another verb. This is much like the equivalent use in English.

rab, *'to want to'*

Bariis báan cúni rabaa.	I want to eat rice.
Barnaámijkií cusúb báan dhegeysán rabaa.	I want to listen to the new programme.

kar, *'to be able to'*

Áf Soomaáliga báan kú hádli karaa.	I can speak in Somali.
Way karín karaan.	They can cook.

waa, *'to fail to'*

Used on its own this verb means 'to fail to get something, miss'. When it is used with an infinitive it means 'to fail to do the action expressed in the infinitive of the other verb'. In addition to this specific meaning the verb is often used to express a negative. Thus, for example

Waan cúni waayay may mean:	I failed to eat it
or	I did not eat it.

This verb is used in this way often in Somali.

When the various endings are added to the verb there are some changes which we must look at. Note that there is no difference in the actual endings; they are all the ones we have seen in relation to the other verbs.

When an ending beginning with a vowel is added to **waa** then the sound **y** is inserted to break up the two vowels:

| waa + ay | waayay | I/he failed to |
| waa + aan | waayaan | they fail to |

| **Waan tégi waayay.** | I failed to go/I did not go. |
| **Wuu akhríyi waayay.** | He failed to read it/he did not read it. |

When a verb ending which begins with a consonant is added to the verb then the form of the verb stem changes from **waa-** to **way-**. For example:

waa + tay	wayday	you/she failed to[1]
waa + teen	waydeen	you (pl.) failed to
waa + naa	waynaa	we fail to

| **Sháaha báy cábbi wayday.** | She failed to drink the tea/she did not drink the tea. |
| **Waannu tégi waynay.** | We failed to go/we did not go. |

Exercise

5 Translate the following sentences into Somali:

1 He failed to see the men.
2 I can take the food but I cannot cook it.
3 Can you cross the road?
4 He didn't call the boys.
5 Does she want to telephone the family?
6 You (pl.) want to learn the lessons.

Use of the impersonal pronoun la

The impersonal pronoun **la** is used often in Somali. We have already seen how it is used in the greeting **Wáa la fiicányahay** (lit.: 'one is well').

The main use of this pronoun is to provide a way to render the passive in Somali. There is no passive form of the verb in Somali, that is to say, there is no way in which the following sentence may be translated word for word into Somali: 'The bread was eaten'.

This type of sentence is rendered in Somali by using the pronoun **la**. Thus the sentence would be translated as follows:

Kibísta wáa la cunay.   Lit.: 'one ate the bread', i.e. 'the bread was eaten'.

This pronoun is always placed immediately before the object verbal pronouns in a sentence.

    Búugií cusúb báa la i tusay.   I was shown the new book (lit.: 'one showed me the new book').

Exercise

6 Translate the following sentences into Somali:

1 The bread was eaten.
2 The mosque was built.
3 Yesterday the milk was brought.
4 The number was dialled.
5 The shoes were made.
6 The camels were grazed.

Reading practice 🎧

Maxamed and Khadra go to buy some clothes

Vocabulary

xáas (m. d4)	wife, wife and children	**xidhántahay**	she is dressed
gado (3B)	to buy	**dhár** (m. d4)	clothes, fabric
maánta	today	**ká eegeeg** (1)	to look around
sháadh (m. d4)	shirt	**dukaánle** (m. d7)	shopkeeper
surwáal (m. d2) **saraawiil** (m.)	trousers	**már** (f. d1)	women's clothing (in plural, as here, it may mean material)
xidhán	dressed		
xidhányahay	he is dressed	**koofiyád** (f. d1)	hat
Khadri	subject form of Khadra	**xataa**	even
		cagaarán	green
guntiíno (f. d6)	woman's dress (like garment made of a cloth wrapped around the body, similar to a sari)	**oo dhán** (subject: **oo dhammi**)	all
		qaáli (m.)	expensive thing
		misé	or (this word for 'or' is only used in questions)

jabán (adj.)	cheap	**meél** (f. d1)	place
iská	fairly, rather	**bulúug** (m. d2)	blue
yahay	it is	**áh**	which is
míd ká jabán	a cheaper one	**waa** (1)	to fail, miss
hayso (3B)	to have	**dhíb** (m. d4)	problem, difficulty
ama	or (this word is used in statements)	**dhíb má léh**	no problem
		haddií Eebbe yidhaahdo	God willing; lit.: if God says it
cás	red	**Eébbe** (m.)	God
má jeclí	I do not like	**kú soó noqo** (3B)	to return to

Maxamed iyo xaaskiisa oo Khadra la yidhaahdo ayaa suuqa tagaya. Waxay rabaan inay dhar gataan. Maxamed shaadh iyo surwaal buu xidhanyahay. Khadrina guntiino bay xidhantahay. Khadri waxay rabtaa inay dhar soo iibsato. Dukaan bay ka eegeegtaa. Dukaanluhu wuxuu iibiyaa dhar badan. Dukaanluhu wuxuu hayaa maryo, surwaallo, shaadhadh, koofiyado, xataa kabo buu iibiyaa. Khadri dhar quruxsan bay aragtaa. Waa dhar cagaaran.
    Khadri dukaanlaha bay weydiinaysaa.

KHADRA: Ma dhar fiican baa?
DUKAANLIHII: Runtii waa dhar fiican. Dharkayga oo dhammi waa fiicanyahay.
KHADRA: Ma qaali baa mise waa jabanyahay?
DUKAANLIHII: Waa iska qaali.
KHADRA: Mid ka jaban ma haysaa?
DUKAANLIHII: Mid cagaaran ma rabtaa?
KHADRA: Haa mid cagaaran ama mid cas.
DUKAANLIHII: Waa yahay. Kan baan hayaa. Wuu ka jabanyahay kii kale.
KHADRA: Laakin kan ma jecli. Meelo kale baan ka eegi doonaa. Mahadsanid walaal, nabad gelyo.
DUKAANLIHII: Waa yahay, mahadsanid, nabad gelyo.

Khadra dhar bay wayday. Maxamedse surwaal buluug ah buu gatay.

MAXAMED: Dhar ma heshay?
KHADRA: Maya waan waayay. Mid quruxsan baan arkay, laakiin qaali buu ahaa.
MAXAMED: Waa yahay. Dhib ma leh. Maalin kale baad heli doontaa, haddii Eebbe yidhaahdo.

Maxamed iyo Khadri gurigii bay ku soo noqdaan.

Maxamed and his wife, Khadra, are going to the market. They want to buy clothes. Maxamed is wearing a shirt and trousers. And Khadra is wearing a guntiino. Khadra wants to buy some material. She looks around in a shop. The shopkeeper sells many clothes. The shopkeeper has material, trousers, shirts, hats, he even sells shoes. Khadra sees beautiful material. It is green material.
   Khadra asks the shopkeeper:

KHADRA:	*Is it good material?*
THE SHOPKEEPER:	*Of course it is good material. All my material is good.*
KHADRA:	*Is it expensive or cheap?*
THE SHOPKEEPER:	*It is quite expensive.*
KHADRA:	*Do you have a cheaper one?*
THE SHOPKEEPER:	*Do you want a green one?*
KHADRA:	*Yes, a green one or a red one.*
THE SHOPKEEPER:	*Right. I have this one. It is cheaper than the other one.*
KHADRA:	*But I don't like this one. I will look around in other places. Thank you, brother, goodbye.*
THE SHOPKEEPER:	*Right, thank you, goodbye.*

Khadra does not find material. But Maxamed has bought some blue trousers.

MAXAMED:	*Did you find some cloth?*
KHADRA:	*No, I didn't find any. I saw a beautiful one, but it was expensive.*
MAXAMED:	*Right. No problem. You will find one another day, God willing.*

Maxamed and Khadra return home.

Note

1   Remember **t** changes to **d** after **y**.

9 Bill lacag buu sariftaa

Bill changes some money

By the end of this lesson you should be able to:

- use the possessive endings
- use prepositional constructions
- use a number of other constructions with the possessive suffixes
- know the negative of the progressive aspect
- use the prefixing verb **yiil**, 'to be situated'

Dialogue

Vocabulary

lacág (f. mass)	money	**hórtíisa**	in front of
sarifo (3B)	to exchange money		(lit.: its front)
doóllar (m. d2)	dollar	**wáddo** (f. d6)	road
kalá yimi	he came from with	**sí tóos áh ú**	directly (lit.: a way which is directness)
ú beddel (1)	to change something for	**tóos** (m. d4)	directness, straightness
bángi (m. d2)	bank	**bidíx** (f.)	left
wáxay kú yaallaan	they are situated in	**midíg** (f.)	right
		ú leexo (3B)	to turn to
farasmagaálo (m.)	city centre, town centre	**ú soco** (3B)	to continue on
		meél lacágta lagú sarifó	a place in which one changes money
má yaqaán	he does not know		
sidaás dárteéd	because of that, therefore	**gabádh** (f. d3)	girl (may also be used for 'young woman')
nín ká míd áh niman	one of the men	**fáran** (m.)	franc
		yidhaahdaa	says
kú yaallaan	they are in	**tiri** (2A)	to count

Bill lacagtiisa buu sarifan doonaa. Landhan doollaro Mareykan ah buu kala yimid. Imminka wuxuu rabaa inuu u beddelo faranka Djibouti. Bangiyadu waxay ku yaalaan farasmagaalaha magaalada Djibouti. Billse meeshaas ma yaqaan. Sidaas darteed wuxuu weydiinayaa nin ka mid ah niman hudheelka hortiisa fadhiya.

BILL: Waryaa. Wax baan ku weydiin rabaa.
NINKII: Waa yahay maxaad i weydiinaysaa?
BILL: Waxaan doonayaa inaan bangiga tago ee ii sheeg xagguu ku yaallo?
NINKII: Bangiyadu waxay ku yaallaan meesha Place Lagarde la yidhaahdo.
BILL: Meeshaasi waa xaggee?
NINKII: Waa yahay waan kuu sheegi doonaa. Waddadan si toos ah u raac dabadeedna xagga bidixda u leexo. Dabadeedna toos u soco ka dibna xagga midigta u leexo. Markaasna waad arki doontaa bangiyo badan.
BILL: Waa yahay. Aad baad u mahadsantahay walaal.
NINKII: Adaa mudan.

Bill bangiyadii buu nelaa. Mid ka mid ah buu galaa. Waxa ku taalla meel lacagta lagu sarifto. Bill wuxuu gabadhii lacagta sarifanaysa ku yidhaahdaa:

BILL: Assaalaamu calaykum.
GABADHII: Calaykum assalaam.
BILL: Doollarkan ayaan rabaa inaan u beddelo faranka Djibouti.
GABADHII: Waa yahay. Waa immisa?
BILL: Waa laba boqol oo doollar.
GABADHII: Waa yahay. Waan tirin doonaa.

Gabadhii lacagtii bay tirisaa.

GABADHII: Waa yahay. Waa tan lacagtaadii.
BILL: Mahadsanid. Nabad gelyo.
GABADHII: Adaa mudan. Nabad gelyo.

Bill wants to change his money. He brought (lit.: he came with) American dollars from London. Now he wants to change it for Djibouti francs. The banks are in the centre of Djibouti town. But Bill does not know that place. Therefore he asks one of the men sitting in front of the hotel.

BILL: *Hey. I want to ask you something.*

THE MAN: *Right, what are you asking me?*
BILL: *I want to go to the bank, tell me where is it?*
THE MAN: *The banks are in a place called Place Lagarde.*
BILL: *Where is that place?*
THE MAN: *Right, I will tell you. Go straight along this street, then turn to the left. Then go straight on, and afterwards turn to the right. Then you will see many banks.*
BILL: *Right. Thank you very much, brother.*
THE MAN: *You're welcome.*

Bill finds the banks. He enters one of them. In it there is a place where one can exchange money. Bill says to the young woman who is changing the money:

BILL: *Peace be with you.*
THE YOUNG WOMAN: *Peace be with you.*
BILL: *I would like to change these dollars for Djibouti francs.*
THE YOUNG WOMAN: *Right, how much is it?*
BILL: *It is two hundred dollars.*
THE YOUNG WOMAN: *Right. I will count it.*

The young woman counts the money.

THE YOUNG WOMAN: *Right. Here is your money.*
BILL: *Thank you. Goodbye.*
THE YOUNG WOMAN: *You're welcome. Goodbye.*

Note on the dialogue: this dialogue contains a number of relative clauses. It is difficult to say much in Somali without sooner or later using a relative clause. We shall deal with relative clauses in more detail later but for the moment you can see that they do not incorporate **wâa** or the focus markers, and the verb form may be different to main clause verb forms. When you have learnt about relative clauses later in the course, come back to these dialogues and you will see then, in detail, how the relative clauses behave.

The possessive suffixes

In Somali possession in phrases such as 'her house', 'their shoes' is indicated by possessive suffixes which are added to the noun possessed.

The suffixes are given in the following table:

	masculine	*feminine*
my	káyga	táyda
your	káaga	táada
his/its (m.)	kíisa	tíisa
her/its (f.)	kéeda	téeda
our (incl.)	kéenna	téenna
our (excl.)	kayága	tayáda
your (pl.)	kíinna	tíinna
their	kóoda	tóoda

dálkóoda	their country
dukáankéenna	our (incl.) shop
lacágtáada	your money

All of the sound changes which affect the definite article suffix also affect these suffixes.

búuggíisa	his book
mágacáyga	my name
warqáddóoda	their letter
haẃsháyda	my work

These suffixes are made up of two parts, the possessive suffix proper and the definite article suffix which is the last part. It is this that shows the difference in case, thus if a possessed noun is the subject of a sentence then the final vowel is **-u**. For example:

Mágacáygu waa Rooble.	My name is Rooble.
Qálinkáygu wáa jabay.	My pen broke.

The **-ii** type definite article endings may also be used in these possessive suffixes where appropriate.

Búuggáygií wúu helay.	He found my book (referred to before).
Macállinkóodii waa ká baxay.	Their teacher left.

When the possessive suffix is added to a noun denoting a relative or a part of the body then the possessive suffix on its own is used without the definite article part at the end.

hooyádaý	my mother
aabbáhaý	my father
fártaý	my finger

These shorter versions are also used in some of the set phrases given below.

Note that the stress-tone pattern of these shorter forms is different to that of the forms with the definite article ending. The forms without the definite article ending are given below; note the difference for absolutive and subject case.

	masculine absolutive	subject	feminine absolutive	subject
my	**kaý**	**káy**	**taý**	**táy**
your	**kaá**	**káa**	**taá**	**táa**
his	**kiís**	**kîis**	**tiís**	**tîis**
her	**keéd**	**kéed**	**teéd**	**téed**
our (incl.)	**keén**	**kéen**	**teén**	**téen**
our (excl.)	**káyo**	**kayo**	**táyo**	**tayo**
your (pl.)	**kiín**	**kîin**	**tiín**	**tîin**
their	**koód**	**kóod**	**toód**	**tóod**

Exercises

1 Add the appropriate possessive suffix to the noun and translate into English:

1 Koob ... waan buuxsaday. (my)
2 Bariis ... ma karin. (their)
3 Baabuur ... cusub buu wadanayaa. (your sg.)
4 Shandado ... baan qaaday. (his)
5 Dameer ... ma ordo. (her)
6 Cunto ... waa cunto wanaagsan. (our incl.)

2 Translate the following sentences into Somali:

1 Their new ambassador visited the president of the country.
2 She read her newspaper yesterday.
3 Their prisoners did not escape.
4 I will meet with your brother tomorrow.
5 Your son broke my leg.
6 He mended his taxi.

Further uses of the possessive suffixes

The possessive suffixes are used with certain words of position and time to form phrases which in English translate as prepositions.

daárta gúdahéeda	inside the house (lit.: the house its inside)
míiska dúshíisa	on top of the table (lit.: the table its surface)

Common phrases of this sort are given below.

gúdihíisa	gúdehéeda	inside, within (a certain time)
debéddíisa	debéddéeda	outside
ágtíisa	ágtéeda	near
dúshíisa	dúshéeda	on top of
hoóstíisa	hoóstéeda	beneath
geéstíisa	geéstéeda	at the side of
hórtíisa	hórtéeda	in front of, before (time)
dabádíisa	dabádéeda	behind, after (time)
dártíisa	dárteeda	because of

Each of the nouns here is a noun that may be used in its own right.

gúdo (m. d6)	inside, interior
debéd (f. d1)	outside, exterior
ág (f. d1)	nearness
dúl (f. d4)	top, surface
hoós (f. d1)	bottom, lower part
geés (f. d4)	side
hór (f. d4)	front part
dábo (f.)	back part, behind
dár (f.)	reason

Note that there is a masculine and a feminine form for each of these, according to the noun going with the phrase.

dhárka dártíisa	because of the clothes

Because **dhar** is masculine the possessive suffix for 'his' is added to **dár**. In the following example the noun going with 'because of' is feminine and therefore the ending is 'her':

daárta dártéeda	because of the house

There is one of these phrases that is often used with 'their' because of its meaning.

dhéxdóoda	among, between
aẃrta dhéxdóoda	among the camels

Exercise

3 Translate the following sentences into Somali:
1 I took your pen from on top of the table.
2 Their house is in the town.
3 My farm is outside the town.
4 They entered the house because of the rain.
5 She found money under the table.
6 The post office is by the side of the mosque.

There are other common phrases which may be formed using the possessive suffixes.

They may be added to numbers, as in the following examples:

labádéenna	the two of us (lit.: our two)
tobánkíina	the ten of you (lit.: your (pl.) ten)
sáddexdóoda	the three of them (lit.: their three)

Also, the following phrases use the shorter version of the possessive suffix without the definite article at the end:

gíddigoód	all of
kúlligoód	all of
qáarkoód	some of
bádidoód	most of

danjirayaásha qáarkoód	some of the ambassadors
guryáha bádidoód	most of the houses

The short versions of the possessive endings are used in the following constructions:

with **kéli** (m.), singleness	**kéligeéd**	on her own
with **gooní** (f.), separateness	**gooníday**	me separately
with **wéli** (m.), still (and a negative verb)	**Wéligay má tegín.**	I still have not been.
with **rún** (f.), truth	**waa rúntaá**	you are right
with **beén** (f.), lie	**waa beéntaá**	you are lying

The final use of the possessive suffixes we shall look at here is in another type of genitive construction. (See Lesson 4 for the general genitive construction type.) The formation with the possessive suffixes is shown in the following examples:

Jawaáhir gúrigéeda   Jawaahir's house (lit.: Jawaahir her house)

macállinka búuggíisa   the teacher's book (lit.: the teacher his book)

The alternative way of saying these is as follows:

gúriga Jawaahír   Jawaahir's house
búugga macállinka   the teacher's book

Both types of genitive constructions are equally used in Somali.

Exercise

4 In the following sentences one of the two genitive constructions is used; change the sentence using the other genitive construction, then translate the sentences into English:

1 Ninka hooyadiis waa tagtay.
2 Qalinka Maxamed ha jebin!
3 Buugga ardeygu waa buug fiican.
4 Shaleyto aabbahay gaadhigiisa ayaan watay.
5 Albaabka daarta ayay furayeen.
6 Inanta magaceedu waa Shamis.

The negative of the progressive

The negative of the progressive (both present and past) is formed in a way that is familiar from the general past and general present.

The present progressive

The present progressive ending ends in the present tense endings:

waan tágayaa,   'I am going', in which the present tense ending is underlined.

One way of forming the negative in the present progressive is to change the positive present tense endings to the negative present tense endings we looked at for the general present tense in Lesson 8. The forms with the negative endings are then used with the negative word **má**.

	verb stem	progressive marker	ending	verb form
I	keen	ay	ó	**keénayó**
you (sg.)	keen	ay	tó	**keénaysó**
			tíd	**keénaysíd**
he, it (m.)	keen	ay	ó	**keénayó**
she, it (f.)	keen	ay	tó	**keénaysó**
we	keen	ay	nó	**keénaynó**
you (pl.)	keen	ay	táan	**keénaysáan**
they	keen	ay	áan	**keénayáan**

Other conjugations are formed in an analogous manner, thus we have the following for conjugation 2B, for example:

	verb stem	progressive marker	ending	verb form
I	sameyn	ay	ó	**sameýnayó**
you (sg.)	sameyn	ay	tó	**sameýnaysó**
			tíd	**sameýnaysíd**
he, it (m.)	sameyn	ay	ó	**sameýnayó**
she, it (f.)	sameyn	ay	tó	**sameýnaysó**
we	sameyn	ay	nó	**sameýnaynó**
you (pl.)	sameyn	ay	táan	**sameýnaysáan**
they	sameyn	ay	áan	**sameýnayáan**

Remember the change of **t** to **s** when it follows the **y** of the progressive marker.

There is another way of forming the negative of the present progressive. This is with an auxiliary form which immediately follows the infinitive of the verb.

The auxiliary form is as follows:

I	**máayó**	we	**máynó**
you (sg.)	**máysó/máysíd**	you (pl.)	**máysáan**
he, it (m.)	**máayo**	they	**máayáan**
she, it (f.)	**máysó**		

You can see the present negative endings in this auxiliary form. Note the difference in vowel length according to whether the ending begins with a consonant or a vowel.

Warqád qóri máayó.	I am not/he is not writing a letter.
Safeýn máayáan.	They are not cleaning it.
Máydin karínaysáan.	You (pl.) are not cooking it.
Má fúrayó.	He is not opening it.

The past progressive

The negative of the past progressive is formed using the negative word **má** and the following verb form, which is the same for all numbers:

conjugation 1:	add **-aýn** or **aynín** to the verb stem
keen + aýn	keénaýn
keen + aynín	keénaynín
Máydin cúnaýn.	You (pl.) were not eating it.
Máydin cúnaynín.	You (pl.) were not eating it.

conjugations 2 and 3:	add **-aýn** or **aynín** to the infinitive
karín + aýn	karínaýn
karín + aynín	karínaynín
qabán + aýn	qabánaýn
qabán + aynín	qabánaynín

Note that the **-ay-** in the negative ending may also be spelt **-ey-**:

Máad samaýnaýn.	You were not making it.
Máy baxsáneynín.	They were not escaping.

Exercise

5 Convert the following sentences into the negative and translate into English:

1 Shan shandadood wuu keenayaa.

2 Warqad way qoraysay.
3 Suuqa way tagayaan.
4 Barnaamijka cusub baan dhegeysanayay.
5 Caano waydin dhamaysaan.
6 Casharkii wuu caddeynayay.

The prefixing verbs

There are five verbs in Somali in which the different tenses and moods are not formed by the addition of suffixes only. These are called prefixing verbs because the person marker is added as a prefix (i.e. at the beginning of the verb stem). The five verbs are:

yiil	to be in a place (inanimate subject)
yimi	to come
yidhi	to say
yiqiin	to know
yahay	to be

Note the citation form of these verbs is the third person masculine singular general past except for **yahay**, which is the third person masculine singular general present.

yiil

The general past

	person marker	stem	number ending	verb form
I	–	iil	–	**iil**
you (sg.)	t	iil	–	**tiil**
he, it (m.)	y	iil	–	**yiil**
she, it (f.)	t	iil	–	**tiil**
we	n	iil	–	**niil**
you (pl.)	t	iil	leen	**tiilleen**
they	y	iil	leen	**yiilleen**

You can see that the person markers are familiar as is the fact that there is an extra number marker on the second and third persons plural and not on the first person plural. Look at some of the other tense tables to compare this.

The reduced verb paradigm used when the subject is focused is as follows:

I	iíl	we	niíl
you (sg.)	yiíl	you (pl.)	yiíl
he, it (m.)	yiíl	they	yiíl
she, it (f.)	tiíl		

Negative general past

The negative of the general past is formed by using **má** with an unchanging negative form of the verb. Both forms mean exactly the same thing.

    oól or **oollín**

The general present

The difference in the tense in the prefixing verbs is marked primarily by a difference in the vowel in the verb stem and the number endings. The forms for **yiil** are given below:

	person marker	stem	number ending	verb form
I	–	aal	–	**aal**
you (sg.)	t	aal	–	**taal**
he, it (m.)	y	aal	–	**yaal**
she, it (f.)	t	aal	–	**taal**
we	n	aal	–	**naal**
you (pl.)	t	aal	liin	**taalliin**
they	y	aal	liin	**yaalliin**

The general present reduced paradigm is as follows:

I	**aál**	we	**naál**
you (sg.)	**yaál**	you (pl.)	**yaál**
he, it (m.)	**yaál**	they	**yaál**
she, it (f.)	**taál**		

There is an optional different form of the general present tense which is given in the following table with the corresponding reduced paradigm:

	full form	reduced form
I	aallaa	aallá
you (sg.)	taallaa	yaallá
he, it (m.)	yaallaa	yaallá
she, it (f.)	taallaa	taallá
we	naallaa	naallá
you (pl.)	taallaan	yaallá
they	yaallaan	yaallá

The negative of the general present is the same as the positive forms except for a different stress-tone pattern. The negative forms are given below and, as usual, are used with the negative word **má**:

I	aál	we	naál
you	taál	you (pl.)	taallíin
he, it (m.)	yaál	they	yaallíin
she, it (f.)	taál		

The infinitive

The infinitive form of **yiil** is **oólli**. This is used with the auxiliary verbs.

    Hálkaás waa oólli jiray.   It used to be there.

The progressive aspect

The only forms that are used in the present progressive of this verb are the third persons. This is because the verb is used only with inanimate objects as explained below. The present progressive forms are:

he, it (m.)	oóllayaa
she, it (f.)	oóllaysaa
they	oóllayaan

The reduced verb paradigm is as follows:

he, it (m.)	oóllayá
she, it (f.)	oóllaysá
they	oóllayá

The past progressive forms are as follows:

he, it (m.)	oóllayay
she, it (f.)	oóllaysay
they	oóllayeen

The reduced verb paradigm is as follows:

he, it (m.)	oóllayaý
she, it (f.)	oóllaysaý
they	oóllayaý

The imperative

The imperative form is   sg.: **óol**   pl.: **oólla**
The negative imperative is   sg.: **ha oóllin**   pl.: **ha oollína**

Using yiil, joog and jir

Each of these words means 'to be in a place'.

Joog is used for people and animals. No preverbal preposition is needed with this word.

Xaggeé báy joogaan?   Where are they?
Gúriga báy joogaan.   They are in the house.

Jir is used for people, animals and inanimate objects. The preverbal preposition **kú** may be used with this verb.

Kábadh báa qólka kú jirá.   There is a cupboard in the room.
Gabádhu dúgsiga kú má jirtó. The girl is not in the school.

Yiil is used for inanimate subjects. The preverbal preposition **kú** may be used with this verb.

Colloquial Somali is also available in the form of a course pack (ISBN 0–415–10011–9) containing this book and two cassettes. The cassettes include pronunciation practice, dialogues and role-playing exercises, recorded by native speakers of Somali and are an invaluable aid to improving your language skills.

If you have been unable to obtain the course pack, the double cassette (ISBN 0–415–10010–0) can be ordered separately through your bookseller or, in case of difficulty, send cash with order to Routledge Ltd, ITPS, Cheriton House, North Way, Andover, Hants SP10 5BE, price (1995) £19.99* including VAT, or to Routledge Inc., 29 West 35th Street, New York, NY 10001, USA, price $24.95*.

The publishers reserve the right to change prices without notice.

CASSETTES ORDER FORM

Please supply one/two/ .... double cassette(s) of

Colloquial Somali, Orwin.
ISBN 0–415–10010–0

Price £19.99* incl. VAT
       $24.95*

☐ I enclose payment with order.
☐ Please debit my Access/Mastercharge/Mastercard/Visa/American Express. Account number:

Expiry date ....

Name ....

Address ....
....
....

Order from your bookseller or from:

ROUTLEDGE LTD
ITPS
Cheriton House
North Way
Andover
Hants
SP10 5BE
ENGLAND

ROUTLEDGE INC.
29 West 35th Street
New York
NY 10001
USA

Kúrsi báa míiska geéstíisa yaallá.	There is a chair at the side of the table.
Kábadhku qólka búu yiil.	The cupboard was in the room.

The difference between **yiil** and **jir** may be summed up as follows: **jir** stresses more that a particular thing exists wherever it might be; **yiil** stresses more that an object is in a particular place.

Exercise

6 Read through the following passage and observe carefully the use of the words **jir**, **joog** and **yiil**:

Reading practice

Vocabulary

yáryahay	it is small
ká koobányahay	it is made up of
mádbakh (m. d2)	kitchen
saarán (adj.)	on top of
fandháal (m. d2)	spoon (wooden Somali spoon)
macalgád (f. d1)	metal spoon
múdac (m. d2)	fork
sáxan (m., **suxuún** (f.))	plate
gidáar (m. d2)	wall
kábadh (m. d2)	cupboard
masálle (m. d7)	prayer mat
siráad (m. d2)	lamp
waálid (m. collec.)	parents

Maryan gurigeedu waa yaryahay. Wuxuu ka koobanyahay musqul, madbakh iyo laba qol. Mid ka mid ah qolalkan waxa ku yaal miis. Miiskan dushiisa waxa saaran buugag, fandhaallo, macalgado, mudacyo iyo suxuun. Gidaarka geestiisa waxa yaal kabadh. Dhar baana kabadhka ku jira. Kabadhka iyo miiska dhexdooda waxa yaal miis yar. Miiskii hoostiisa waxa yaal masalle. Miiska dushiisa waxa saaran siraad.

Maryani waxay joogtaa qolka. Waxay ku fadhisaa kursi, kursiguna miiska agtiisa ayuu yaal. Maryani warqad bay qoraysaa; warqadda waalidkeeda bay u diri doontaa.

Maryan's house is small. It is made up of a bathroom, a kitchen and two rooms. In one of these rooms is a table. On this table are books, wooden spoons, metal spoons, forks and plates. At the side of the wall is a cupboard. And clothes are in the cupboard. Between the cupboard and the table is a small table. Under the table is a prayer mat. On the table is a lamp.

Maryan is in the room. She is sitting on a chair and the chair is by the table. Maryan is writing a letter; she will send the letter to her parents.

10 Safarka baa la bilaabayaa

The beginning of the journey

> By the end of this lesson you should:
> - know the verb **yimi**, 'come'
> - know the verb **yidhi**, 'say'
> - know how to focus a noun phrase with the **wáxa** construction

Dialogue

Bill and Sue prepare for their journey

Vocabulary

sí uu ú	in order to
bilaab (1)	to begin
sháqo (f. d6)	work
kulá	**kú** + **lá** in (e.g. Djibouti) + with (e.g. Sue)
kulan (1, **kulmaa**)	to meet
gaádhi raac (1)	to go by car
oo tégi doontá	who will go
iyádana	and she
safar (1, **safraa**)	to travel
gaádhi (m. d2)	car
sáfar (m. d2)	journey
loó yaqaanó	known as (lit.: who one knows as)
watá	who drives
tabábbar (m.)	training
dheeráad (m. d2)	extra
Jármal (m.)	Germany

baansíin (m. d2 mass)	petrol
raáshin (m. d2 collec.)	provisions
soó gado (3B)	to buy
waa ín la qaadó	one must take
ká fóg (adj.)	far from
sí wanaagsán	a good way; well
ú diyaargarow (1, diyaargaroobaa, diyaargarowdaa)	to prepare for
loogú	**la** + **ú** + **ú** one + in (e.g. **sí wanaagsán**) + for (e.g. the journey)
waa ín . . . diyaargaroobó	one must prepare
wáqti (m.)	time
dhowow (3, dhowaaday, dhowaatay)	to move close
diyaár (adj.)	prepared, **ú**: for
má tahay	are you
kú shub (1)	to pour in
sháag (m. d4)	tyres
jeeg garee (2B)	to check
garee (2B)	this is a verb that is used with words from other languages (such as **jeeg**, 'check') to form a verb not otherwise found in Somali. Another example is **telefoongaree**, 'make a telephone call'
kií dheeráad	the extra one
timi	came
meéday	where? (f.)
imánaysaa	she is coming
habaryár (f. d1)	maternal aunt
soó nabadgelyee (2B)	to say goodbye to
kici (2A)	to start up

Bill wuxuu tegi doonaa magaalada Burco si uu u bilaabo shaqadiisa. Af ingiriisiga ayuu dhigi doonaa. Djibouti wuxuu kula kulmi doonaa gabadh Sue la yidhaahdo oo tegi doonta magaalada Gaalkacyo oo dalka Soomaaliya ku taal. Sue iyaduna af ingiriisiga bay dhigi doontaa. Sue iyo Bill way wada safri doonaan. Waxay raaci doonaan gaadhi, maanta ayayna safarka bilaabi doonaan.

Waxa raaci doonta gabadh Idil loo yaqaano iyo nin gaadhi wata oo Maxmuud la yidhaahdo. Maxmuud waa dhakhtar oo tababbar dheeraad ah ku sameeyay dalka Jarmalka. Baansiin buu soo iibsaday raashinna buu soo gatay. Biyuhuna waa in la qaado. Biyo buu ka soo iibsaday dukaan. Burco waa meel Djibouti ka fog waana in si wanaagsan loogu diyaargaroobo safarka.

MAXMUUD:	Waryaa, Bill. Ma nabad baa?
BILL:	Waa la wanaagsanyahay. Bal iska warran adigu? Waqtigii wuu soo dhowaaday. Maanta baa la baxayaa.
MAXMUUD:	Haa, diyaar ma tahay? Gaadhiga bensiin waan ku shubay. Shaagaggana waan jeeg gareeyay. Kii dheeraadka ahaana wuu fiicanyahay.

Sue ayaa timi.

MAXMUUD:	Sue, is ka warran? Idil meeday?
SUE:	In yar u kaadi way imanaysaa. Habaryarteed bay soo nabadgelyaynaysaa.
MAXMUUD:	Waa inaynu tagno. Bustayaashii ma keentay?
SUE:	Haa, waan keenay. Eeg, waa tan Idil. Idilay is ka warran?
IDIL:	Hayye, waa la wanaagsanyahay. Is ka warrama idinku?
SUE, MAXMUUD iyo BILL:	Waa la wanaagsanyahay.

Dabadeedna Maxmuud gaadhiga buu kiciyaa safarkoodana way bilaabaan. Bill iyo Idil waxay tegi doonaan ilaa Burco. Maxmuud iyo Suena ilaa Gaalkacyo bay sii socon doonaan.

Bill is going to go to the town Burco in order to begin his work. He will teach English. In Djibouti he is to meet a young woman called Sue who will go to the town Gaalkacyo which is in the country of Somalia. And Sue also will teach English. Sue and Bill will travel together. They will go by car and today they will begin the journey.

A young woman called Idil will be going with them and a man who drives the car, called Maxmuud. Maxmuud is a doctor who did further training in Germany. He bought petrol and he bought provisions. And water must be taken. He bought some water from a shop. Burco is a place far from Djibouti and one must prepare well for the journey.

Maxmuud:	Hey, Bill. How are you?	
Bill:	I am well. And how are you? The time has come near. Today we're going.	
Maxmuud:	Yes, are you ready? I have put petrol in the car. And I checked the tyres. The spare one is fine.	

Sue has come.

Maxmuud:	Sue, how are you? Where is Idil?
Idil:	Wait a little, she is coming. She is saying goodbye to her aunt.
Maxmuud:	We must go. Did you bring the blankets?
Sue:	Yes, I brought them. Look here is Idil. Idil, how are you?
Idil:	Hi, I am well. How are you all?
Sue, Maxmuud and Bill:	Well.

Then Maxmuud starts the car and they begin their journey. Bill and Idil will go up to Burco. And Maxmuud and Sue will continue on to Gaalkacyo.

The verb yimi

The verb **yimi** is another prefixing verb which means 'to come'.

The general past

The forms for the general past meaning 'I came', 'you came' etc. are given in the following table:

	person marker	stem	number ending	verb form
I	-	imi	-	**imi**
you (sg.)	t	imi	-	**timi**
he, it (m.)	y	imi	-	**yimi**
she, it (f.)	t	imi	-	**timi**
we	n	imi	-	**nimi**
you (pl.)	t	imi	aaddeen	**timaaddeen**
they	y	imi	aaddeen	**yimaaddeen**

Note that when the ending for the second and third person plural is added the final -**i** of the verb stem is deleted.

There is an optional different form for this tense in all except the second and third person plural forms. This has an additional **d** added to the end of the verb form.

I	**imid**	we	**nimid**
you (sg.)	**timid**	you (pl.)	**timaaddeen**
he, it (m.)	**yimid**	they	**yimaaddeen**
she, it (f.)	**timid**		

The reduced paradigm, used when the subject is focused, is as follows:

I	**imí**	or	**imíd**
you (sg.)	**yimí**	or	**yimíd**
he, it (m.)	**yimí**	or	**yimíd**
she, it (f.)	**timí**	or	**timíd**
we	**nimí**	or	**nimíd**
you (pl.)	**yimí**	or	**yimíd**
they	**yimí**	or	**yimíd**

The negative of the general past is formed by using **má** with an unchanging negative form of the verb: **imán** or **imanín**.

The verbal pronouns may be used with **má** as with the other verbs we have seen.

The general present

The general present forms for **yimi**, meaning 'I come', 'you come', are given below:

	person marker	stem	ending	verb form
I	–	imaad	daa	**imaaddaa**
you (sg.)	t	imaad	daa	**timaaddaa**
he, it (m.)	y	imaad	daa	**yimaaddaa**
she, it (f.)	t	imaad	daa	**timaaddaa**
we	n	imaad	naa	**nimaadnaa**
you (pl.)	t	imaad	daan	**timaaddaan**
they	y	imaad	daan	**yimaaddaan**

The general present reduced paradigm is as follows:

I	imaaddá	we	nimaadná
you (sg.)	yimaaddá	you (pl.)	yimaaddá
he, it (m.)	yimaaddá	they	yimaaddá
she, it (f.)	timaaddá		

The negative of the general present is formed in a similar way to the suffixing verbs, as can be seen in the following example. That is to say, the long vowel **-aa** changes to **-ó** and the ending **-aan** changes to **-áan**. As usual, the negative word **má** is used with these forms.

I	imaaddó	we	nimaadnó
you (sg.)	timaaddó	you (pl.)	timaaddáan
he, it (m.)	yimaaddó	they	yimaaddáan
she, it (f.)	timaaddó		

The infinitive

The infinitive form of **yimi** is **imán**. This is used with the auxiliary verbs, for example:

Waan imán doonaa.   I will come.

It is also the base form for the progressive aspect. The present progressive is given in the following table; it is formed from the familiar progressive verb endings with the infinitive **imán** as the verb stem:

	verb stem	progressive marker	ending	verb form
I	imán	ay	aa	**imánayaa**
you (sg.)	imán	ay	taa	**imánaysaa**
he, it (m.)	imán	ay	aa	**imánayaa**
she, it (f.)	imán	ay	taa	**imánaysaa**
we	imán	ay	naa	**imánaynaa**
you (pl.)	imán	ay	taan	**imánaysaan**
they	imán	ay	aan	**imánayaan**

The reduced paradigm is made in the same way as other verbs, and is given in the following example:

I	imánayá	we	imánayná
you (sg.)	imánayá	you (pl.)	imánayá
he, it (m.)	imánayá	they	imánayá
she, it (f.)	imánaysá		

The negative of the present progressive is formed in the same way as that of the prefixing verbs using the auxiliary forms: **máayó**, **máysó** etc. with the infinitive.

Imán máayáan. They are not coming.

Also, forms of the type **má imánayó**, 'I/he am/is not coming'; **má imánaysó**, 'you (sg.)/she are/is not coming'; **má imánaysáan**, 'you (pl.) are not coming' etc. may be used. These are given in the following example:

I	imánayó	we	imánaynó
you (sg.)	imánaysó/síd	you (pl.)	imánaysáan
he, it (m.)	imánayó	they	imánayáan
she, it (f.)	imánaysó		

The past progressive

This is formed in the same way as the present progressive except that the past tense endings are used.

	verb stem	progressive marker	ending	verb form
I	imán	ay	ay	**imánayay**
you (sg.)	imán	ay	tay	**imánaysay**
he, it (m.)	imán	ay	ay	**imánayay**
she, it (f.)	imán	ay	tay	**imánaysay**
we	imán	ay	nay	**imánaynay**
you (pl.)	imán	ay	teen	**imánayseen**
they	imán	ay	een	**imánayeen**

The reduced paradigm is as expected:

I	imánayaý	we	imánaynaý
you (sg.)	imánayaý	you (pl.)	imánayaý
he, it (m.)	imánayaý	they	imánayaý
she, it (f.)	imánaysaý		

The negative of the past progressive is formed with the negative word **má** and the following form of the verb, which does not change for person or number:

imánaýn or **imánaynín**

Múu imánaynín.   He was not coming.

The imperative

The imperative form is   sg.: **kaálay**   pl.: **kaaláya**
The negative imperative is   sg.: **ha íman** or **ímanin**   pl.: **ha imanína**

Exercise

1 Translate the following sentences into Somali; focus the noun phrases in italics:

1 They will come tomorrow.
2 Come (pl.) here!
3 The students came from *the school* yesterday.
4 *The students* came from the school yesterday.
5 I will not come tomorrow. I am going to my brother's house.
6 They came here in January.

yidhi, 'to say'

The forms of the verb **yidhi** are similar to the forms of **yimi** to a certain extent although there are some differences; all the forms for the tenses and moods we have met so far are given in this section.

The general past

The forms for the general past, meaning 'I said', 'you said' etc., are given in the following table:

	person marker	stem	number ending	verb form
I	–	idhi	–	**idhi**
you (sg.)	t	idhi	–	**tidhi**
he, it (m.)	y	idhi	–	**yidhi**
she, it (f.)	t	idhi	–	**tidhi**
we	n	idhi	–	**nidhi**
you (pl.)	t	idhi	aahdeen	**tidhaahdeen**
they	y	idhi	aahdeen	**yidhaahdeen**

Note that when the ending for the second and third person plural is added the final -**i** of the verb stem is deleted.

The reduced paradigm used when the subject is focused is as follows:

I	**idhí**	we	**nidhí**
you (sg.)	**yidhí**	you (pl.)	**yidhí**
he, it (m.)	**yidhí**	they	**yidhí**
she, it (f.)	**tidhí**		

The negative of the general past is formed by using **má** with an unchanging negative form of the verb:

odhán or **odhanín**.
Máy odhán.   She/they did not say.

The general present

The general present forms for **yidhi**, meaning 'I say', 'you say' etc., are given below:

	person marker	stem	ending	verb form
I	–	idhaah	daa	**idhaahdaa**
you (sg.)	t	idhaah	daa	**tidhaahdaa**
he, it (m.)	y	idhaah	daa	**yidhaahdaa**
she, it (f.)	t	idhaah	daa	**tidhaahdaa**
we	n	idhaah	naa	**nidhaahnaa**
you (pl.)	t	idhaah	daan	**tidhaahdaan**
they	y	idhaah	daan	**yidhaahdaan**

The general present reduced paradigm is as follows:

I	**idhaahdá**	we	**nidhaahná**
you (sg.)	**yidhaahdá**	you (pl.)	**yidhaahdá**
he, it (m.)	**yidhaahdá**	they	**yidhaahdá**
she, it (f.)	**tidhaahdá**		

The negative of the general present is formed in the same way as with other verbs as can be seen in the following example; as usual, the negative word **má** is used with these forms:

I	**idhaahdó**	we	**nidhaahnó**
you (sg.)	**tidhaahdó**	you (pl.)	**tidhaahdáan**
he, it (m.)	**yidhaahdó**	they	**yidhaahdáan**
she, it (f.)	**tidhaahdó**		

The infinitive

The infinitive form of **yidhi** is **odhán**. This is used with the auxiliary verbs.

    'Háa' búu odhán jiray.   He used to say 'Yes'.

It is also the base form for the progressive aspect. The present progressive is given in the following table; it is formed from the familiar progressive verb endings with the infinitive **odhán** as the verb stem:

	verb stem	progressive marker	ending	verb form
I	odhán	ay	aa	**odhánayaa**
you (sg.)	odhán	ay	taa	**odhánaysaa**
he, it (m.)	odhán	ay	aa	**odhánayaa**
she, it (f.)	odhán	ay	taa	**odhánaysaa**
we	odhán	ay	naa	**odhánaynaa**
you (pl.)	odhán	ay	taa	**odhánaysaan**
they	odhán	ay	aan	**odhánayaan**

The reduced verb paradigm is formed in a predictable way:

I	**odhánayá**	we	**odhánayná**
you (sg.)	**odhánayá**	you (pl.)	**odhánayá**
he, it (m.)	**odhánayá**	they	**odhánayá**
she, it (f.)	**odhánaysá**		

The negative of the present progressive is formed in the same way as that of other verbs you have met using the auxiliary forms: **máayó, máysó** etc. with the infinitive.

Odhán máayáan.   They are not saying.

Also, forms of the type **má odhánayó**, 'I/he am/is not saying'; **má odhánaysó**, 'you (sg.)/she are/is not saying'; **má odhánaysáan**, 'you (pl.) are not saying' etc. may be used.

I	**odhánayó**	we	**odhánaynó**
you (sg.)	**odhánaysó/síd**	you (pl.)	**odhánaysáan**
he, it (m.)	**odhánayó**	they	**odhánayáan**
she, it (f.)	**odhánaysó**		

The past progressive

This is formed in the same way as the present progressive except that the past tense endings are used.

	verb stem	progressive marker	ending	verb form
I	odhán	ay	ay	**odhánayay**
you (sg.)	odhán	ay	tay	**odhánaysay**
he, it (m.)	odhán	ay	ay	**odhánayay**
she, it (f.)	odhán	ay	tay	**odhánaysay**
we	odhán	ay	nay	**odhánaynay**
you (pl.)	odhán	ay	teen	**odhánayseen**
they	odhán	ay	een	**odhánayeen**

The reduced paradigm is formed in the predictable manner:

I	**odhánayaý**	we	**odhánaynaý**
you (sg.)	**odhánayaý**	you (pl.)	**odhánayaý**
he, it (m.)	**odhánayaý**	they	**odhánayaý**
she, it (f.)	**odhánaysaý**		

The negative of the past progressive is formed with the negative word **má** and the following form of the verb, which does not change:

odhánaýn or **odhánaynín**

The imperative

The imperative form is   sg.: **dhéh**   pl.: **dháha**
The negative imperative is   sg.: **ha ódhan**   pl.: **ha odhanína**
                      or **ódhanin**

The use of yidhi

The verb **yidhi** is used only with direct speech. This means that when it is used with a phrase that has been said by someone then the phrase is basically a quotation of what the person said.

'Wáan tagay' báy tidhi.   She said, 'I went'.

Indirect speech is generally introduced by the verb **sheeg** and a subordinate clause which will be discussed in the next chapter.

To translate 'to' as in 'I said to him ...' the preverbal preposition **kú** is used.

'Háa' báan kú idhi.   I said 'Yes' to him.

Using the waxa . . . focus construction

In Lesson 6 we looked at the use of the focus markers **báa** and **ayáa**. In this section we shall look at another way of focusing a noun phrase in a sentence. This is done by using the noun **wáx**, 'thing', as in the examples given below:

    Wáxaan cúnayaa kibís.   I am eating *bread*.

This sentence may be broken down in the following way:

wáxa	aan	cúnayaa	kibís
the thing	I	am eating	bread

    Wáxay ká yimaaddeen dúgsiga.   They came from *the school*.

wáxa	ay	ká	yimaaddeen	dúgsiga
the thing	they	from	came	the school

As you can see from these examples the word **wáxa** comes before the verb and is used with the subject verbal pronouns we have met already. The form of the verb is just as it is in any other sentence.

The meaning of this construction is the same as the meaning of a sentence which uses one of the focus markers **báa** or **ayáa**. So if somebody asks the question,

    Maxáad cúnaysaa?   What are you eating?

you may reply in one of two ways:

    Baríis báan cúnayaa.   I am eating *rice*.

or

    Wáxaan cúnayaa baríis.   I am eating *rice*.

It has been suggested that this particular focus construction is used when the noun phrase is particularly long, for example when it incorporates a relative clause.

    Wáxaan arkay nínka oo labá iyo tobán sanadoód ká hór macállinkáyga ahaan jiraý.
    I saw the man who used to be my teacher twelve years ago.

This is preferable to the following:

    Nínka oo labá iyo tobán sanadoód ká hór macállinkáyga ahaán jiraý baan arkay.

In the latter sentence the focus marker **báa** is used. Note that these sentences incorporate a relative clause. We shall look at relative clauses in detail in a later lesson.

Word order

As you can see from the above examples the word order of sentences with the **wáxa**-focus construction is different to the word order you are used to.

We may set out the basic word order as follows:

WÁXA (+verbal pronoun)   VERB   FOCUSED NOUN PHRASE

Any other words in the sentence are generally placed before **wáxa**, or if they are adverbial phrases they may also be placed after the focused noun phrase.

Berríto ardéydu wáxay tégi doonaan jaamacádda.

or

Ardéydu wáxay tégi doonaan jaamacádda berríto.
Tomorrow the students will go to *the university*.

Focusing the subject

You will remember from Lesson 6 that when the subject is focused then there are certain characteristics that hold. Since the **waxa**-construction is also a focus construction, then, when the subject is focused in this way these characteristics also hold.

Kibísta wáxa cuná shimbiráha.   *The birds* eat the bread.

In this example the subject of the sentence is **shimbiráha**, 'the birds'. Note, however, the following three characteristics because the subject is focused:

- the subject **shimbiráha** is in the absolutive form;
- the verb is from the reduced paradigm: **cuná** instead of **cunaan**;
- the focus word **wáxa** does not have the subject verbal pronoun attached to it.

All these characteristics are the same as when the subject is focused using **báa** or **ayáa**, as discussed in Lesson 6.

Warqáddii wáxa qortaý Canab   *Canab* wrote the letter a year
sanád ká hór.   ago.

Aẃrta wáxa daajinayá Maxámed.   *Maxamed* is grazing the burden camels.

Exercises

2 Translate the following sentences into Somali:
1 They said, 'We will not come tomorrow, we shall come in an hour.'
2 What did he say? He said, 'Take the food for Canab.'
3 Did you say 'Yes'?
4 I am not saying, 'They cannot buy the meat.'
5 Say 'How are you?'!
6 They are going to the house of the teacher and will say 'Good morning'.

3 The following sentences use the focus markers **báa** and **ayáa** in them. Change the sentences to ones which use the **wáxa . . .** type focus construction, then translate them into English. For example:

Kalluun baan cunay changes to **Waxaan cunay kalluun**, I ate *fish*.

1 Kubbad baan ku siiyay.
2 Baraha cusub ee dugsiga baa masaajidka ka yimi.
3 Sonkor bay shaaha ku shubtay.
4 Warqad dheer saaxiibaddeeda bay u dirtay.
5 Odayaasha baa danjirayaasha la kulmay.
6 Albaabka kale buu furay.

4 The following sentences use the **wáxa . . .** type focus construction. Change the sentences so that they use the **báa** or **ayáa** type focus construction, then translate them into English. For example:

Waxaan qaaday kabihiisa cuscusub changes to **Kabihiisa cuscusub baan qaaday**, I took his new shoes.

1 Wuxuu tusay basaboorkiisa.
2 Waxa ka yimi odayaasha.
3 Berrito waxaan wadan doonaa gaadhiga cusub.
4 Waxay caddeynayaan buugga cusub ee madaxweynaha.
5 Maanta waxaan karin doonaa bariis, hilib iyo khudrad badan.
6 Waxa awrta daajin doona inammada.

Reading practice 🔊

dád (m. collec.)	people
dádka Soomaaliyeéd	the Somali people
noól (adj.)	living
noólyihiin	they live
dál (m. d4)	country
qaýb (f. d1)	part
xoolaléy (f. collec.)	livestock keepers
beeraléy (f. collec.)	farmers
réer (m. d1)	family, group of people
réer magaál	townspeople
ugú badán	most
ugú jecéshahay	like the most
adkaýsi (m. d7)	endurance
ugá	ú + ká
harráad (m.)	thirst
gaájo (f.)	hunger
ká maaran (1, maarmaa)	to manage without something
cásho (f. d6)	day
lis (1)	to milk (tr.)
waa lagá lisaa	one gets milk from (lagá: one + from)
núxur (m. collec.)	nourishment
núxurléh	nourishing (lit.: possessing nourishment)
macaán (adj.)	sweet
saán (f. d1, saamo)	hide
wáx (m. waxyaabo (m.))	things
wáxtar (m.)	usefulness
wáxtar léh	useful
ká samee (2B)	to make from
ádhi (m. collec.)	caprines (sheep and goats)
ú qaybsan (1, qaybsamaa)	to be divided into
ído (m. collec.)	sheep
rí (f. d1)	nanny goat
riyo (plural of rí)	goats in general
cáan (m. d4)	fame
madoẃ (adj.)	black
lagá jecélyahay	one likes more than
beer (1)	to cultivate
galláy (f.)	maize
hadhúudh (m.)	sorghum

moórdi (m.)	red sorghum
sisín (f.)	sesame
bocór (f.)	pumpkin
moxóggo (f. d6)	cassava
qásab (m.)	sugar cane
cámbe (m. d7)	mango
bábbay (m. d2)	papaya
iyo wíxií lá míd áh	etcetera, abbreviated to: **iwm.**
kháas ahaán	especially
ká dhexee (2B)	to be in between
ee	and (used here to join the attributive adjective **kalé** with the relative clause **lagú beeraa**. It is used because the head noun is a defined noun with an adjective following it.)

Dadka Soomaaliyeed [1]

Dadka Soomaaliyeed waxay ku noolyihiin dalalka geeska Afrika: Soomaaliya, Soomaaliland, Jabuuti, Kiiniyaa iyo Itiyoobiya. Soomaalidu waa saddex qaybood: xoolaley, beeraley iyo reer magaal. Xoolaleyda ayaa ugu badan. Soomaalidu geela ayay xoolaheeda ugu jeceshahay. Waayo isagu xoolaha kale wuu uga adkeysi badan yahay harraadka iyo gaajada. Geelu wuxuu biyaha ka maarmi karaa ilaa labaatan casho. Geela waa la lisaa, caanaha geelana waa cunto nuxurleh oo macaan. Geela saantiisa ayaana waxyaabo badan oo waxterleh laga sameyn karaa. Adhigu wuxuu u qaybsamaa ido iyo riyo. Idaha Soomaaliyeed waxay caan ku yihiin madax madow. Riyaha iyo idahaba caano baa laga lisaa, hilibkoodana waa la cunaa waana laga jecelyahay kii lo'da iyo geelaba.

Beeraleydu waxay beeraan galley, hadhuudh, moordi, sisin, bocor, moxoggo, qasab, muus, cambe, babaay iyo wixii la mid ah. Dadka beerlayda ahi khaas ahaan waxay ku noolyihiin meelaha u dhexeeya labada webi ee Shabeelle iyo Jubba. Meesha kale ee wax lagu beeraa waa gobolka waqooyi galbeed.

The Somali people

The Somali people live in the countries of the Horn of Africa: Somalia, Somaliland, Djibouti, Kenya and Ethiopia. The Somalis are divided into three groups: pastoralists, agriculturalists and townspeople. The pastoralists are the most numerous. Of their livestock the Somalis like the camels the most, because they are more enduring of thirst and hunger than the other livestock. Camels can go without water for up to twenty days. Camels are milked, and camels' milk is a nourishing and sweet food; and one can make many useful things from the hide of camels. Caprines are divided into sheep and goats. The sheep of the Somalis are famous for having black heads. Nanny goats and sheep are milked and their meat is eaten; it is liked more than that of cattle and camels.

The agriculturalists grow maize, sorghum, red sorghum, sesame, pumpkins, cassava, sugar cane, bananas, mangos, papayas etc. The agriculturalists live especially in the places between the two rivers Shabeelle and Jubba. The other place that is cultivated is the north-west region.

Note

1 This passage is an edited version of a passage in *Af Soomaali Fasalka Labaad*, a book published for schools in 1976 in Mogadishu by the then Ministry of Education and Training.

11 Tuulo baa la joogaa
Staying in a village

By the end of this lesson you should:

- know the verb **yiqiin**, 'to know'
- know something about subordinate clauses, particularly 'that' clauses
- know how to use **sheeg**, 'to tell'
- know how to say 'in order to' and 'must'
- know about pronoun and preposition clusters

Dialogue

Bill and his friends arrive at a small village

Vocabulary

tuúlo (f. d6)	village
kú bari (1)	to spend the night in/at (infinitive: **baryi**)
ká míd áh	who is of
socóto (f. d6 collec.)	travellers
martiqaad (1)	to entertain (guests)
sideé	how (lit.: which way)
ahaa	it was
xiíso (f. d6)	interest, fascination
xiíso léh	interesting, fascinating
waraábe (m. d7)	hyena
geeltoosíye (m. d7)	a type of vulture
habardugáag (m. collec.)	wild animals
háad (m. d5)	birds of prey
halkaásoó	where

basbáas (m. d2)	chilli pepper
jeclayso (3B)	to like
caáwa	this evening
timír (f. mass)	dates
soór (f. collec.)	porridge type food made from different grains
dhan (1, dhamaa)	to drink (used only with milk)
aád báan ú jeclahay	I like very much
xawáash (m. collec.)	spices
sí (f., siyaabo (m.))	way
loó	la + ú one + in (i.e. the way)
sída loó sameeyó	how it is made
dambé	next
sameýnayaý	who was making
márka horé	firstly
ú baahán	needing
wáxaad ú baahántahay	you need
kíldhi (m. d2)	kettle
dáb (m. d4)	fire
kala	separately
qórfe (m. d7)	cinnamon
xabbád (f.)	unit (of something), piece
héyl (m. d4)	cardamom
dhegayáre (m. d7)	clove
filfíl (f. mass)	black pepper
moóye (m. d7)	mortar
kál (f. d1)	pestle
tun (1)	to grind
tumán (adj.)	ground
karayá	which is boiling
há karo	let it boil
qaáddo (f. d6)	spoon
kú dar (1)	to add to
daqiiqád (f. d1)	minute
íntaánu sháahu karín	before the tea has boiled
diiri (2A)	to heat (tr.)
diirán (adj.)	heated
termúus (m. d2)	thermos flask
iskú day (2A)	to try

Bill iyo saaxiibbadiisu waxay yimaaddeen tuulo yar. Halkaasna way ku baryi doonaan. Nin Cabdullaahi la yidhaahdo oo reerka Maxmuud ka mid ah ayaa socotadaas martiqaada.

CABDULLAAHI: Soo dhowaada. Is ka warrama.

Waxay wada yidhaahdaan 'Waa la wanaagsanyahay'.

CABDULLAAHI: Safarkana ka warrama. Sidee buu ahaa?
SUE: Safar wanaagsan buu ahaa. Waxaannu aragnay waxyaabo badan oo xiiso leh. Waraabayaal baannu aragnay iyo geeltoosiyayaal iyo habardugaag kale. Haad iyo shimbirona waannu aragnay.
BILL: Haa waxaannuna marnay tuulo yar halkaasoo aannu wax ka cunnay. Cuntadase basbaas badan baa ku jiray, mana jeclaysan.
CABDULLAAHI: Caawa waxaynu cuni doonnaa hilib riyaad, bariis, timir iyo soor. Caano geel baynuna dhami doonnaa shaah baynuna cabbi doonnaa.
SUE: Shaah Soomaali aad baan u jeclahay. Waa macaan oo xawaash leh. Waxaan rabaa inaan barto sida loo sameeyo.

Maalintii dambe Sue way toostaa. Aqalka bay ka baxdaa in yarna tuulada bay wareegtaa. Waxay eegtaa nin shaah sameynaya.

SUE: Walaal, subax wanaagsan. Ma nabad baa?
NINKA: Hayye waa nabad. Iska warran adigu?
SUE: Waan fiicanahay. Ma shaah baad sameynaysaa?
NINKA: Haa wax ma cabbi rabtaa?
SUE: Haa mahadsanid. Wax baan ku weydiin rabaa. Sidaad shaah xawaash leh u sameyso i bar.
NINKA: Waan ku barayaa. Marka hore waxaad u baahantahay kildhi, biyo, dab, caleen shaah, sonkor, caano iyo xawaash. Xawaashku wuxuu kala yahay in yar oo qorfe ah, saddex xabbadood oo heyl ah, xabbad dhegayare ah, iyo laba xabbadood oo filfil ah. Xawaashka mooye ku shub oo kal ku tun. Dabadeedna xawaashka tuman biyo karaya ku dar. Shan daqiiqadood ha karo dabadeedna laba amba saddex qaaddo yar oo caleen shaah ah ku dar. Shan daqiiqadood kari. Intaanu shaahu karin caano diiri. Dabadeedna sonkor iyo caanaha diiran shaaha ku dar. Dabadeedna termuus ku shub. Kaasuna wuxuu sameeyaa afar koob oo shaah ah.
SUE: Mahadsanid. Markaan Gaalkacyo gaadho baan isku dayn doonaa.

Bill and his friends have come to a small village. They will spend the night there. A man called Cabdullaahi, who is part of Maxmuud's family, entertains the travellers.

CABDULLAAHI: Welcome. How are you?

They say together: 'We are well.'

CABDULLAAHI: Tell me about the journey. How was it?
SUE: It was a good journey. We saw many interesting things. We saw hyenas and vultures and other wild animals. And we saw birds of prey and birds.
BILL: Yes, and we passed by a small village where we ate something. But there was a lot of chilli in the food, and I didn't like it.
CABDULLAAHI: This evening we shall eat goat's meat, rice, dates and soor. And we will drink camel's milk and tea.
SUE: I like Somali tea very much. It is sweet and spicy. I would like to learn how it is made.

The next day, Sue gets up. She leaves the house and walks around the village a little. She sees a man who is making tea.

SUE: Brother, good morning. How are things?
THE MAN: Hi, fine. How are you?
SUE: I am well. Are you making tea?
THE MAN: Yes, do you want to drink some?
SUE: Yes, thank you. I would like to ask you something. Teach me how you make spicy tea.
THE MAN: I will teach you. Firstly you need a kettle, water, fire, tea leaves, sugar, milk and spices. The spices are a little cinnamon, three cardamom pieces, a clove and two peppercorns. Pour the spices in a mortar and grind them with a pestle. Then add the ground spices to boiling water. Let it boil for five minutes then add two or three small spoons of tea leaves. Boil for five minutes. Before the tea has boiled warm up some milk. Then add sugar and the hot milk to the tea. Then pour it into a thermos flask. And that makes four cups of tea.
SUE: Thank you. When I reach Gaalkacyo I will try it.

The verb yiqiin

The verb **yiqiin** is another prefixing verb which means 'know' or 'recognize'.

The general past

The forms for the general past, meaning 'I knew', 'you knew' etc., are given in the following table:

	person marker	stem	number ending	verb form
I	–	iqiin	–	**iqiin**
you (sg.)	t	iqiin	–	**tiqiin**
he, it (m.)	y	iqiin	–	**yiqiin**
she, it (f.)	t	iqiin	–	**tiqiin**
we	n	iqiin	–	**niqiin**
you (pl.)	t	iqiin	neen	**tiqiinneen**
they	y	iqiin	neen	**yiqiinneen**

The reduced verb paradigm, used when the subject is focused, is as follows:

I	**iqiín**	we	**niqiín**
you (sg.)	**yiqiín**	you (pl.)	**yiqiín**
he, it (m.)	**yiqiín**	they	**yiqiín**
she, it (f.)	**tiqiín**		

The negative of the general past is formed by using **má** with an unchanging negative form of the verb.

oqoón or **oqoonín** (these may also be spelt **aqoón** or **aqoonín**)

Máydin oqoonín.   You (pl.) did not know.

The general present

The general present forms for **yiqiin**, meaning 'I know', 'you know', are given below:

	person marker	stem	ending	verb form
I	–	aqaan		**aqaan**
you (sg.)	t	aqaan		**taqaan**
he, it (m.)	y	aqaan		**yaqaan**
she, it (f.)	t	aqaan		**taqaan**
we	n	aqaan		**naqaan**
you (pl.)	t	aqaan	niin	**taqaanniin**
they	y	aqaan	niin	**yaqaanniin**

The general present reduced paradigm is as follows:

I	**aqaán**	we	**naqaán**
you (sg.)	**yaqaán**	you (pl.)	**yaqaán**
he, it (m.)	**yaqaán**	they	**yaqaán**
she, it (f.)	**taqaán**		

As with the verb **yiil** there is an optional different form of the general present of **yiqiin**, which is given below:

	person marker	stem	ending	verb form
I	–	aqaan	naa	**aqaannaa**
you (sg.)	t	aqaan	naa	**taqaannaa**
he, it (m.)	y	aqaan	naa	**yaqaannaa**
she, it (f.)	t	aqaan	naa	**taqaannaa**
we	n	aqaan	naa	**naqaannaa**
you (pl.)	t	aqaan	niin	**taqaanniin**
they	y	aqaan	niin	**yaqaanniin**

The reduced paradigm of this variation is as follows:

I	**aqaanná**	we	**naqaanná**
you (sg.)	**yaqaanná**	you (pl.)	**yaqaanná**
he, it (m.)	**yaqaanná**	they	**yaqaanná**
she, it (f.)	**taqaanná**		

The negative of the general present is formed, as with other verbs, with the negative word **má** and the following negative verb forms:

I	**aqaán**	we	**naqaán**
you (sg.)	**taqaán**	you (pl.)	**taqaanníin**
he, it (m.)	**yaqaán**	they	**yaqaanníin**
she, it (f.)	**taqaán**		

The infinitive

The infinitive form of **yiqiin** is **aqoón**. This is used with the auxiliary verbs. For example:

Wáan ku aqoón doonaa.   I will recognize you.

The progressive aspect

The infinitive is also used as the base for the progressive aspect. When this verb is used in the progressive, present or past, then it means 'recognize' rather than 'know'. The forms are given in the following table, meaning 'I recognize', 'you recognize' etc.

	verb stem	progressive marker	ending	verb form
I	aqoón	ay	aa	**aqoónayaa**
you (sg.)	aqoón	ay	taa	**aqoónaysaa**
he, it (m.)	aqoón	ay	aa	**aqoónayaa**
she, it (f.)	aqoón	ay	taa	**aqoónaysaa**
we	aqoón	ay	naa	**aqoónaynaa**
you (pl.)	aqoón	ay	taan	**aqoónaysaan**
they	aqoón	ay	aan	**aqoónayaan**

The reduced paradigm of the verb is given below:

I	**aqoónayá**	we	**aqoónayná**
you (sg.)	**aqoónayá**	you (pl.)	**aqoónayá**
he, it (m.)	**aqoónayá**	they	**aqoónayá**
she, it (f.)	**aqoónaysá**		

The past progressive form is, as you would expect, analogous to the present progressive form, but with the past tense endings; note that in this tense also the verb has more of the meaning 'recognize' than 'know'.

	verb stem	*progressive marker*	*ending*	*verb form*
I	aqoón	ay	ay	**aqoónayay**
you (sg.)	aqoón	ay	tay	**aqoónaysay**
he, it (m.)	aqoón	ay	ay	**aqoónayay**
she, it (f.)	aqoón	ay	tay	**aqoónaysay**
we	aqoón	ay	nay	**aqoónaynay**
you (pl.)	aqoón	ay	teen	**aqoónayseen**
they	aqoón	ay	een	**aqoónayeen**

The reduced paradigm of the verb is also as you would expect:

I	**aqoónayaý**	we	**aqoónaynaý**
you (sg.)	**aqoónayaý**	you (pl.)	**aqoónayaý**
he, it (m.)	**aqoónayaý**	they	**aqoónayaý**
she, it (f.)	**aqoónaysaý**		

The negative of the present progressive is constructed in a predictable manner. The infinitive may be used with the **máayó** forms or the negative present tense endings may be used.

Má aqoónayó.   I do not recognize her.
Oqoón máayó.   I do not recognize her.

In the past progressive the invariable form **oqoónaynín** is used with the negative word **má**:

Má oqoonaynín.   I didn't recognize her.

The imperative

The imperative form is   sg.: **oqóow**   pl.: **oqoóda**
The negative imperative is   sg.: **ha óqoon**   pl.: **ha oqoonína**
    or **óqoonin**

Exercise

1 Translate the following sentences into Somali:

1 I know him.
2 They did not know me.
3 You (pl.) will recognize the new ambassador tomorrow. He will come with the president.
4 Did you know the elder?
5 I didn't recognize him but I recognized his brother.
6 I don't know that story.

Subordinate clauses

Up to now all the sentences we have dealt with have been main clauses. We shall now begin to look at subordinate clauses which will allow you to say much more. The difference between a subordinate and a main clause is simple:

- a main clause is a clause that may stand on its own as a sentence;
- a subordinate clause is a clause that may *not* stand on its own as a sentence.

There are some characteristics of subordinate clauses in Somali that it is useful to know about now in order to understand how subordinate clauses function in the language:

1 Subordinate clauses are all essentially noun phrases. That is to say, the various roles a noun phrase plays in a Somali sentence can also be played by a subordinate clause. Thus, as we shall see, certain verb forms in subordinate clauses have absolutive and subject forms according to the role the subordinate clause plays within the sentence.
2 The mood classifier and focus markers are not used in subordinate clauses, and the negative word is different, **aán** instead of **má** (we shall deal with negative relative clauses in a later lesson).
3 There are special forms of the verbs which are used in subordinate clauses.
4 All subordinate clauses are essentially relative clauses, although we shall divide them into three convenient groups.

ín-clauses or complement clauses

In this section we shall look at the type of clause we shall call an **ín**-clause. This is the sort of clause which in English would be mostly introduced by the word 'that'.

Waxáy ií sheegtay ínay imán doonáan. She told me that they will come.

In this sentence we have the subordinate clause **ínay imán doonáan**, 'that they will come'.

In this sentence the subordinate clause is the object of the sentence. Because of this the clause must show the absolutive case. We have seen in other noun phrases that the case marking goes on the final part of the noun phrase. This is true also of subordinate clauses and since the last part of a subordinate clause is the verb, then it is the verb that has the case marking. Note that the word order in a subordinate clause is basically the same as in a main clause, hence the verb is invariably at the end.

Wáxaan aqaan ínuu tagaý. I know that he went.
Wáxay ú maleýnaysaa ínay cúnayáan. She supposes that they are eating.
Wúxuu sheégayaa ínuu siín doonó. He is saying that he will give it.

As you can see from these examples the subject verbal pronoun is added to the word **ín**. This is the same word we have met before which in general usage means 'amount'. The following example gives all of the forms when the subject verbal pronoun is added to **ín**.

I	ín + aan	ínaan
you (sg.)	ín + aad	ínaad
he, it (m.)	ín + uu	ínuu
she, it (f.)	ín + ay	ínay
we (incl.)	ín + aynu	ínaynu
we (excl.)	ín + aannu	ínaannu
you (pl.)	ín + aydin	ínaydin
they	ín + ay	ínay

You will notice from the example sentences above that the stress-tone on the verb of the **ín**-clause is not the same as that of the main clause verb form, which has no stress-tone at all; compare the following two sentences:

Wúu tagay. He went.
Ínuu tagaý búu sheegay. He said that he went.

Subordinate verb forms

The verb forms in subordinate clauses are different to the main clause verb forms. The difference should not pose too much of a problem, as the forms are similar to ones you have already met. In this section we shall look at the verb forms used with **ín**-clauses.[1]

First, the general present and the present progressive forms are the same as the main clause negative forms, that is to say the ending **-aa** changes to **-ó** and the ending **-aan** changes to **-áan**.

The form for the general present is given in full below for the verb **keen**:

	verb stem	ending	verb form
I	keen	ó	**keenó**
you (sg.)	keen	tó	**keentó**
he, it (m.)	keen	ó	**keenó**
she, it (f.)	keen	tó	**keentó**
we	keen	nó	**keennó**
you (pl.)	keen	táan	**keentáan**
they	keen	áan	**keenáan**

All of this should be familiar to you from the negative general present.

Examples

Wáxaan maqlay ínay keénayáan. I heard that they are bringing it.
Wáxaan ú maleýnayaa ínuu tagó. I suppose he goes.

As for the general past and the past progressive, the only difference between the main clause forms and the subordinate clause forms is in the stress-tone of the verb. The pattern is given below for the general past of the verb **keen**:

	verb stem	ending	verb form
I	keen	aý	**keenaý**
you (sg.)	keen	taý	**keentaý**
he, it (m.)	keen	aý	**keenaý**
she, it (f.)	keen	taý	**keentaý**
we	keen	naý	**keennaý**
you (pl.)	keen	téen	**keentéen**
they	keen	éen	**keenéen**

The forms for the past progressive are formed in the same way with the stress-tone on the final or penultimate vowel.

Prefixing verbs

The subordinate forms of the prefixing verbs are formed in the same way as with the suffixing verbs. Thus in the general present and the present progressive the forms that end in **-aa** change to forms ending in **-ó** and the forms ending in **-aan** change to **-áan**. The past tense forms show the same stress-tone pattern as the suffix verbs. That is to say there is a stress-tone on the final vowel, except for the second and third person plural forms which end in **-n**, which have a stress-tone on the penultimate vowel.

Wáxay sheegeen ínay yimaaddéen. They said they came.
Wáxaan ú malaýnayaa ínaan imán doonó. I suppose that I will come.

Focus and classifiers and subordinate clauses

As we mentioned above, there are no classifiers or focus markers in subordinate clauses.

Since subordinate clauses are essentially noun phrases, however, they may be focused in main clauses. Look at the following examples (look back also at the examples above):

Wáxay sheegeen ínay keéni doontó. They said that she will bring it.

This may also be said as follows:

Ínay keéni doontó báy sheegeen.

The **wáxa** type construction, however, is generally used more often in these cases since the subordinate clause tends to be somewhat longer than a simple noun phrase.

Note that when an **ín**-clause is part of a sentence, then it is very often focused.

Word order

The word order in **ín**-clauses is generally the same as in main clauses, namely SUBJECT OBJECT VERB. Note, however, that the object may also come after the verb.

| Wáxay sheegeen ínay cuntó keéni doonáan. | They said that they will bring food. |

This may also be given as follows:

| Wáxay sheegeen ínay keéni doonáan cuntó. | They said that they will bring food. |

The use of sheeg

We mentioned in Lesson 10 that the verb **yidhi** was only used for direct speech. The verb used mostly for conveying indirect speech is **sheeg**, 'tell, say'. **Sheeg** is never used with direct speech, always indirect speech; the clause including the indirect speech is an **ín**-clause.

| Wáxaan kuú sheégayaa ínaan ku siín doonó berríto. | I am telling you that I will give you it tomorrow. |
| Wáxay sheegtay ínay áf Soomaáliga barán rabtó. | She said that she wants to learn Somali. |

Exercise

2 The following is a list of clauses. Keep the first clause as a main clause and make the second clause into a subordinate clause. For example:

I know. He will come tomorrow.
Waan aqaan inuu berrito iman doono.

1 Do you know? The fool has brought the shoes.
2 The boys told them. They will go to the school.
3 The girl heard. The prisoners escaped.

4 I heard. The president will come here in three hours.
5 They think. They will drink tea.

'In order to'

The phrase 'in order to' is rendered in Somali by using an **ín**-clause and the preverbal preposition **ú**.

    Wáxaan ú tagay ínaan áf   I went in order to learn Somali.
    Soomaáliga bartó.
    Wáxay ú keentay ínay cuntó.   She brought it in order to eat it.

Note that **ú** comes before the main clause verb and refers to the **ín**-clause.

'Have to, must'

The expression 'have to, must' is rendered in Somali by an **ín**-clause used in conjunction with the classifier **wâa**.

    Waa ín la cunó.   One must eat it.

In this particular construction the main clause verb form may also be used. Thus the following is also correct:

    Waa ín la cunaa.   One must eat it.

Another example is:

    Waa ínaan tagó. or **Waa ínaan tagaa.**   I must go.

Exercise

3 Translate the following sentences into Somali:

1 Tell them that they can bring the suitcases tomorrow.
2 I am going to the restaurant to have lunch.
3 You will go to the school to learn.
4 I went to the teacher's house to tell him that my brother will go to the school tomorrow.
5 They went to the shop to buy new pencils.
6 You must go to the restaurant.
7 I must find my passport.

Preposition and pronoun clusters

You have learnt to use the preverbal prepositions and the object pronouns in Somali.

Wáan ku túsi doonaa. I will show you it.
Ma lá tágaysaan? Are you going with them?

In this section we shall look at the way these short words fit together when more than one of them is used in a sentence at the same time.

There are two aspects to this:

- the order in which the words are used is fixed
- sound changes occur when certain combinations arise.

The order is always as follows:

PRONOUN followed by PREPOSITIONS (always in the order U KU KA LA)

When these words are used in combination they are generally written as one word, as you can see in these examples:

Wuu kulá cúni doonaa. He will eat with you.
Waan kuú qoray. I wrote it for you.

Pronoun and preposition clusters

Remember the pronoun always comes first.

	+ *ú*	+ *kú*	+*ká*	+*lá*
i	**ií**	igú	igá	ilá
ku	**kuú**	kugú	**kaá**	kulá
na	**noó**	nagú	nagá	nalá
ina	**inoó**	inagú	inagá	inalá
idin	**idiín**	idinkú	idinká	idinlá

As you can see there are no particular rules that may be given for the sound changes in the pronoun and preposition clusters, although you may see certain patterns in some of the forms, such as the change from **k** to **g** between vowels. The clusters that are not so predictable have been underlined.

Note also the lack of third person pronouns; remember there are no third person object pronouns in Somali.

Examples of sentences with these clusters:

Way inoó keéni jireen. They used to bring it for us.
Waan kulá hadli doonaa. I will talk with you.

When two preverbal prepositions come together, they also undergo some changes; these clusters are given in the following table:

	+ ú	+ kú	+ká	+lá
ú	**ugú**	ugú	ugá	ulá
kú		**kagá**	**kagá**	kulá
ká			kagá	kalá

You can see that there are certain impossible forms given the rigid order in which these preverbal prepositions must be. Note also the fact that there is only one stress-tone in these clusters. Whenever a preverbal preposition is in a cluster with pronouns or other preverbal prepositions then there is only ever one stress-tone on the final vowel of the cluster.

Again the clusters that are less predictable are underlined.

As to clusters of a pronoun + a preverbal preposition cluster, these are given in the following table:

	ugú	ugá	ulá	kagá	kulá	kalá
i	iigú	iigá	iilá	igagá	igulá	igalá
ku	kuugú	kaagá	kuulá	kaagá	kugulá	kaalá
na	noogú	noogá	noolá	nagagá	nagulá	nagalá
ina	inoogú	inoogá	inoolá	inagagá	inagulá	inagalá
idin	idiinkú	idiinká	idiinlá	idinkagá	idinkulá	idinkalá

Waan kaagá qaaday. I took it from him for you.

kaagá is made up of the following parts:
ku	you
ú	for
ká	from

Caanáha kóobka búu iigú shubay. He poured the milk in the cup for me.

iigú is made up of the following parts:
i	me
ú	for
kú	in

Way inoogá warrámi jireen.   They used to give us news about it.

inoogá is made up of the following parts: **ina**   we (incl.)
 ú   to
 ká   about

Jawaáhir gúrigéeda báannu idinkulá kúlmi doonnaa.   We will meet with you at Jawaahir's house.

idinkulá is made up of the following parts: **idin**   you (pl.)
 kú   in, at
 lá   with

The use of preverbal prepositions is not easy to learn quickly. Experience is the best teacher. If you use Somali regularly you will find that certain clusters crop up much more often than others. As with anything, practice is the key.

Exercise

4 Insert the appropriate pronoun and preposition clusters. For example:

Waan _____ hadli doonaa.   I will talk with you.
Waan kula hadli doonaa.

1 Wuu _____ sheegay.   He told me.
2 Maxamed baa dukaanka _____ keenay.   Maxamed took it from the shop for me.
3 Lacagta buu _____ qaadey.   He took the money from us.
4 Koobka _____ shub.   Pour it in the cup for me.
5 Way _____ qaadeen.   They took it from you.
6 Way _____ warrantay.   She told me about it.

Reading practice

How to make **soor.**[2]

Vocabulary

wáxay ká míd tahay	is one of	**walbá**	each, every
cuntáda joogtáda áh	staple food	**búdo** (f. d6)	flour

sída	like (lit.: the way)	**sídatán**	this way
sarréen (m. mass)	wheat	**bisleýn** (f.)	cooking
iskú dar (1)	to put in together	**nadiifi** (2A)	to clean
qúmbe (m. d7)	coconut	**jarjar** (1)	to chop up
digír (f. collec.)	beans, peas	**diir** (1)	to peel
caádi (m. d2)	ordinary, normal	**ilaá**	until
caádi áh	normal	**guduudo** (3B)	to become reddish brown
iskú karís áh	cooked together (i.e. lots of things)	**iskú walaaq** (1)	to stir together
haddií la sameýn doonó	if one wants to do it	**aád ú yar**	very small
		bislow (3B, bislaaday, bislaatay, bislaanayaa)	to be cooked
rúbuc (m. d2)	quarter		
basál (f. collec.)	onion		
xubín (f. d3)	member, segment		
toón (f.)	garlic	**sanuunád** (f. d1)	gravy
yaányo (f. d6)	tomato	**dúfan** (m. d2)	grease
saliíd (f. mass)	oil	**dabool** (1)	to cover
bádh (m. d4)	half	**dhuxúl** (f.)	charcoal
cúsbo (f. mass)	salt	**saar** (1)	to put on top of something
tumán (adj.)	ground		
shiilán (adj.)	fried	**íntií**	for the duration
háddií	if	**ama=amba**	or

Soortu waxay ka mid tahay cuntada joogtada ah ee maalin walba la cuno. Soorta waxa laga sameyn karaa budo kasta sida galleyda, bariiska, sareenka ama laba waa la isku dari karaa sida gallay iyo qumbe, sarreen iyo digir iwm.

Waxa la sameyn karaa soor caadi ah ama soor isku karis ah. Haddii la sameyn rabo soorta isku karis ah waxa loo baahanyahay:

saddex koob oo budo ah
rubuc kiilo oo hilib ah
basal
laba xubnood oo toon ah
afar yaanyo oo waaweyn
afar qaaddo oo yar oo saliid ah ama subag ah
qaaddo yar iyo badh oo cusbo ah
qaaddo yar oo heyl iyo qorfe tuman ama shiilan ah haddii la doono

Habka bisleynta soorta isku karis ahi waa sidatan:
Hilibka nadiifi oo jarjar, basasha diir oo jarjar, yaanyooyinka diir oo jarjar. Budada nadiifi, saliidda kululee oo basasha shiil ilaa ay

guduudato. Hilibka ku dar oo in yar isku shiil. Yaanyooyinka, cusbada iyo koob biyo ah ku dar. Labaatan daqiiqadood kari. Budada iyo xawaashka ku dar oo isku walaaq. Dab aad u yar ku kari ilaa iyo intay budada iyo hilibkuba bislaanayaan. In yar oo sanuunadda ah ama dufan (subag ama saliid) korka ku shub, dabool oo dhuxul korka ka saar intii shan iyo toban daqiiqadood ah.
Dabadeedna waa la cunaa.

Soor is one of the staple foods which are eaten every day. Soor *can be made from every flour such as maize, rice or wheat, or two can be added together, like maize and coconut, wheat and peas etc.*

One can make normal soor *or* soor *cooked together [with other things]. If one wants to make* soor *with other things one needs:*

three cups of flour
a quarter of a kilo of meat
an onion
two cloves of garlic
four large tomatoes
four small spoons of oil or butter
one-and-a-half small spoons of salt
a small spoon of ground or fried cardamom and cinnamon, if desired

The way of cooking soor *is this way:*
Clean the meat and cut it up, peel the onion and chop it up, peel the tomatoes and chop them up. Rinse the flour and heat the oil, and fry the onion until it is brownish. Add the meat and fry it a little. Add the tomatoes, the salt and a cup of water. Cook for twenty minutes. Add the flour and spices and stir together. Cook on a very low heat until the flour and meat is cooked. Pour a little gravy or grease (butter or oil) on the top, cover and put on charcoal for twenty-five minutes.
Then it is eaten.

Notes

1 You will see in the next chapter that these are the forms used in a relative clause when the head noun is not the subject of the relative clause and the relative clause plus head noun is not the subject of the sentence.
2 This recipe is an edited version taken from a book called *Diyaarinta Cuntada Xaaska*, 'Preparation of the family's food', published in Mogadishu by the former Ministry of Education and Training.

12 Ma xanuunsan-tahay?

Are you ill?

> By the end of this lesson you should:
> - know about and be able to use relative clauses
> - use some 'wh-' question words and answer them
> - be able to use the independent pronouns

Dialogue

Bill feels unwell

Vocabulary

kú noqo (3B)	to return
kú faraxsán (adj.)	happy about
xanuun (1)	to be in pain
warwareer (1)	to feel dizzy
dhibaáto naqás	difficulty breathing
náqas (m.)	breath; unhealthy air
cúne (m. d7)	throat
cunáháasé	cunáha + báa + sé 'but the throat + focus'
qufac (1, qufcaa)	to cough
caloól (f. d1)	stomach
shúban (m.)	diarrhoea
dúrey (m.)	cold (note: in Somali a cold 'falls on you': **Dúray báa igú dhacaý**, lit.: 'A cold fell on me', I have a cold)
xún (adj.)	bad
má xumá	it is not bad
ká tallaal (1)	to vaccinate against

intaánad imán	before you came (ínta + aán + ad; aán is the negative marker for subordinate clauses, it is dealt with in a later lesson)
laygá	la + i + ká, 'one + me + against'
daacúun (m.)	cholera
jadeecó (f.)	typhoid (this seems also to be used for yellow fever)
teetáne (m.)	tetanus
kiniíni (m. d2)	tablet, pill
kaneéco (f. d6 collec.)	mosquito
kiniíniga kaneecáda (duúmo (f.)	malaria pills malaria)
kú dhac (1)	to happen to, afflict
ilaali (2A)	to look after
mood (1)	to think
xáal (m., axwaal (f.))	state, condition
xumow (3A, xumaadaa, xumaataa)	to become worse
hargabsán (adj.)	having a cold
madaxáa	mádaxa + báa
aynu quraacánno	let us have breakfast (the optative form)

Sue waxay ku noqatay gurigii Cabdullaahi. Markay guriga gaadhay Bill bay eegtay. Wuxuu la hadlayay Maxmuud.

BILL: Waan ku faraxsanahay inaad dhakhtar tahay. Madaxa ayaa i xanuunaya in yarna waan warwareerayaa.
MAXMUUD: Dhibaato naqas ma jiraa?
BILL: U maleyn maayo. Cunahaase in yar i xanuunaya.
MAXMUUD: Ma qufcaysaa?
BILL: In yar.
MAXMUUD: Calooshana ka warran, shuban ma jiraa?
BILL: Maya. Calooshu way fiicantahay.
MAXMUUD: Waxaan u maleynayaa in durey kugu dhacay. Ma xuma. Ma lagu tallaalay intaanad iman geeska Afrika?
BILL: Haa. Waxa layga tallaalay daacuun, jadeeco iyo teetane. Maalin kastana waxaan cunaa kiniiniga kaneecada.
MAXMUUD: Waa inaad caafimaadkaaga ilaaliso. Cunahaa i tus. Afkaa fur.

Maxmuud Bill cunihiisa buu eegay.

MAXMUUD: Waxaan moodayaa in durey yari kugu dhacay. Wax xun ma aha, laakiin haddii xaalkaagu xumaado waa inaad ii soo sheegto.
BILL: Waa yahay. Mahadsanid.

Idil baa gurigii ka baxday.

SUE: Idilay, subax wanaagsan, bal iska warran.
IDIL: Waan iska wanaagsanahay. Waxaanse u maleynayaa inaan hargabsanahay, waayo madaxaa i xanuunaya.
SUE: Waan ka xumahay, Idil. Duray baana Bill ku dhacay.
MAXMUUD: Kaalaya aynu quraacanno. Maanta ilaa meel fog baynu u safri doonnaa, haddii Eebbe yidhaahdo.

Sue returned to Cabdullaahi's house. When she reached the house she saw Bill. He was speaking with Maxmuud.

BILL: *I am happy that you are a doctor. I have a sore head and I feel a little dizzy.*
MAXMUUD: *Do you have difficulty breathing?*
BILL: *I don't think so. But my throat is a little sore.*
MAXMUUD: *Are you coughing?*
BILL: *A little.*
MAXMUUD: *How is the stomach, is there diarrhoea?*
BILL: *No. My stomach is fine.*
MAXMUUD: *I think that you have a cold. It is not serious. Were you vaccinated before you came to the Horn of Africa?*
BILL: *Yes, I was vaccinated against cholera, typhoid and tetanus. And every day I take pills against malaria.*
MAXMUUD: *You must look after your health. Show me your throat. Open your mouth.*

Maxmuud looked at Bill's throat.

MAXMUUD: *I think that you have a slight cold. It is nothing serious, but if your condition gets worse you must tell me.*
BILL: *Right, thank you.*

Idil came out of the house.

SUE: *Idil, good morning, how are you?*
IDIL: *I'm not too bad. But I think I have a cold, because I have a headache.*
SUE: *I am sorry, Idil. Bill also has a cold.*
MAXMUUD: *Come, let us have breakfast. Today we shall travel to a far place, God willing.*

Relative clauses

In this section we shall look at another type of subordinate clause, the relative clause. An example of a relative clause in English is the following:

The bread <u>which I ate</u> is sweet.

The underlined clause 'which I ate' is a relative clause referring to the noun phrase 'the bread'. The noun phrase 'the bread' is called the head noun of the relative clause.

There are two types of relative clauses: appositive and restrictive clauses.

appositive: these clauses simply provide some extra information about the head noun. This type is also sometimes called a 'commenting' clause.

restrictive: these clauses, as the name implies, restrict the head noun, that is to say the head noun is specifically identified by the relative clause. This type is also sometimes called a 'defining' clause.

This distinction is shown in the examples below.

appositive: 'I read the book, which Canab wrote'. In this example Canab simply happened to have written the book. The important thing is not who wrote it.

restrictive: 'I read the book Canab wrote'. In this example the book is singled out; it is important that it is the one Canab wrote.

In English the distinction between the two is only apparent in the intonation and stress pattern of the sentence in speech. In writing it is possible to distinguish between the two by the use of the comma, as above.

In Somali the distinction between appositive and restrictive clauses is made by using the word **oo**. This is used between the head noun and the relative clause when it is an appositive clause. When the clause is a restrictive clause, no other word is used and the clause just follows the head noun.

Búugga oo Canabi qortaý báan akhriyay.	I read the book, which Canab wrote.
Búugga Canabi qortaý báan akhriyay.	I read the book Canab wrote.

Note that the word **oo** is not a relative pronoun ('which, who etc.'); there is no relative pronoun in Somali. It is important to remember that **oo** does not translate the word 'which' of the English. Its only purpose is to distinguish between these two types of relative clause.

It is important to note that in Somali appositive relative clauses cannot be used with undefined head nouns. Also, restrictive relative clauses may not be used with names.

As you can see from these examples a relative clause is similar in structure to a main clause but has all of the characteristics we set out in the last lesson as the characteristics of subordinate clauses in general.

Using the subject verbal pronouns in relative clauses

In relative clauses when the subject is a pronoun then the subject verbal pronouns are used on their own since there is no mood classifier or focus marker in any subordinate clause in Somali.

Búugga oo ay qortaý báan akhriyay.	I read the book, which she wrote.
Búugga ay qortaý báan akhriyay.	I read the book she wrote.

Since relative clauses are subordinate clauses, we use the subordinate clause verb forms in them. There is, however, more than one form covering all relative clauses. Remember that subordinate clauses are noun phrases, thus they may be subjects, objects or adverbials of main clauses. The particular role a relative clause plays in a sentence is therefore marked on the relative clause, i.e. it is marked absolutive or as subject. Regarding relative clauses, there is a further factor in play: the head noun of a relative clause may be the subject of that relative clause or not. These two factors determine the form of the verb in a relative clause. We shall look at these various possibilities individually.

Relative clause verb forms when the head noun is not the subject of the relative clause

There is an important distinction which must be made with regard to the head noun of a relative clause in Somali. It is either the subject of the relative clause or not.

The woman <u>who bought the stamps</u> sent the letter.

In this sentence the relative clause is underlined. The head noun of the relative clause is 'the woman'. In addition to this the relative pronoun is the subject of the relative clause. Thus, we may say that the head noun is the subject of the relative clause.

I sent the letter <u>which she wrote</u>.

In this sentence the relative clause is underlined. The head noun of the relative clause is 'the letter' and, as you can see, this is not the subject of the relative clause. The subject of the clause 'which she wrote' is 'she'. The head noun in this case is the object of the relative clause.

In this section we shall look at the case when the head noun is *not* the subject of the relative clause.

There are two possibilities for such clauses:

- the head noun + relative clause may not be the subject of the sentence;
- the head noun + relative clause may be the subject of the sentence.

When the head noun plus relative clause is not the subject of the sentence

In this section we shall look at what happens when the head noun + relative clause is not the subject of the sentence. In these cases the subordinate clause verb is in the absolutive case. Two examples of such sentences are the following:

| **Macállinku wúxuu kariyay cuntáda <u>ínanku cúnayó</u>.** | The teacher cooked the food <u>the boy is eating</u>. |
| **Baríiska <u>oo gabádhu soó iibsataý</u> báy karisay.** | She cooked the rice <u>which the girl bought</u>. |

In each sentence the subject of the sentence is not the relative clause and head noun. Note also the fact that the head noun in each case is not the subject of the relative clause.

As you can see from these examples the forms of the verb are the same as the **ín**-clause forms we gave in the last lesson. It is these forms that are used in these cases. Go back over these verb forms, as they are used in all subordinate clauses in which the head noun is not the subject of the relative clause and in which the head noun + subordinate clause is not the subject of the sentence.

When the head noun plus relative clause is the subject of the sentence

Let us now look at the second possibility given above. If the head noun plus relative clause is the subject of the main sentence, then the relative clause verb will be in the subject form. This form of the verb is easy because it is the same as the main clause form in all respects.

Saacádda uu keenay wáa jabay.   The clock which he brought broke.

In the past tense, as here, the only difference to the absolutive verb form is in the stress-tone. In the present tense, however, the vowel is also different to the absolutive form of the subordinate clause verb form.

Áwrka uu keénayaa wáa cúni doonaa.   The camel which he is bringing will eat it.

This may be compared with the following sentence in which the relative clause plus head noun is not the subject:

Áwrka uu keénayó wuu cúni doonaa.   He will eat the camel which he is bringing.

Before going on to the next set of relative clause possibilities here is an exercise to practise what you have just learned.

Exercise

1 Translate the following sentences into Somali:

1 I spoke with the man I saw in the cafe.
2 They brought the camels the boy is grazing.
3 They listen to the programme which the BBC transmits. (transmit: wartebi (2A); BBC: BBCda)
4 He threw the spear which I made.
5 Are you eating the food which I cooked?
6 Will he bring the books which the teacher bought?
7 They go to the school which was built in Burco.
8 The camel I bought is grazing today.
9 Canab, whom they met in the cafe, goes to the new school.
10 The house he is building is in the centre of the town.

Relative clause verb forms when the head noun is the subject of the relative clause

We shall now look at the case when the head noun of the relative clause is also the subject of the relative clause. In these cases the important thing to remember is that the reduced verb paradigm is used. When the head noun + relative clause is not the subject of the main sentence then the reduced verb forms are the same as those given in Lesson 6, i.e. those used when the subject of a sentence is focused.

Again there are two possibilities for clauses of this type:

- when the head noun + relative clause is not the subject of the sentence;
- when the head noun + relative clause is the subject of the sentence.

When the head noun plus relative clause is not the subject of the sentence

An example of this type is the following sentence:

Nimánka <u>keenayá</u> wáan arkay.   I saw the men <u>who are bringing it</u>.

In this sentence the relative clause has been underlined. Note that the subject of the relative clause is also its head noun: **nimánka**, 'the men'. In this case the reduced paradigm is used, that is the same verb form as is used in main clauses when the subject is focused. Compare this with the following sentence in which the head noun of the relative clause is not the subject of it:

Nimánka ay raácayaan wáa danjirayaal.   The men they are accompanying are ambassadors.

We shall call this form the reduced paradigm (absolutive) from now on to distinguish it from the reduced paradigm (subject) below.

Another point that must be remembered when the head noun is the subject of the relative clause, is that there is no subject pronoun in the relative clause. Look at the two examples, and you can see that in the first one there is no pronoun, because the subject of the relative clause is the head noun. In the second example, however, the head noun is the direct object, thus a pronoun may be used as it is here.

When the head noun plus relative clause is the subject of the sentence

We now have one more possibility to look at. The case when the head noun is the subject of the relative clause and the head noun + relative clause is also the subject of the main sentence. In this case the reduced paradigm is also used since the head noun of the relative clause is also the subject of the relative clause. However, since the head noun + relative clause is also the subject of the sentence then the relative clause as a whole must be marked as the subject. This marking is on the final part, the verb.

Examples of relative clauses with these forms are:

Naagáha imánayaa wáa raáci doonaan. The women who are coming will accompany them.
Nínka warqádda diray wáa tagay. The man who sent the letter went.

As you can see, these forms look like the main clause forms except that we have the limited set of forms for person and number of the reduced verb paradigm. In other words the reduced paradigm is used in terms of the restricted number of distinctions for person and number, but the endings are not as in the absolutive forms. Despite this the endings are very easy to remember since they are basically the main verb endings. We shall call this verb form the reduced paradigm (subject). The full set is given below:

General past

	verb stem	ending	verb form
I	keen	ay	**keenay**
you (sg.)	keen	ay	**keenay**
he, it (m.)	keen	ay	**keenay**
she, it (f.)	keen	tay	**keentay**
we	keen	nay	**keennay**
you (pl.)	keen	ay	**keenay**
they	keen	ay	**keenay**

General present

	verb stem	ending	verb form
I	keen	aa	**keenaa**
you (sg.)	keen	aa	**keenaa**
he, it (m.)	keen	aa	**keenaa**
she, it (f.)	keen	taa	**keentaa**
we	keen	naa	**keennaa**
you (pl.)	keen	aa	**keenaa**
they	keen	aa	**keenaa**

The present and past progressives are formed in the way you would expect with the restricted set of forms but the main clause type endings.

Focusing a relative clause

You will remember that when we looked at the **in**-clauses we saw that the clause itself, being a noun phrase, could be focused. This is, of course, also the case with relative clauses.

You must remember, however, that when the subject of a sentence is focused, then the subject is not in the subject case but in the absolutive. This naturally also holds for subject relative clauses which are focused as in the example below:

Naagáha imánayá báa raáci doaná.   *The women who are coming* will accompany them.

Compare this with the following sentence in which the relative clause is not focused:

Naagáha imánayaa wáa raáci doonaan.   The women who are coming will accompany them.

Note the difference in the verb forms in the two sentences. In the first sentence the verb is not marked as a subject because the relative clause is focused.

The subject of relative clauses in Somali is not an easy one. Below is a table that sets out the principles in a concise way which, it is hoped, will be of help.

	HN subject of RC	HN not subject of RC
RC subject of sentence	reduced agreements but verb forms as in main clause, reduced paradigm (subject)	as main clause verb forms
RC not subject of sentence	reduced form verbs just as when the subject in a sentence is focused reduced paradigm (absolutive)	present tense same as main clause negative verbs; past tense with stress tone on final vowel, otherwise the same as the main clause forms

HN = head noun
RC = relative clause

Exercise

2 Translate the following sentences into Somali; focus the noun phrases in italics:

1 The girl who cooked the food is my sister.
2 Do you hear Axmed, who is grazing the camels?
3 Show me the boys who broke it.
4 *The lions that growled yesterday* killed a camel. (to growl: **ci** (1))
5 I will buy the chair which he is making.
6 The women who met the ambassadors returned to the town.
7 The boy who broke the radio ran to his house.
8 The two men, who came yesterday, are elders.
9 I saw *the woman who cooked the food.*
10 I have found *the passport you lost.*

'Wh-' questions and answers

These are questions in which a specific question word is used, such as: 'when', 'who', 'where', 'how' etc. We shall take the English question words in turn and see how they are rendered in Somali. Note we have already dealt with the **max . . .** construction meaning 'what . . .?' in Lesson 6.

'When'

The question word 'when' in Somali is **goórma**.

This is used in conjunction with the focus marker **báa** and the subject verbal pronouns, but all of these become one word as shown in the following examples:

Goórmáad tágaysaa?	When are you going?
Goórmáy yimaaddeen?	When did they come?

The full complement of forms is as follows:

	goórma	báa	subject pronoun	full form
I	goórma	báa	aan	**goórmáan**
you (sg.)	goórma	báa	aad	**goórmáad**
he, it (m.)	goórma	báa	uu	**goórmúu**
she, it (f.)	goórma	báa	ay	**goórmáy**
we (excl.)	goórma	báa	aannu	**goórmáannu**
we (incl.)	goórma	báa	aynu	**goórmáynu**
you (pl.)	goórma	báa	aydin	**goórmáydin**
they	goórma	báa	ay	**goórmáy**

Note when a subject pronoun is not needed with **goórma** + **báa** then the form is simply **goórmáa**.

Goórmáa la qaaday?	When did one take it? When was it taken?

To answer this type of question you use the appropriate time word in the answer; but remember to focus the time that has been asked!

Goórmáy tégi doontaa?	When will she go?
Saacád ká díb báy tégi doontaa.	She will go in an hour.

'Why'

There are two ways of saying 'why' in Somali. When you are asking the question 'Why?' on its own, without any verb then you use the word **wáayo**. For example if somebody says:

Sháleyto má imán.	Yesterday I didn't come.

you may respond with:

Wáayo?	Why?'

Note that in this case this might be translated in English as 'Why not?'

If you wish to use the word 'why' with a verb, then you use the construction **maxáa . . . ú**

Maxáad ú sameysay?	Why did you make it?
Muxúu ú tégi doonaa?	Why will he go?

You can see that this construction is somewhat similar to the expression 'for what, what for' in English.

There are a number of ways in which this question may be answered. We have met one already, the possessive construction **dartiís** or **awgiís**; this may be used in conjunction with the preverbal preposition **ú**:

Gúriga maxáad ú gashay?	Why did you enter the house?
Róobka áwgiís báan ú galay.	I entered it because of the rain.

Another way is to use the preverbal preposition with a focus construction and a relative clause. Such clauses translate the English 'in order to', 'so that'.

Qólka maxáad ú gashay?	Why did you enter the room?
Qólka wáxaan ú galay ínaan heló shandáddáyda.	I entered the room in order to find my suitcase.
Áf Soomaáliga maxáad ú baránaysaa?	Why are you learning Somali?
Áf soomaáliga wáxaan ú baránayaa ínaan suugaánta Soomaaliyeéd gartó.	I am learning Somali in order to understand Somali literature.

The relative clause in these cases may also begin with the word **sí**, but this must be accompanied by the preverbal preposition **ú** in the subordinate clause also.

Qólka wáxaan ú galay sí aan ú heló shandáddáyda.	I entered the room in order to find my suitcase.
Áf soomaáliga wáxaan ú baránayaa sí aan suugaánta Soomaaliyeéd ú gartó.	I am learning Somali in order to understand Somali literature.

'Who'

There are two ways of translating 'who' into Somali: **yáa** or **kúma/túma**.

When **yáa** is the subject of the sentence then the reduced paradigm of the verb is used.[1]

Yáa ku booqdaý?	Who visited you?
Yáa ká keéni dooná?	Who will bring it from there?

Remember to focus the person in the reply to such questions; the following are possible replies to the above questions:

Canab báa ku booqataý.	Canab visited you.
Baráha báa ká keéni dooná.	The teacher will bring it from there.

When the person referred to by **yáa** is not the subject of the sentence then the subject pronoun is added to **yáa**.

Yáad aragtay?	Whom did you see?
Cáli báan arkay.	I saw Cali.
Yáydin lá tégi doontaan?	Whom will you go with?
Maxámed qóyskíisa báannu lá tégi doonnaa.	We will go with Maxamed's family.

The other way of saying 'who' is using the words **kúma** in the masculine and **túma** in the feminine. Note that in questions these words are focused, as with **goórma**.

Kúma báad booqán doontaa?	Whom will you visit?
Túma báad lá hádlaysay?	Whom were you speaking with?

The focus marker is very often contracted in these cases, giving:

Kúmáad booqán doontaa?	Whom will you visit?
Túmáad lá hádlaysay?	Whom were you speaking with?

The word **kúma** or **túma** is used with **wâa** in the phrase 'Who is it?':

Waa kúma?	Who is it?
Waa túma?	Who is it?

'How'

The question 'how?' is asked in Somali with the word **sideé**, which literally means 'which way?'.

Sideé báad tahay?	How are you? (**tahay** = you are)

Sideé, 'which way', may also be used with the preverbal preposition **ú** to ask how something is done.

Bíyo sideé báad ú karisaa? How do you boil water?
Kíldhi báan kú kariyaa. I boil it in a kettle.

Exercise

3 Translate the following questions into English and give answers:

1 Goormay ka yimaaddeen?
2 Maxaydin ugu noqoteen?
3 Yaa ku booqday shaleyto?
4 Kumaad la hadli rabtaa?
5 Goormay ku noqon doonaan?
6 Maxaad u sameysay?
7 Sidee bay u yimaaddeen?

Independent pronouns

The independent pronouns are pronouns which may stand on their own in a sentence. We have seen in this lesson how the subject verbal pronouns are able to stand on their own in a relative clause, but this is a restricted situation. The independent pronouns on the other hand may play the role of any noun phrase in a sentence or a subordinate clause.

Aníga báa cunaý. I ate it.
Iyága báan lá tagay. I went with them.

You may ask what the difference is between the use of the independent pronouns and the verbal subject and object pronouns we have already met. The independent pronouns may be used for emphasis, in which case they may be used in addition to the verbal pronouns.

Miyáy tágaysaa iyádu? Is *she* going?
Is ká warráma idínku. Give news about yourselves/How are *you* (pl.)?

Another important way in which the independent pronouns are used is when you wish to focus a pronoun. Look again carefully at the first examples and you can see that the independent pronouns are focused. We are able to focus the independent pronouns because they are basically nouns with the definite article suffix attached to them (note that all are masculine except **iyáda**).

The full set of independent pronouns is given below:

I	aníga	we (incl.)	innága
		we (excl.)	annága
you (sg.)	adíga	you (pl.)	idínka
he, it (m.)	isága	they	iyága
she, it (f.)	iyáda		

You can see that the definite article suffixes in these words are in the absolutive case. If the independent pronoun is the subject of a sentence (and is not focused), then the subject form of the definite article is used.

Iságu wáa tagay.   He went.

Shorter versions of these independent pronouns, without the definite article, are also used in certain circumstances. One of these situations is when a word is attached to the pronoun such as a contracted focus marker or the suffix meaning 'and' **-na**. The forms **an**, **ad** and **is** are used when a suffix is added to these particular shortened pronouns. Compare the following two sets of sentences:

Aníga báa cunaý.   I ate it.
Iyága báan lá tagay.   I went with them.

These may also be written:

Anáa cunaý.   I ate it.
Iyáan lá tagay.   I went with them.

The following gives all of the shortened forms:

I	ani/an	we (incl.)	inna
		we (excl.)	anna
you (sg.)	adi/ad	you (pl.)	idin
he, it (m.)	isa/is	they	iya
she, it (f.)	iya		

'While'

The independent pronouns are used in a construction meaning 'while'.

Anígoo jídka soó márayaý waláalkaý báan lá kulmay. While I was walking along the street I met my brother.

This construction is made up of the independent pronoun of the subject of the subordinate clause verb, here **aníga**, plus an appositive relative clause with the independent pronoun as head noun. Note the word **oo** invariably becomes joined together with the independent pronoun as one word.

Iyágoo keénayaý heés báy qaádayeen. While they were bringing it they were singing a song.

Exercise

4 Translate the following sentences into Somali, focusing the words in italics:

1 *I* brought the books.
2 *You* sent them letters.
3 I took the three lamps to *them*.
4 While they were singing they were laughing.
5 While I was at the hotel I met with Maxamed.
6 While she was cooking the boy ate the bread.

Reading practice

A folktale

Vocabulary

talogélyo (f.)	seeking advice
béri (m. d1)	day, time
ína	son of
Sánweyne	nickname meaning 'big-nose'
adéer (m. d2)	paternal uncle; can also be used as a term of address to someone either much older or younger than the speaker

lá tali (2A)	to advise somebody
-ye	a suffix linking an imperative with a declarative
taladáad	**talada** + **aad**
tálo (f. d6)	advice, decision
áfo (f. d6)	wife
fur	open, also means divorce
sí xún ú eegay	looked at him in a bad (i.e. angry) way
cadhow (3B, cahdaaday, cadhaatay)	to get angry (**ú**: with)
iigú	**í** + **ú** + **ú** from **maxaad . . . ú** and **i . . . ú**
oo	'and' joining clauses of equal status
laygá	**la** + **i** + **ká**
baabbi'i (2A)	to destroy
talo geli (2A)	to seek advice (**ká**: from)

Talogelyo

Ninka Ina Sanweyne la odhan jiray buu beri nin u yimi. Markaasuu ninkii Ina Sanweyne ku yidhi: 'Adeer, inaad ila talisaa baan kaa doonayaaye, ila tali!' Markaasuu Ina Sanweyne yidhi: 'Oo waa maxay taladaad iga doonaysaa?'

Markaasaa ninkii yidhi: 'Inaan afadayda furaa baan doonayaaye, ila tali!' Markaasuu ina Sanweyne ninkii si xun u eegay. Markaasaa ninkii ina Sanweyne ku yidhi: 'Adeer miyaad ii cadhootay? Maxaad sidaa xun iigu eegtay?'

Markaasaa ina Sanweyne yidhi: 'Haa, waan kuu cadhooday.' Markaasaa ninkii yidhi: 'Oo maxaad iigu cadhootay?'

Markaasuu ina Sanweyne yidhi: 'Oo aniga reer la dhisayo baa layga talo geliyaaye; ma reer la baabbi'inayo baa layga talo geliyaa?'

Seeking advice

One day a man came to the man who used to be called Ina Sanweyne. Then the man said to Ina Sanweyne: 'Sir, I want you to advise me, advise me!' Then Ina Sanweyne said: 'And what advice do you want from me?'

Then the man said: 'I want to divorce my wife, advise me!' Then Ina Sanweyne looked at the man in an angry way. Then the man said to Ina Sanweyne: 'Sir, are you angry with me? Why did you look at me in that angry way?'

Then Ina Sanweyne said: *'Yes, I was angry with you.'* Then the man said: *'And why were you angry with me?'*

Then Ina Sanweyne said: *'People ask advice from me about a family which is being built; am I being asked for advice about a family which is being destroyed?'*

Notes

1 This is because the word **yáa** incorporates the focus marker **báa**.

13 Jariidadda

The newspaper

> **By the end of this lesson you should be able to:**
> - use the verb **yahay**, 'to be'
> - use adjectives with **yahay**
> - form the comparative, superlative and the construction meaning 'very'
> - use some more 'wh-' question words
> - use mass and collective nouns

Reading practice

These are slightly edited versions of Somali newspaper articles on Liberia and Japan, taken from a newspaper called Midnimo *['Unity'] printed 16 June 1992 in Mogadishu*

Vocabulary

wasíir (m. d2)	minister
arrín (f. d1, **arrimo**)	matter
dibád (f.)	outside, abroad
wasíirka arrimáha dibádda	foreign minister
wáddan (m. d2, **waddamo**)	country, nation
xarún (f. d1, **xarumo**)	capital
yeelo (3B)	to hold
shír (m. d4)	meeting
qalalaáse (m. d7)	disturbance
ká taagán (adj.)	facing
hannáan (m. d2)	appearance, system
dambee (2B)	to come after

iská horimáad (m. d2)	confrontation
la soó dhaafaý	one has passed, last
dhaaf (1)	to pass by
ká tirsán (adj.)	belonging to, member of
askári (m. **askar** (f.))	soldier
ciidammo (f. pl.)	forces
ilaalín (f.)	watching over
nabád ilaalín (f.)	peace keeping
góbol (m. d2)	area
wár (m. d4)	news
ká soó daadguree (2B)	to evacuate
goób (f. d4)	site, position
dagáal (m. d2)	fighting, war
gacánta ugú jir (1)	to be in the hands of
xóog (m. d4)	force, army
oggolow (3B, **oggolaaday**, **oggolaatay**)	to allow, approve, ratify
shárci (m. d2)	law
haẃl (f. d1)	work, activity
isbahaýsi (m. d2)	alliance
ká koobán (adj.)	comprised of
xísbi (m. d2)	party
taláda hayá	in power
xulufo (f.)	allies
isbahayso (3B)	to make an alliance
hortag (1)	to oppose
baaji (2A)	to prevent, postpone
kú saabsán (adj.)	concerning
mucaárad (m. d2)	opposition (political)
balladhán (adj.)	wide
xayir (1)	to block
xayíri lahaa	it would block
go'áan (m. d2, **go'aammo**)	decision

Liberia

Wasiirada Arrimaha Dibadda ee waddamada galbeedka Afrika ayaa ku kulmaya xarunta dalka Liberia ee Monrovia, waxana halkaas ay ku yeelanayaan shir ay kaga wada hadlayaan qalalaasaha ka taagan hannaanka nabadda ee dalka Liberia.

Arrintaasi waxay ka dambeysay iska horimaadyadii bishii la soo dhaafay markii la dilay lix ka tirsan askarta Senigaal oo qayb ka ahaa ciidamada nabad ilaalinta ee gobolkaas.

Wararkii ugu danbeeyeyna waxay sheegayaan in qeyb ka mid ah ciidamada Senigaal laga soo daadgureeyey goobtaasi woqooyiga dalka oo ah meesha dagaaladu ay ka dheceen.

Iyo Jabaan . . .

Barlamaanka Jabaan waxaa uu oggolaaday sharci oggolaanaya in dalkaasi Jabaan in uu u diro waddamada dibadda si ay qayb uga qaataan hawlaha nabad ilaalinta, sharciga waxa oggolaaday isbahaysi ka kooban xisbiga talada haya iyo xulufo yaryar oo way isbahaystaan si looga hortago in la baajiyo go'aan ku saabsan sidii mucaaradka ballaaran ee dalkaasi uu u xayiri lahaa. Sharciguna waxaa uu oggolaanayaa in Jabaan ciidamo nabad ilaalin ah ay u dirto dibadda.

Liberia

The foreign ministers of the states of west Africa are meeting in the capital of Liberia, Monrovia; they are holding a meeting there at which they are talking about the disturbances facing the peace plan in Liberia.

This matter follows clashes last month when six soldiers from Senegal who were part of the peace-keeping force of the region were killed.

The latest news says that part of the Senegalese force has been evacuated from that northern region of the country which is the place where the fighting happened.

And in Japan . . .

The parliament of Japan has ratified a law which allows the country of Japan to send them (i.e. troops) to foreign countries so that they take part in peace-keeping activities; the law was approved by an alliance comprised of the ruling party and [some] small allies, and they are combining to prevent opposition to a decision which widespread opposition in the country would have blocked. The law [now] allows Japan to send peace-keeping troops abroad.

The verb yahay, 'to be'

We have already met some words that can be translated as 'to be' in English: **joog**, **yiil** and **jir**. The verb **yahay**, however, is used to translate the verb 'to be' when it is used not as 'to be situated somewhere', but when something has some particular property. One example you are already well familiar with is the following phrase:

 Wáa la fiicányahay.   I am well. (lit.: one is well)

or

 Waan fiicanáhay.   I am well.

The underlined parts are from the verb **yahay**.

As with 'to be' in many languages, **yahay** in Somali is a somewhat irregular verb. In this section we shall look at the forms of the verb and its usage in main clauses. We shall look at its use with adjectives and nouns separately, as the behaviour differs a little in each case.

The forms of the verb yahay

The verb **yahay** is one of the prefixing verbs, thus certain aspects of its forms will be familiar to you.

The general past

The forms for the general past, meaning 'I was', 'you were' etc., are given in the following table:

	stem	person marker	number ending	verb form
I	ah	aa		**ahaa**
you (sg.)	ah	ayd		**ahayd**
he, it (m.)	ah	aa		**ahaa**
she, it (f.)	ah	ayd		**ahayd**
we	ah	ayn		**ahayn**
you (pl.)	ah	ayd	een	**ahaydeen**
they	ah	aa	een	**ahaayeen**

As you can see in this tense there is no person marker prefix. The person marker appears as a suffix.

The reduced verb paradigm is as follows (remember these forms are used when the subject is focused or when the head noun of a relative clause is the subject of that clause):

I	**ahaá**	we	**ahaýn**
you (sg.)	**ahaá**	you (pl.)	**ahaá**
he, it (m.)	**ahaá**	they	**ahaá**
she, it (f.)	**ahaýd**		

You can see that this reduced paradigm is roughly the same as you would expect, but note that the vowel does not change to a short vowel.

The negative of the general past is formed by using **má**, with or without the subject verbal pronouns, with an unchanging negative form of the verb: **ahaýn**.

As you can see the endings on this tense are similar to the endings of the general present tense in the suffixing verbs. Remember, though, that in this verb the endings are the past tense endings.

Danjíre búu ahaa. He was an ambassador.
Gúriga wéyni má ahaýn. It was not a big house.

The general present

The general present forms for **yahay**, meaning 'I am', 'you are' etc., are given below:

	stem	person marker	ending	verb form
I	-	ah	ay	**ahay**
you (sg.)	t	ah	ay	**tahay**
he, it (m.)	y	ah	ay	**yahay**
she, it (f.)	t	ah	ay	**tahay**
we	n	ah	ay	**nahay**
you (pl.)	t	ah	iin	**tihiin**
they	y	ah	iin	**yihiin**

These forms of the verbs do use the person marker prefixes. Note the change in the stem from **a** to **i** in the second and third person plural. The ending **-ay** will be familiar to you by now as the past tense ending in the suffixing verbs. Remember that in the verb **yahay** here it is a present tense ending.

The general present reduced paradigm is very easy to learn as it is an invariable form, that is to say it does not change for person or number. The form is **áh** in the absolutive and **ihi** in the subject case. This will be used when it is the final part of a relative clause which, along with its head noun, is the subject of the sentence (and when at the same time the head noun is the subject of the relative clause), as well as when the subject is focused.

absolutive	subject
áh	**ihi**

The negative forms of the general present are not as one would necessarily expect, so learn these forms carefully. As usual, the negative word **má** is used with these forms:

I	**ihí**	we	**ihín**
you	**ihíd**	you (pl.)	**ihidín**
he, it (m.)	**ahá**	they	**ahá**
she, it (f.)	**ahá**		

Ardéy báannu nahay.	We are students.
Wáxay yihiin shandado.	They are suitcases.
Iyáda báa danjiráha áh.	*She* is the ambassador.
Dhákhtar má ahá.	He is not a doctor.

The infinitive

The infinitive form of **yahay** is **ahaán**.
There is no progressive form of the verb **yahay**; this is because it is a type of verb known as a stative verb, but the infinitive is used in the constructions with verbs that take the infinitive.

Dhákhtar báan ahaán doonaa.   I will be doctor.

The imperative

The imperative form is	sg.: **aháw**	pl.: **ahaáda**
The negative imperative is	sg.: **ha ahaánin**	pl.: **ha ahaanína**

This form is used in the useful expression **igá raálli aháw**, 'Excuse me', or simply **raálli aháw** (**raálli** means 'willing, agreeable').

Subordinate clause forms

The subordinate clause forms of the verb **yahay** are the same as the main clause verb forms (except the reduced paradigm past tense). Thus there are no new forms which need to be learnt but you must remember to use the reduced paradigm in the appropriate places as you learnt in the lesson on relative clauses.

Note that the subject form of the reduced paradigm of the past tense is without a stress-tone, unlike the absolutive form.

Nínka macállinka áh báan arkay.	I saw the man who is the teacher.
Naagáha oo dhakhtarado áh báy lá kúlmi doonaan.	They will meet with the women who are doctors.
Nínka macállinka ihi wáa yimi.	The man who is the teacher came.
Naagáha oo dhakhtarado ihi waa imán doonaan.	The women who are doctors will come.
Adéerkaý oo dhákhtar ahaá wáan booqday.	I visited my paternal uncle who was a doctor.
Naagáha oo dhakhtarado ahaá way lá kulmeen.	They met with the women who were doctors.
Adéerkaý oo dhákhtar ahaa wáa na booqán doonaa.	My uncle who is a doctor will visit us.
Naagáha oo dhakhtarado ahaa way lá kúlmi doonaan.	The women who are doctors will meet with them.

Exercise

1 Translate the following sentences into Somali:

1 She is a doctor. She was a doctor.
2 The boys are good students. The boys were good students.
3 She sees the man who is a doctor. She saw the man who was a doctor.
4 The man who is a teacher visits me. The man who was a teacher visited me.
5 They are camels which are grazing. They were camels which were grazing.
6 The women who are ambassadors meet with the minister. The women who were ambassadors met with the minister.

Adjectives and their use with the verb yahay

Before we look at adjectives it is important to point out that in older textbooks on Somali, adjectives were regarded as being a type of verb. If you use any of these older books you will see that the endings are all the same as those you will meet here, but the explanation is different.

The use of the verb **yahay** differs when we use it with adjectives. With nouns it is used in the same way as any verb you have met. The use of **yahay** with adjectives, however, is a little different, and will be dealt with in this section.

There are two types of adjectives in Somali: *predicative* and *attributive*.

Predicative adjectives are, strictly speaking, always used with one form or another of the verb **yahay**. Even in cases such as **gúriga cusúb** there is a form of the verb! This will be explained in a short while. There are two main points to remember when using **yahay** with predicative adjectives:

- the adjective and **yahay** are written together, often as one word;
- there are some shortened versions of the forms of **yahay** which are used with adjectives.

The attributive adjectives do not occur with the verb **yahay** but simply follow immediately the noun they are describing on their own. There are only a few examples of this type of adjective, and we shall return to them below.

Usage in main clauses

We shall look at the use of **yahay** in main clauses first. In a main clause the verb **yahay** always immediately follows the adjective and is, in general, written with the adjective.

The general past tense

When the general past tense is used with an adjective then the shortened forms of the tense must be used. Note also there is no stress-tone in the adjective and **yahay** suffix form.

Barnaámijku wúu wanaagsanaa. The programme was good.
Gabádhu wáy quruxsanayd. The girl was beautiful.

The full set of shortened forms of the general past is as follows:

	person marker	number ending	verb form
I	aa		**-aa**
you (sg.)	ayd		**-ayd**
he, it (m.)	aa		**-aa**
she, it (f.)	ayd		**-ayd**
we	ayn		**-ayn**
you (pl.)	ayd	een	**-aydeen**
they	aa	een	**-aayeen**

As you can see, the forms of these shortened versions are not difficult to learn. They may be derived from the long version by simply deleting the **ah** from the full version. Note also that these forms are always added onto the adjective. Here is the adjective **wanaagsán**, 'good', with all of these shortened forms:

I	**wanaagsanaa**	we	**wanaagsanayn**
you (sg.)	**wanaagsanayd**	you (pl.)	**wanaagsanaydeen**
he, it (m.)	**wanaagsanaa**	they	**wanaagsanaayeen**
she, it (f.)	**wanaagsanayd**		

Note that the final vowel of an adjective is deleted when it ends in the pattern VCVC, for example: **wúu fiicnaa** (from: **fiicán + aa**). Compare this with the discussion of declension 3 nouns.

The negative shortened form of the general past tense is formed in the same way as in the positive. That is to say **ah** is deleted, giving the form **-aýn**.

Má dheeraýn. I was not tall.
Má cusbaýn. It was not new.

The general present tense

In the general present tense the shortened versions of the verb **yahay** are optional when used with adjectives. That is to say you do not have to use them as is the case with the past tense forms.

Nínku waa dhéeryahay. The man is tall.
Mindídu waa cusúbtahay. The knife is new.

Note that in these cases where the full form of the verb is used then the verb may be written separately from the adjective:

Nínku waa dhéer yahay. The man is tall.
Mindídu waa cusúb tahay. The knife is new.

Using the optional short forms these sentences may also be as follows; note that when the short forms are used then they must be written with the adjective as here:

Nínku waa dhéeryay. The man is tall.
Mindídu waa cusúbtay. The knife is new.

As you can see from these examples the way in which the form of the verb **yahay** is shortened is, again, by deleting the **ah** part in the middle. Thus the full set of shortened forms of the general present tense is as follows:

	person marker	ending	verb form
I	–	ay	**-ay**
you (sg.)	t	ay	**-tay**
he, it (m.)	y	ay	**-yay**
she, it (f.)	t	ay	**-tay**
we	n	ay	**-nay**
you (pl.)	t	iin	**-tiin**
they	y	iin	**-yiin**

In the negative the shortened version is also optional and is formed by deleting the **ah** from the full version of the negative general present form.

Má kulúlá. It is not hot.
Má dheregsání. I am not full.

The full set of shortened forms of the negative is given here:

I	**-í**	we	**-ín**
you	**-íd**	you (pl.)	**-idín**
he, it (m.)	**-á**	they	**-á**
she, it (f.)	**-á**		

Exercise

2 Translate the following sentences into Somali:

1 The house is new.
2 Axmed, who is a student, is tall.
3 They are well.
4 I was hungry but I have eaten and now I am satisfied.
5 He belongs to the school.
6 The airport is wide.

The verb yahay *used with adjectives in subordinate clauses*

In the previous section you learnt about the use of **yahay** with adjectives in main clauses. In this section you will look at the way **yahay** is used with adjectives in subordinate clauses.

The main point to remember when the verb **yahay** is used with adjectives in subordinate clauses is that the contracted form of the verb is *always* used, that is, in both the present tense and in the past tense. The only shortened forms you have not yet met are those of the reduced paradigm. These are formed in the same way as the other forms, that is, the **ah** part of the verb is deleted.

You will remember that the reduced paradigm of the present tense is simply **áh** in the absolutive and **ihi** in the subject case. When **ah** is deleted from these forms nothing remains of the **áh** form and **-i** remains from the subject form. Thus, zero or nothing is the absolutive form and **-i** is the subject form of the verb which goes with adjectives in relative clauses in which the head noun is the subject of the relative clause.

You can see that what is described here is simply the behaviour of adjectives which you learnt in Lesson 4, although you are now able to understand this behaviour.

Gaádhi cusúb báan soó iibsaday.	I bought a new car. (lit.: a car which is new)
Naágta dheeri wáy timi.	The tall woman came. (lit.: the woman who is tall)
Nínka xanuunsanaa waa ií keenay.	The man who was ill brought it for me.

Exercise

3 Translate the following sentences into Somali:

1 The new teacher is good.
2 I showed them my large house.
3 We went to the town, which is far.
4 The tall man could not open the closed door.
5 The boy, who was a member of the school, ate the food I made.
6 I added it to the water which was hot.

Comparative and superlative of adjectives and 'very'

The comparative form of an adjective is the form such as 'drier' used when comparing two noun phrases. The superlative is the name given to forms such as 'driest', 'heaviest' etc.

There are no specific forms of the adjective to express the comparative and the superlative in Somali. Both are expressed through the use of preverbal prepositions.

The comparative

This is formed using the preverbal preposition **ká** with the adjective.

Shandáddani shandáddíisa way ká culústahay.	This suitcase is heavier than his suitcase.
Canabi hooyádeéd way ká dheértahay.	Canab is taller than her mother.

Ká can also be used in this way with adjectives on their own to express the comparative in general. (Remember that, strictly speaking, these adjectives are not on their own but with the form **áh** of **yahay** which has been deleted.)

Shandádda ká culús noó kéen.	Bring the heavier suitcase for us.
Nínkií ká dhéer báan lá hadlay.	I spoke with the taller man.

The superlative

The superlative in Somali is expressed using the preverbal preposition cluster **ugú** with the adjective.

Hudhéelkanu waa ugú weýnyahay.	This hotel is the largest.

Cásharkani waa ugú fududaa. This lesson was the easiest.

Also, **ugú** may be used on its own with adjectives.

Dálka ugú fóg báan booqán doonaa.	I will visit the furthest country.
Búuggíisa ugú cusúb báan akhríyayay.	I was reading his newest book.

'Very'

There is no specific word for 'very' in Somali. The way to express this is to use the word **áad** in conjunction with the preverbal preposition **ú**. When this is used the word **áad** is always focused using **báa** or **ayáa**.

Áad báan ú fiicánahay.	I am very well.
Áad báa hálkaás ugá fógyahay.	It is very far from there.

For further emphasis the expression **áad iyo áad** may be used.

Áad iyo áad báa ú kululaa.	It was very, very hot.

Now that you are able to use adjectives with the verb 'to be' we shall look at some of the most common adjectives. These are set out in pairs of adjectives with opposite meanings. Note that the stress-tone pattern of adjectives is almost always stress-tone on the final vowel.

wéyn	big	**yár**	small
dhéer	long, tall	**gaabán**	short
kulúl	hot	**qabow**	cold
dhow	near	**fóg**	far
culús	heavy	**fudúd**	light, easy
wanaagsán	good	**xún**	bad
macaán	sweet	**qadhaádh**	bitter
buurán	fat	**dhuubán**	thin
quruxsán	beautiful	**foolxún**	ugly
harraadsán	thirsty	**gaajaysán**	hungry
toosán	straight, upright	**qalloocán**	curved, bent
jirrán, xanuusán	sick, ill	**ladán**	healthy
jilicsán	soft	**adág**	hard, difficult
qoyán	wet	**engegán**	dry
dheregsán	full		

Exercise

4 Translate the following sentences into Somali:

1 These shoes are wet.
2 She is well now but yesterday she was very ill.
3 That man is taller than me.
4 I think that I am taking the heaviest suitcase.
5 Sugar is very sweet.
6 That hat is cheaper than that one I bought yesterday.

'Which?'

The word 'which' is expressed in Somali with the suffix **-keé/-teé**. As you will realize, **-keé** is added to masculine nouns and **-teé** is added to feminine nouns.

Búuggeé báad heshay?	Which book did you find?
Baréheé báa ku baraý?	Which teacher taught you?

As with other suffixes that are added to nouns this suffix may stand on its own. In this case it means 'which one?', or 'which ones?' in the plural.

keé	which one (m.)?
teé	which one (f.)?
kuweé	which ones?
Kuweé báad heshay?	Which ones did you find?

Note that when this suffix is used in a sentence, either with a noun or on its own, then it is usually focused. This is because specific information is being asked for. In the light of this you can see that when an answer is given to a question of this type then the thing which has been asked for is always focused. Here are some examples of questions and answers:

Baabúurkeé báad wadatay?	Which car did you drive?
Baabúurka Maxaméd báan watay.	I drove Maxamed's car.
Keé ma qaádayaan?	Which one are they taking?
Káyga báy qaádayaan.	They are taking mine.

'Where?'

The way to express 'where' in Somali is to use a word meaning 'place' with the **-keé/-teé** suffix. There are two words which are particularly used in this context:

xág (m. d4), place, direction
hál (m.), place (remember **hálkán** and **hálkaás**)

Xággeé báydin tégi doontaan?	Where will you (pl.) go?
Hálkeé báy joogtaa?	Where is she?

Remember that when you answer one of these questions you must focus the information asked for in the question. Thus possible answers for the two questions above are the following:

Macállinka gúrigíisa báannu tégi doonnaa.	We will go to the teacher's house.
Dúgsiga báy joogtaa.	She is at the school.

These question words may also be used with **wâa** as in the following:

Dúgsigu waa xággeé?	Where is the school?

Another word for 'where' is **meé**, which is used with noun phrases on its own.

Dúgsigu meé?	Where is the school?

There are also the following forms of this particular question word, which are used on their own or with an appropriate subject:

meéyey	where is he?
meédey	where is she?
meéye	where are they?

'How much?', 'How many?'

To ask about an amount you use one of the following expressions: **ímmisa**, **meéqa**, **inteé**.

Ímmisa báad siisay?	How many did you give?
Meéqa báa la dhisay?	How many were built?

These words may both also be used with nouns. In this case they behave in the same way as numbers.

Ímmisa kaboód báad soó iibsatay?	How many shoes did you buy?
Meéqa buúg búu akhriyay?	How many books did he read?
Inteé báy keeneen?	How many did they bring?

'How long?'

The expression used for 'how long' is **inteé** (lit.: 'which amount').

Inteé báad joógaysaa?	How long are you staying?
Inteé báy eégayeen?	How long were they looking?

Exercise

5 Provide questions to the following answers:

1 Waxaan ka imi Burco.
2 Laba bay ka keentay.
3 Waxaan joogayaa laba toddobaad.
4 Kii ugu culus baan kuu qaadi doonaa.
5 Makhaayadda buu joogaa.
6 Saddex koob buu jabiyay.

Vocabulary building: attributive adjectives

The following is a list of the most common attributive adjectives:

horé	first, previous
dhexé	middle, between
dambé	next, last, behind
kalé	other
kastá	each, every
wálba	each, every
koré	upper
saré	upper, top
hoosé	lower
shishé	far
soké	near

Mass nouns and collective nouns

Most nouns in Somali are countable. For example, the noun **káb**, 'shoe', may be counted: **labá kaboód**, 'two shoes'.

Mass nouns are nouns that refer to something which may not be counted, such as **caáno**, 'milk', or **sonkór**, 'sugar'. These nouns may be used with particular measures but must be used with a form of the verb **yahay**, 'to be'. Basically, a relative clause is being used in these cases and the verb form most often used is **áh**.

kóob sháah áh	a cup of tea (lit.: a cup which is tea)
kiílo súbag áh	a kilo of butter (lit.: a kilo which is butter)

Note that if a number is used with the unit of measure then the word **oo** is used, as in the following examples:

shán koób oo sháah áh	five cups of tea
labá kiiló oo súbag áh	two kilos of butter

Some common mass nouns are the following:

súbag (m.)	butter (especially clarified butter)
caáno (m.)	milk
sháah (m.)	tea
bíyo (m.)	water
búr (m.)	flour
salíid (f.)	oil
sonkór (f.)	sugar

Collective nouns

Collective nouns indicate, as the name implies, 'collections'; they are nouns that are used for a set of things. We have already met the word **carruúr**, 'children'. Collective nouns behave in the same way as mass nouns.

sáddex carruúr áh	three children
labá dúmar áh	two women

Other common collective nouns are the following:

dád (m.)	people
dúmar (m.)	women
rág (m.)	men
géel (m.)	camels
ló' (f.)	cattle

ádhi (m.) sheep and goats
ído (m.) sheep

The word **géel** is a collective noun, and also the only word in Somali that has an irregular definite article.

géela 'the camels' (note the lack of **k** in the definite article)

Exercise

6 Translate the following sentences into Somali:

1 I drank four cups of tea today.
2 Bring a kilo of sugar from the market for me.
3 Bring me a cup of water!
4 The people who came here are Arabs.
5 Three children went to the school yesterday.
6 I shall take the sheep and goats in order to graze them.

Reading practice

A folktale

go' (1)	to cut (intr.)
xidhan (1, **xidhmaa**)	to become closed, tied
béri (m. d1)	day, time
más (m. d4)	snake
deg (1)	to live, reside
márkaasúu	then he (**márkaás** + **báa** + **uu**)
daállin (m., **daallimiín** (f.))	oppressor, nasty thing
dhéxdóodúu	**dhexdooda** + **búu**
maalín dambé	a later day
tasho (3A)	to consider
yáanu cúnin	may he not eat
hádh (m. d4)	shade
seéf (f. d4)	sword
qoór (f. d4)	neck
kú dhufo (3B)	to hit with
kagá	**kú** + **ká** (with + from)
jirríd (f. d1)	tree trunk
carar (1)	to run away

gód (m. d4)	hole (especially in the ground)
seexseexo (3B)	to sleep (of a number of people)
seexo (3B)	to sleep
cúrad (m. d2 or f. d1)	firstborn child
qaniin (1)	to bite, sting
dhimo (3B, **dhintaa**)	to die
wacatan (1, **wacatamaa**)	to make a pact
is	oneself
day (2A)	to look at, examine
wáar	version of **waryáa**
wáa taynu	**waa ta** + **aynu** (emphasising expression)
wáa taynu nabádda ahayn	we were at peace
goy (2A)	to cut (tr.)
xabáal (f. d1)	grave

Nabad go'day ma xidhanto

Nin baa beri guri mas ku jiro degay. Markaasuu maskii arkay; maskuse mas daallin ah ma ahayn. Casho walba carruurta iyo xoolaha dhexdooduu mari jiray oo waxba ma yeeli jirin.

Maalin dambe baa ninkii tashaday oo is yidhi: 'Maskanu yaanu xoolaha iyo carruurta cunin'. Markaasuu maskii oo geed hadhkiisa ku hurda u yimi oo is yidhi: 'Seef qoorta kaga dhufo!' markaasuu la waayay oo seeftii jirriddii ku dhacday. Markaasaa maskii toosay oo cararay oo god galay.

Habeenkii, markii la seexseexday buu maskii soo baxay oo ninka inankiisii curad qaniinay. Markaasaa inankii dhintay.

Subixii baa ninkii maskii u yimi oo ku yidhi: 'Waar, masyohow, aan wacatanno oo is deyno!' markaasaa maskii yidhi: 'Waar, ninyohow, berigii horeba waa taynu nabadda ahayn ee aad goysay. Imminkana markaan anna seeftii jirridda ku taal arkayo, adna inankaa xabaashiisa arkayso, wacad inoo xidhmi maayo. Aynu kexeenno.'

Peace that has been broken does not become mended (lit.: closed).

Once a man lived in a house in which a snake [also] lived. Then he saw the snake; but the snake was not nasty. Each day it used to pass among the children and the livestock and did not [used to] do anything.

On a later day the man considered and said to himself: 'May this snake not eat the livestock and the children'. Then he went to the snake who was sleeping in the shade of a tree and said to himself: 'Cut his neck off with a sword;' and he missed and the sword stuck into the tree. Then the snake woke up and ran away, and went into a hole.

In the evening, when [people] were sleeping the snake came out and bit the firstborn son of the man. Then the child died.

In the morning the man came to the snake and said to it: 'O snake, let us make a pact and look at ourselves!' Then the snake said: 'O man, we were at peace which you broke (lit.: cut) it. And now while I see the sword in the trunk of the tree and you see the grave of your son a pact cannot be made between us. And so let us part.'

14 Raydiyowga
The radio

> **By the end of this lesson you should be able to:**
> - use adverbial relative clauses, thus translate 'when . . .', 'after' etc.
> - use negative subordinate clauses
> - use focus in questions
> - form negative questions
> - use the optative form, e.g. 'let us go'
> - use the potential form and say 'maybe'
> - use the conditional form 'I would have gone'

Reading practice

A report in the style of language used on the radio

Vocabulary

hoggaamíye (m. d7)	leader
dhaqdhaqáaq (m. d2)	movement
ká soó horjeed (1)	to oppose, be in conflict with
xukumád (f. d1)	government
ú xagli (2A)	to tend towards
síi wad (1)	to continue
wadahádal (m. d2)	talks
dawlád (f. d1)	government
rasaás joojín (f.)	ceasefire
wareýsi (m.)	interview
yeelo (3B)	to have, hold
telefíshan (m.)	television

dagáal sokeeyé	civil war
cíd (f.)	someone
cídna	no one (when used with a negative verb, **cidina**, no one marked as subject)
aánay	negative word in subordinate clauses + **-ay**
kú guuleyso (3B)	to succeed in
islá márkaási	at the same time
qabso (3A)	to take hold
weérar (m. d2)	attack
weérar qaad	to make an attack
madaxbannaán (adj.)	independent
xaqiiji (2A)	to confirm

Dalka Angola

Hoggaamiyaha dhaqdhaqaaqa UNITA ee ka soo horjeeda xukumadda Angola, Jonas Savimbi, ayaa waxa uu sheegay inuu isu xaglinayo dhinaca in la sii wado wadahadalada dawladda uu kula jiro ee rasaas joojinta ah. Wareysi uu la yeeshay telefishanku Savimbi waxa uu sheegay in dagaal sokeeye cidina aanay ku guuleysanaynin, isla markaasi telefishanka waddanka Angola ayaa waxa uu sheegay UNITA inay ku guuleysan waayeen inay qabsadaan magaalo ku taalla koonfurta waddanka oo la yidhaahdo Kibungo oo maalintii jimcihii weerar ay ku soo qaadeen. Warar madaxbannaan oo xaqiijinaya weerarkaas una ma jiraan.

Angola

Jonas Savimbi, the leader of the UNITA movement which is in conflict with the government of Angola, has said that he is in favour of continuing the talks he is having with the government on a ceasefire. In an interview he had on television Savimbi said that no one would win the civil war; at the same time the television of the state of Angola said that UNITA did not succeed in capturing a town called Kibungo in the south of the country on Friday when they launched an attack. There is no independent news confirming this attack.

Adverbial relative clauses

Such words as 'when', 'if' etc., when they are used as conjunctions, are translated into Somali by relative clauses with specific head nouns which may be thought of as functioning like conjunctions.

You have met some of these already in the dialogues and reading passages. We shall look at the most common of these in this section.

'When'

This is rendered in Somali by: **márka** (lit.: 'the time') and a relative clause.

| **Márkaan karínayaý kóob báan jabiyay.** | When I was cooking it I broke a cup. |
| **Márkay timí cuntáda báy qaadday.** | When she came, she took the food. |

As you can see the subordinate clause is the same type as the **ín**-clause you have already met and the subject verbal pronoun is added to the head noun **márka** (lit.: 'the time'). This is the same with all the other adverbial clauses we shall meet in this section. Note that as with all subordinate clauses in Somali these clauses are also relative clauses. Since you now know the way the verb behaves in these clauses we shall not refer to this in particular here. You will see that everything in these clauses is regular and predictable from what you have already learnt.

The word **már** with the **-kií** definite article may also be used.

Márkií ay ká tagtaý 'Nabád gélyo' báy tidhi.
When she went away from there she said, 'Goodbye'.

Note that when this form is used the subject verbal pronoun is not added to **márkií**, but is written separately.

Other head nouns may be used to mean 'when':

| **goór** (f.) | time (remember **goórma**) |
| **kól** (m.) | time |

These are used in exactly the same way as **márka**.

Kólkay magaaláda heléen áad báy ú faraxsanaayeen.
When they found the town they were very happy.

Qólka wáy gashay goórtaan cashaýnayaý.
She entered the room when I was having dinner.

'After'

The word **káddib**, 'after' (made up of **ká** and **díb**), may be placed before **márka** to express the notion 'after . . .'.

Káddib márkuu cunaý ayúu gacmíhiís dhaqay.
After he ate he washed his hands.

Káddib márkaan noqdaý shaqáda báan bilaabay.
After I returned I began the work.

'As soon as'

The word **islá** may be used with **márka** to mean 'as soon as'.

Islá márkaan makhaayádda gaadhó sháah báan cábbi doonaa wáayo waan haraadsánahay.
As soon as I reach the cafe I will drink tea because I am thirsty.

Islá márkay yimaaddéen wáy cuneen.
As soon as they came they ate.

'Since'

'Since' is expressed in Somali by the phrase **tán iyo goórtií** (lit.: this and the time) along with a relative clause.

Warqado badán búu qoray tán iyo goórtií uu bartaý qorídda áfka.
He has written many letters since he learnt to write the language.

'Although'

This is expressed in Somali with the words **ín kastá** plus an appositive relative clause.

Ín kastá oo aan tagaý isága má arkín.
Although I went I did not see him.

Ín kastá oo ardeydu yidhaahdéen 'Máya' wáxaan ú maleýnayaa ínay imán doonáan.
Although the students said 'No' I suppose they will come.

Note that this expression may also be used in the contracted form: **ín kastóo**.

Ín kastóo aan tagaý isága má arkín. Although I went I did not see him.

'While'

'While' is expressed using the word **intií** with a relative clause. Remember also the use of the independent pronouns with **oo** to mean 'while'. As with other of these expressions the head noun may beome one word along with the pronoun.

> **Íntií aan warqádda qórayaý sháah báan cábbayay.**
> While I was writing the letter I was drinking tea.

> **Íntií uu bángiga joogaý nín búu lá hadlay.**
> While he was at the bank he spoke with a man.

> **Íntuu bángiga joogaý nín búu lá hadlay.**
> While he was at the bank he spoke with a man.

'If'

The conditional 'if . . .' is expressed in Somali using the word **háddií** (lit.: 'the time').

> **Háddií ay keéni doonáan waan faraxsánaán doonaa.**
> If they bring it I will be happy.

> **Haddií uu baabúurka hagaajiyó waannu tégi karraa.**
> If he mends the car we can go.

This construction may also be contracted.

> **Hádday keéni doonáan waan faraxsánaán doonaa.**
> If they bring it I will be happy.

Exercise

1 Translate the following sentences into Somali:

1 If you go to the restaurant you will meet my brother.
2 When the minister met with the ambassador they were happy.
3 After she left they told him.
4 While I was giving him the news he ran away from me.
5 As soon as she sees him she will give him the money.
6 When he lit the fire they sat down.

Negative subordinate clauses

In this section we shall look at the use of the negative in subordinate clauses. One main difference we have already mentioned is that the negative word used in subordinate clauses is **aán**, as opposed to the word **má** used in main clauses. The word **aán** immediately follows the head noun and is attached to it if the head noun ends in a short vowel. If it occurs in an appositive relative clause then **aán** immediately follows **oo**.

If there is a subject verbal pronoun in the clause then this is attached immediately to **aán**; furthermore it is a shortened form of the subject verbal pronoun which is added. These shortened forms are as follows:

I	-an	we (incl.)	-aynu
you (sg.)	-ad	we (excl.)	-aannu
he, it (m.)	-u	you (pl.)	-aydin
she, it (f.)	-ay	they	-ay

As you can see it is only the first three pronouns that are different, although in cases when the short pronouns are used the singular short versions are very often used for the first and second person plural.

Let us see now how all these different parts go together. Look at the following sentence:

Wáxaan ú maleýnayaa ínaánu imán doonó.
I suppose he will not come.

Here you can see that the **ín**-clause is introduced by **ín** (the head noun of this clause) followed by the negative word **aán** followed by the shortened form of the subject verbal pronoun: **ín – aán – u**.

Another example is the following:

Wáxay ií sheegtay ínaánay keéni karáan.
She told me that they cannot bring it.

In this example we have the following sequence: **ín – aán – ay**.

The negative verb forms

From the examples above you can see that the negative form of the verb is, in these cases, the same as the main clause negative verb form. This is the case for all of the tenses except for the present progressive. In this tense the negative form using **máayó** cannot be used in relative clauses.[1] The other present progressive negative forms **keénayó**, **keénaysó** etc. may be used. Or, the same invariable form used with the past progressive may be used in the present: **keénaýn** or **keénaynín**.

Nínka oo aán báre ahá báa yimi.	The man who is not a teacher came.
Cuntáda aánay cunín báan keenay.	I took the food she did not eat.
Soórta aánu walaaqín má macaánaýn.	The *soor* he did not stir was not tasty.

Exercise

2 Translate the following sentences into Somali:

1 I made the tea he did not drink.
2 The car which she did not mend was new.
3 She wrote the letter which they did not send.
4 I think that I will visit the boy who doesn't come to the school.
5 Bring me the one which is not red.
6 I went when he did not come.

Focusing in 'yes–no' questions

In previous sections you have learnt how to use the focus constructions in declarative sentences. It is also possible to focus a noun phrase in a 'yes–no' question (as well as the 'wh-' questions already dealt with). There are two ways of doing this by using **báa** or **ayáa**.

Báa is used in the following way:

Roóble ma aẃrtií Maxaméd búu daajiyay?
Did Rooble graze *Maxamed's burden camels?*
Ma cuntádaás báad cuntay?
Did you eat *that food?*

Note that when the subject is focused then all the characteristics that prevail in a statement also prevail in a question.

Ma Roóble báa daajiyaý?   Did *Rooble* graze them?

The other way of focusing a noun phrase in a question is to use the **miyáa** form.

Gúriga miyáad tágaysaa?   Are you going to *the house*?
Cuntádaás miyáad cunteen?   Did you eat *that food*?

Note again that if the subject is focused in this way then the familiar characteristics are present.

Cáli miyáa ká keenaý?   Did *Cali* bring it from there?

This use of **miyáa** does not discount the general use you learnt in Lesson 2. Compare, for example, the two following sentences:

Inammádu miyáy dúgsiga tegeen?   Did the children go to the school?
Inammáda miyáa dúgsiga tegeý?   Did *the children* go to the school?

The difference between these two sentences is in the emphasis. As you can see in the second sentence the subject is focused, therefore the emphasis is on 'the children'. In the first sentence on the other hand there is no particular emphasis.

Exercise

3 Change the following statements into questions so that the noun phrase in italics is focused in the question.

  Example: *Cali* **waa tagay**   gives **Ma Cali baa tagay?**

1 *Isaga* waad aragtay.
2 *Tuulada yar* waydin gaadheen.
3 *Adhiga* wuu daajiyay.
4 *Danjirayaashu* way madaxweynaha la kulmeen?
5 *Gacantu* waa ku xanuunaysaa.
6 *Muqdisho* way tagaysaa.

Negative questions

In this section we shall look at the way in which negative questions are formed, that is such questions as: 'Did you not go yesterday?'

There are two ways of forming negative questions according to whether a noun phrase in the question is focused or not. In a sentence without noun phrase focus the construction: **sów ... má** is used in the following way:

Jawaahir sów má cunín?	Didn't Jawaahir eat it?
Sów máad tegín?	Didn't you go?

These correspond to the following declarative statements:

Jawaáhir wáa cuntay.	Jawaahir ate it.
Wáad tagtay.	You went.

Note that the word **sów** may be separated from **má** by intervening noun phrases.

Sów Jawaahir má cunín?	Didn't Jawaahir eat it?
Sów albáabka máad xidhín?	Didn't you shut the door?

If a particular noun phrase is focused in a negative question then the negative word **aán** is used and it is added to the focus marker in a focused question of the type mentioned above.

Awrta miyaán daaqín?	Did *the camels* not graze?

or

Ma awrta baán daaqín?	Did *the camels* not graze?

Note the stress-tone in these examples. It is the stress-tone from the negative **aán** that prevails.

If there is a subject verbal pronoun on one of the negative + focus marker combinations then it is the shortened version that is used, the same form as is used in a negative relative clause given above.

Ma awrta baánad daajín?	Did you not graze the camels?

These short versions are also used with **miyáa**.

Miyaánu tágayó?	Is he not going?

Exercise

4 Put the following questions into the negative:

1 Hilib miyuu cunin?
2 Cali ma ka yimi?
3 Berrito dugsiga miyaad tegi doontaa?
4 Miyaad tagaysaa?
5 Farasmagaalada miyuu degganyahay?
6 Maxaabiistu ma ka baxsadeen?

The optative

The optative is a mood of the verb which is used when you wish to give commands in the first or third person.

Aan cúnno!   Let us eat!
Há qaado!   May he take it!

It is also used to express something that is wished.

Sháah aynu cábno.   Let us have some tea.

The forms of this mood are given in the following table for the verb **keen**, meaning 'let me bring', 'may you bring' etc. Note that in this mood the pronoun is an inherent part of the form for all the persons except the third person. In the third person the word **há** is used instead of a pronoun.

	pronoun	verb stem	ending	verb form
I	aan	keen	-o	**aan keéno**
you (sg.)	aad	keen	-to	**aad keénto**
he, it (m.)	-	keen	-o	**há keeno**
she, it (f.)	-	keen	-to	**há keento**
we (incl.)	aynu	keen	-no	**aynu keénno**
we (excl.)	aannu	keen	-no	**aannu keénno**
you (pl.)	aad	keen	-teen	**aad keénteen**
they	-	keen	-een	**há keeneen**

This pattern is the same for conjugations 2 and 3, in which the appropriate sound changes are made. The forms for the verb **joogso** are given below:

	pronoun	verb stem	ending	verb form
I	aan	joogso	-o	**aan joogsádo**
you (sg.)	aad	joogso	-to	**aad joogsáto**
he, it (m.)	–	joogso	-o	**há joogsado**
she, it (f.)		joogso	-to	**há joogsato**
we (incl.)	aynu	joogso	-no	**aynu joogsánno**
we (excl.)	aannu	joogso	-no	**aannu joogsánno**
you (pl.)	aad	joogso	-teen	**aad joogsáteen**
they	–	joogso	-een	**há joogsadeen**

As you can see from the tables the stress-tone pattern of the optative is: stress-tone on the vowel immediately before the ending, except in the third person. In the third person there is no stress-tone on the verb form itself, but there is one on the word **há**. Note also the use of the singular second person pronoun **aad** in the plural.

The optative mood may also be used in the negative. In these forms an invariable form of the verb is used. This is the same as the negative general past form, except that in conjugation 1 the stress-tone is on the final vowel of the verb stem, as opposed to the final vowel of the negative form.

keénin karín sameýn joogsán furán

These invariable forms are immediately preceded by the following negative words which incorporate the subject verbal pronouns:

I	**yáanan**	we (incl.)	**yáynu**
you (sg.)	**yáanad**	we (excl.)	**yáanan** or **yáanannu**
he, it (m.)	**yáanu**	you (pl.)	**yáanad**
she, it (f.)	**yáanay**	they	**yáanay**

The potential and 'maybe'

The potential mood is used to express possibility; it therefore translates the English words 'maybe', or 'perhaps'.

Shów qaadnee. Maybe we shall bring it.
Shów ú sheegeen. Perhaps they will tell him.

The classifier **shów** is always present with this mood. The forms of the verb are as follows:

	verb stem	ending	verb form
I	keen	ee	**keenee**
you (sg.)	keen	tee	**keentee**
he, it (m.)	keen	ee	**keenee**
she, it (f.)	keen	tee	**keentee**
we	keen	nee	**keennee**
you (pl.)	keen	teen	**keenteen**
they	keen	een	**keeneen**

The forms for the other conjugations are formed in the same way with the appropriate sound changes and so on. The potential of the verb **samee**, 'to make' is given below as an example:

	verb stem	ending	verb form
I	samee	ee	**sameeyee**
you (sg.)	samee	tee	**sameysee**
he, it (m.)	samee	ee	**sameeyee**
she, it (f.)	samee	tee	**sameysee**
we	samee	nee	**sameynee**
you (pl.)	samee	teen	**sameyseen**
they	samee	een	**sameeyeen**

Another way of expressing 'maybe, perhaps'

There is another way of expressing 'maybe, perhaps' in Somali. This is with the following phrase:

wáxa lagá yaabaa   lit.: 'what one is amazed by'

or

waa lagá yaabaa   lit.: 'one is amazed by it'

This is used with **in**-clauses as in the following examples:

Wáxa lagá yaabaa ináan tégi doonó.   Perhaps I will go.
Waa lagá yaabaa ínuu sameeyeý.   Perhaps he made it.

Conditional

The formation of conditional clauses has been dealt with above. Here we shall look at a verb formation which translates the English expression 'would', as in 'I would have gone'. The infinitive is used, followed by the verb forms given below. These are the word **léh** with the contracted adjective forms of the verb **yahay**. Note there is no distinction for tense in this mood.

I	**lahaa**	we	**lahayn**
you (sg.)	**lahayd**	you (pl.)	**lahaydeen**
he, it (m.)	**lahaa**	they	**lahaayeen**
she, it (f.)	**lahayd**		

Way keéni lahaayeen.   They would have brought it.

In the negative the negative word **má** is used, along with the following verb forms:

	verb stem	*ending*	*verb form*
I	keen	eén	**keeneén**
you (sg.)	keen	teén	**keenteén**
he, it (m.)	keen	eén	**keeneén**
she, it (f.)	keen	teén	**keenteén**
we	keen	neén	**keenneén**
you (pl.)	keen	teén	**keenteén**
they	keen	eén	**keeneén**

Exercise

5 Translate the following sentences into Somali:

1 Let us go to the cafe.
2 I would have brought it but he took it from me.
3 Maybe I will see you tomorrow.
4 If they saw him they would not have told me.
5 Let me look.
6 I would have made it for you but you were not there.

Reading practice 🔊

Another report in the style used on the radio

Vocabulary

koóx (f. d1)	group	faraggeli (2A)	to intervene
ká dagaallan (1, dagaallamaa)	to fight	kú tilmaan (1, tilmaamaa)	to describe as
ká míd áh	one of	masiíbo (f. d6)	calamity
ká soco (3B)	to continue in	bani aadnimó (f.)	humanitarianism, humanity
kú dhawaaq (1)	to announce, call for	fidi (2A)	to expand
adduunwéyne (m. d7)	international community		

Dalka Suudaan

Hogaamiyaha koox ka mid ah kooxaha ka dagaallamaya koonfurta dalka Suudaan ee dawladda ka soo horjeeda Riek Machar ayaa waxa uu sheegay xukumadda waddanka Suudaan inay qaadday weerarkii ugu weynaa ee tobankii sano ee dagaalka sokeeye dalkaa ka soconayay. Waxana uu markaas ku dhawaaqay in adduunweynuhu ay soo faraggeliyaan sidii loo joojin lahaa waxa uu ku tilmaamay masiibo dhinaca bani aadminnimo ah oo timaadda.

Sudan

Riek Machar, the leader of one of the groups fighting in the south of Sudan in opposition to the government has said that the state government of Sudan has launched the biggest attack [yet] in the ten years in which the civil war has continued. And he then called for the international community to intervene to stop what he described as a calamity which had befallen humanity.

Note

1 This is because the negative word **má** is part of the **máayó** form and is not allowed in subordinate clauses.

Grammatical tables

In order for these tables not to be too long only the verb forms of conjugations 1, 2 and 3 are given here. These are scattered throughout the book. The forms of the prefixing verbs and the verb **yahay**, on the other hand, are all together in the following lessons and thus are not repeated here:

yiil	Lesson 9
yiqiin	Lesson 11
yidhi	Lesson 10
yimi	Lesson 10
yahay	Lesson 13

Imperative   *Imperative negative*

kéen	keéna	ha keénin	ha keenína
kári	karíya	ha karín	ha karinína
samée	sameéya	ha ha sameýn	ha sameynína
joogsó	joogsáda	ha joogsán	ha joogsanína
furó	fúrta	ha furán	ha furanína

Infinitive

keéni	karín	sameýn	joogsán furán

General past

keenay	kariyay	sameeyay	joogsaday	furtay
keentay	karisay	sameysay	joogsatay	furatay
keenay	kariyay	sameeyay	joogsaday	furtay
keentay	karisay	sameysay	joogsatay	furatay
keennay	karinnay	sameynay	joogsannay	furannay

| keenteen | kariseen | sameyseen | joogsateen | furateen |
| keeneen | kariyeen | sameeyeen | joogsadeen | furteen |

Reduced paradigm; all verbs follow the same pattern, as given below:

keenaý
keenaý
keenaý
keentaý
keennaý
keenaý
keenaý

General past negative

| keenín | karín | sameýn | joogsán | furán |

General present

keenaa	kariyaa	sameeyaa	joogsadaa	furtaa
keentaa	karisaa	sameysaa	joogsataa	furataa
keenaa	kariyaa	sameeyaa	joogsadaa	furtaa
keentaa	karisaa	sameysaa	joogsataa	furataa
keennaa	karinnaa	sameynaa	joogsannaa	furannaa
keentaan	karisaan	sameysaan	joogsataan	furataan
keenaan	kariyaan	sameeyaan	joogsadaan	furtaan

Reduced paradigm; all verbs follow the same pattern, as given below:

keená
keená
keená
keentá
keenná
keená
keená

General present negative

keenó	kariyó	sameeyó	joogsadó	furtó
keentó	karisó	sameysó	joogsató	furató
keenó	kariyó	sameeyó	joogsadó	furtó

keentó	karisó	sameysó	joogsató	furató
keennó	karinnó	sameynó	joogsannó	furannó
keentáan	karisáan	sameysáan	joogsatáan	furatáan
keenáan	kariyáan	sameeyáan	joogsadáan	furtáan

There is an optional variant form for the second person singular -tíd, e.g. keentíd.

Present progressive

keénayaa	karínayaa	sameýnayaa	joogsánayaa	furánayaa
keénaysaa	karínaysaa	sameýnaysaa	joogsánaysaa	furánaysaa
keénayaa	karínayaa	sameýnayaa	joogsánayaa	furánayaa
keénaysaa	karínaysaa	sameýnaysaa	joogsánaysaa	furánaysaa
keénaynaa	karínaynaa	sameýnaynaa	joogsánaynaa	furánaynaa
keénaysaan	karínaysaan	sameýnaysaan	joogsánaysaan	furánaysaan
keénayaan	karínayaan	sameýnayaan	joogsánayaan	furánayaan

Reduced paradigm; all verbs follow the same pattern, as given below:

keénayá
keénayá
keénayá
keénaysá
keénayná
keénayá
keénayá

Present progressive negative

1 Use the infinitive with the following forms, which immediately follow the infinitive:

máayó
máysó / máysíd
máayo
máysó
máynó
máysáan
máayáan

2 Use the following forms:

keénayó	karínayó	sameýnayó	joogsánayó	furánayó
keénaysó	karínaysó	sameýnaysó	joogsánaysó	furánaysó
keénayó	karínayó	sameýnayó	joogsánayó	furánayó
keénaysó	karínaysó	sameýnaysó	joogsánaysó	furánaysó
keénaynó	karínaynó	sameýnaynó	joogsánaynó	furánaynó
keénaysáan	karínaysáan	sameýnaysáan	joogsánaysáan	furánaysáan
keénayáan	karínayáan	sameýnayáan	joogsánayáan	furánayáan

There is an optional variant form for the second person singular -tíd, e.g. keénaysíd.

Past progressive

keénayay	karínayay	sameýnayay	joogsánayay	furánayay
keénaysay	karínaysay	sameýnaysay	joogsánaysay	furánaysay
keénayay	karínayay	sameýnayay	joogsánayay	furánayay
keénaysay	karínaysay	sameýnaysay	joogsánaysay	furánaysay
keénaynay	karínaynay	sameýnaynay	joogsánaynay	furánaynay
keénayseen	karínayseen	sameýnayseen	joogsánayseen	furánayseen
keénayeen	karínayeen	sameýnayeen	joogsánayeen	furánayeen

Reduced paradigm; all verbs follow the same pattern, as given below:

keénayaý
keénayaý
keénayaý
keénaysaý
keénaynaý
keénayaý
keénayaý

Past progressive negative

keénaýn / keénaynín   karínaýn / karínaynín
sameýnaýn / sameýnaynín joogsánaýn / joogsánaynín
furánaýn / furánaynín

Optative

aan keéno	aan karíyo	aan joogsádo	aan fúrto
aad keénto	aad karíso	aad joogsáto	aad furáto
há keeno	há kariyo	há joogsado	há furto
há keento	há kariso	há joogsato	há furato
aynu keénno	aynu karínno	aynu joogsánno	aynu furánno
aannu keénno	aannu karínno	aannu joogsánno	aannu furánno
aad keénteen	aad karíseen	aad joogsáteen	aad furáteen
há keeneen	há kariyeen	há joogsadeen	há furteen

There is an optional variant form for the second person singular -tid, e.g. **aad keéntid**.

Negative optative

The following invariable forms are immediately preceded by the negative forms (given below), incorporating the subject verbal pronouns:

keénin   karín   sameýn   joosgán   furán

yáanan
yáanad
yáanu
yáanay
yáynu
yáanan or yáanannu
yáanad
yáanay

Conditional

Use the infinitive of the verb with the following forms:

lahaa
lahayd
lahaa
lahayd
lahayn
lahaydeen
lahaayeen

Conditional negative

keeneén	kariyeén	sameeyeén	joogsadeén	furteén
keenteén	kariseén	sameyseén	joogsateén	furateén
keeneén	kariyeén	sameeyeén	joogsadeén	furteén
keenteén	kariseén	sameyseén	joogsateén	furateén
keenneén	karinneén	sameyneén	joogsanneén	furanneén
keenteén	kariseén	sameyseén	joogsateén	furateén
keeneén	kariyeén	sameeyeén	joogsadeén	furteén

Potential

In this mood the classifier **shów** is used with the following verb forms:

keenee	kariyee	sameeyee	joogsadee	furtee
keentee	karisee	sameysee	joogsatee	furatee
keenee	kariyee	sameeyee	joogsadee	furtee
keentee	karisee	sameysee	joogsatee	furatee
keennee	karinnee	sameynee	joogsannee	furannee
keenteen	kariseen	sameyseen	joogsateen	furateen
keeneen	kariyeen	sameeyeen	joogsadeen	furteen

Subordinate clause verb forms

In this section we shall give the subordinate clause verb forms for **keen**; the equivalent forms for the other conjugations are easily derived.

Full paradigm (absolutive) (used when the head noun is not the subject of the relative clause and the head noun plus relative clause is not the subject of the sentence or main clause):

General present	*General past*
keenó	keenaý
keentó	keentaý
keenó	keenaý
keentó	keentaý
keennó	keennaý
keentáan	keentéen
keenáan	keenéen

Present progressive   *Past progressive*

    keénayó   **keénayaý**
    keénaysó   **keénaysaý**
    keénayó   **keénayaý**
    keénaysó   **keénaysaý**
    keénaynó   **keénaynaý**
    keénaysáan   **keénayséen**
    keénayáan   **keénayéen**

Full paradigm (subject) (used when the head noun is not the subject of the relative clause and the head noun plus relative clause is the subject of the sentence); these forms are the same as the main clause verb full paradigm:

General present   *Present progressive*

    keenaa   **keénayaa**
    keentaa   **keénaysaa**
    keenaa   **keénayaa**
    keentaa   **keénaysaa**
    keennaa   **keénaynaa**
    keentaan   **keénaysaan**
    keenaan   **keénayaan**

General past   *Past progressive*

    keenay   **keénayay**
    keentay   **keénaysay**
    keenay   **keénayay**
    keentay   **keénaysay**
    keennay   **keénaynay**
    keenteen   **keénayseen**
    keeneen   **keénayeen**

Reduced paradigm (absolutive) (used when the head noun is the subject of the relative clause and the head noun plus relative clause is not the subject of the sentence or main clause); this is the same as the reduced paradigm used in main clauses when the subject is focused:

General present   *Present progressive*

    keená   **keénayá**
    keená   **keénayá**
    keená   **keénayá**
    keentá   **keénaysá**
    keenná   **keénayná**
    keená   **keénayá**
    keená   **keénayá**

General past   *Past progressive*

    keenaý   **keénayaý**
    keenaý   **keénayaý**
    keenaý   **keénayaý**
    keentaý   **keénaysaý**
    keennaý   **keénaynaý**
    keenaý   **keénayaý**
    keenaý   **keénayaý**

Reduced paradigm (subject) (used when the head noun is the subject of the relative clause and the head noun plus relative clause is the subject of the sentence or main clause):

General present   *Present progressive*

    keenaa   **keénayaa**
    keenaa   **keénayaa**
    keenaa   **keénayaa**
    keentaa   **keénaysaa**
    keennaa   **keénaynaa**
    keenaa   **keénayaa**
    keenaa   **keénayaa**

General past   *Past progressive*

    keenay   **keénayay**
    keenay   **keénayay**
    keenay   **keénayay**
    keentay   **keénaysay**
    keennay   **keénaynay**
    keenay   **keénayay**
    keenay   **keénayay**

Subject verbal pronouns

I	-aan	we (incl.)	-aynu
you (sg.)	-aad	we (excl.)	-aannu
he, it (m.)	-uu	you (pl.)	-aydin
she, it (f.)	-ay	they	-ay

Note that **-aad** is used sometimes in place of **-aydin**.

Subject verbal pronouns short versions

I	-an	we (incl.)	-aynu
you (sg.)	-ad	we (excl.)	-aannu
he, it (m.)	-u	you (pl.)	-aydin
she, it (f.)	-ay	they	-ay

Object verbal pronouns

i	me	**na**	us (excl.)
ku	you	**ina**	us (incl.)
		idin	you (pl.)

Possessive suffixes

	masculine	feminine
my	káyga	táyda
your (sg.)	káaga	táada
his / its (m.)	kíisa	tíisa
her / its (f.)	kéeda	téeda
our (incl.)	kéenna	téenna
our (excl.)	kayága	tayáda
your (pl.)	kíinna	tíinna
their	kóoda	tóoda

Possessive suffixes (short versions)

	masculine absolutive	subject	feminine absolutive	subject
my	**kaý**	**káy**	**taý**	**táy**
your (sg.)	**kaá**	**káa**	**taá**	**táa**
his	**kiís**	**kíis**	**tiís**	**tíis**
her	**keéd**	**kéed**	**teéd**	**téed**
our (incl.)	**keén**	**kéen**	**teén**	**téen**
our (excl.)	**káyo**	**kayo**	**táyo**	**tayo**
your (pl.)	**kiín**	**kíin**	**tiín**	**tíin**
their	**koód**	**kóod**	**toód**	**tóod**

Pronoun and preposition clusters

Pronoun plus preposition

	+ *ú*	+ *kú*	+*ká*	+*lá*
i	**ií**	**igú**	**igá**	**ilá**
ku	**kuú**	**kugú**	**kaá**	**kulá**
na	**noó**	**nagú**	**nagá**	**nalá**
ina	**inoó**	**inagú**	**inagá**	**inalá**
idin	**idiín**	**idinkú**	**idinká**	**idinlá**

Note that the pronoun **la**, 'one', behaves in the same way as **na** in clusters but must come before any object pronoun.

Preposition plus preposition

	+ *ú*	+ *kú*	+*ká*	+*lá*
ú	**ugú**	**ugú**	**ugá**	**ulá**
kú		**kagá**	**kagá**	**kulá**
ká			**kagá**	**kalá**

Pronoun plus prepostion cluster

	+ ugú	+ ugá	+ ulá	+ kagá	+ kulá	+ kalá
i	iigú	iigá	iilá	igagá	igulá	igalá
ku	kuugú	kaagá	kuulá	kaagá	kugulá	kaalá
na	noogú	noogá	noolá	nagagá	nagulá	nagalá
ina	inoogú	inoogá	inoolá	inagagá	inagulá	inagalá
idin	idiinkú	idiinká	idiinlá	idinkagá	idinkulá	idinkalá

Key to exercises

1 Is ka warran!

1

1 Waa nabad. 2 Waa la fiicanyahay.

2

1 Maryanay, Zaynabay, Jawaahiray 2 Cartanow, Maxmuudow, Cabdinuurow

3 The stress-tone patterns are as follows:

1 Kéen! plural: Keéna! 2 Tág! plural: Tága! 3 Cún! plural: Cúna! 4 Joóji! plural: Joojíya! 5 Súg! plural: Súga!

4

1 Read it! Read them! 2 Eat it! Eat them! 3 Look at him! Look at her! Look at it! Look at them! 4 Write it! Write them! 5 Open it! Open them!

5

1 Ma shaah baa? 2 Waa shaah. 3 Ma nabad baa? 4 Waa nabad. 5 Ma sonkor baa? 6 Waa sonkor.

6

1 diiday, diidday, diiday, diidday, diidnay, diiddeen, diideen
2 baaqay, baaqday, baaqay, baaqday, baaqnay, baaqdeen, baaqeen

3 go'ay, go'day, go'ay, go'day, go'nay, go'deen, go'een 4 akhriyay, akhriday, akhriyay, akhriday, akhrinay, akhrideen, akhriyeen 5 dilay, dishay, dilay, dishay, dillay (or dilnay), disheen, dileen 6 tegey, tagtay, tegey, tagtay, tagnay, tagteen, tegeen

7

1 Way heleen. 2 Way dirtay. 3 Waad keentay. 4 Waydin qaaddeen. 5 Wuu baxay. 6 Waannu gallay (or galnay).

8

1 Haa, waan akhriyay. 2 Haa, way heshay. 3 Haa, waannu ka baxnay. 4 Haa, way heleen. 5 Haa, wuu galay.

9

1 Miyay direen? or Ma direen? 2 Miyaydin heshen? or Ma hesheen? 3 Miyuu keenay? or Ma keenay? 4 Miyay gashay? or Ma gashay? 5 Miyaad ka baxday? or Ma ka baxday?

2 Subax wanaagsan

1

1 Shandad miyaa? 2 Haa, waa shandad. 3 Kubbad miyaa? 4 Haa, waa kubbad.

2

1 Ma koob baa? Haa, waa koob. 2 Warqad miyaa? Haa, waa warqad. 3 Guri miyaa? Haa, waa guri. 4 Ma dukaan baa? Haa, waa dukaan.

3

1 xidhayaa, xidhaysaa, xidhayaa, xidhaysaa, xidhaynaa, xidhaysaan, xidhayaan 2 dhigayaa, dhigaysaa, dhigayaa, dhigaysaa, dhigaynaa, dhigaysaan, dhigayaan 3 barayaa, baraysaa, barayaa, baraysaa, baraynaa, baraysaan, barayaan 4 doonayaa, doonaysaa, doonayaa, doonaysaa, doonaynaa, doonaysaan, doonayaan 5 gaadhayaa,

gaadhaysaa, gaadhayaa, gaadhaysaa, gaadhaynaa, gaadhaysaan, gaadhayaan 6 akhriyayaa, akhriyaysaa, akhriyayaa, akhriyaysaa, akhriyaynaa, akhriyaysaan, akhriyayaan

4

1 Haa, guriga way ka baxayaan. 2 Haa, Landhan waannu tagaynaa. 3 Haa, buug way akhriyaysaa. 4 Haa, shandadda waan furayaa. 5 Haa, warqad wuu qorayaa.

5

1 Maxamed waa cunayaa. 2 Ruqiya guriga way galaysaa. 3 Cali waa akhriyayaa. 4 Laybreeriga way gaadheen. 5 Kursiga miyuu qaaday? 6 Guriga way dhisayaan.

6

1 beero, 2 sababo, 3 daaro, 4 kabo, 5 qaybo, 6 saaxiibado

7

1 saacad, 2 jidh, 3 dayuurad, 4 su'aal, 5 dhakhtarad, 6 bil

8

1 gidaarro, 2 barnaamijyo, 3 madaxyo, 4 bangiyo, 5 subaxyo, 6 laybreeriyo

9

1 dukaan, 2 kursi, 3 cashar, 4 dhakhtar, 5 baabuur, 6 laabbis

10

1 gabdho, 2 gacan, 3 garbo, 4 jilbo, 5 kibso, 6 waran

11

1 Dariiqyo way dhiseen. 2 Maanta suuqyo way tagayaan. 3 Kursiyo way qaadeen. 4 Laabbisyo way keentay. 5 Kabo ma keenaysaa?

12

1 buug iyo qalin; a book and a pen 2 Guriga waan galay shaahna waan cabbay; I entered the house and I drank tea. 3 Hargeysa, Muqdishu, Baydhaba iyo Harar; Hargeysa, Mogadishu, Baidoa and Harar. 4 Guriga waydin ka baxdeen albaabkana waydin xidheen; You (pl.) left the house and you (pl.) closed the door. 5 Buug waan akhriyay warqadna waan qoray; I read a book and I wrote a letter. 6 kibis, subag, shaah iyo sonkor; bread, butter, tea and sugar

3 Bill iyo Zaynab

1

1 bare, 2 af, 3 Soomaali, 4 naagi, 5 shaah, 6 gabadhi

2

1 habéen, 2 baríis, 3 mágac, 4 qalmo, 5 hílib, 6 warqád

3

1 Caano dhan. 2 Guriga waan tagayaa. 3 Canabi warqad way qortay. 4 Dugsiga tag. 5 Maxamed albaabka waa furay. 6 Kibis keen! 7 Naagi hilib way cuntay. 8 Maxamed dukaanka wuu gaadhayaa. 9 Dhakhtaradi buug way akhriday. 10 Shimbiri warqad waa qaadday.

4

1 magaca, 2 shimbirtii, 3 shaahu, 4 kubbadda, 5 subaxdu, 6 kursigii

5

1 Inammadu hasha way qaadeen. 2 Baruhu ardeyga ma barayaa? 3 Gidaarka waydin dhisteen. 4 Dukaanka tag! 5 Gabadhu kabaha way heshay. 6 Naaguhu kibista way cuneen, shaahana way cabbeen.[1]

6

1 dabab, 2 buug, 3 koobab, 4 roob, 5 dalal, 6 san

7

1 mádax, 2 eý, 3 aẃr, 4 háad, 5 Cárab, 6 díbi

8

1 Buugagga akhri. 2 Koobabka wuu keenay. 3 Ardeydu jaamacadda way galeen. 4 Dalka way gaadheen. 5 Haaddu way sugayaan. 6 Dhakhtaraddu warqadda way diidday.

9

1 bixiyay, bixisay, bixiyay, bixisay, bixinnay, bixiseen, bixiyeen; bixinayaa, bixinaysaa, bixinayaa, bixinaysaa, bixinaynaa, bixinaysaan, bixinayaan 2 joojiyay, joojisay, joojiyay, joojisay, joojinnay, joojiseen, joojiyeen; joojinayaa, joojinaysaa, joojinayaa, joojinaysaa, joojinaynaa, joojinaysaan, joojinayaan 3 dhoofiyay, dhoofisay, dhoofiyay, dhoofisay, dhoofinnay, dhoofiseen, dhoofiyeen; dhoofinayaa, dhoofinaysaa, dhoofinayaa, dhoofinaysaa, dhoofinaynaa, dhoofinaysaan, dhoofinayaan

10

1 Naagtu inanka way toosisay. 2 Ninku awrta wuu daajinayaa. 3 Maxamed miiska wuu jabiyay. 4 Canabi way bixisay. 5 Naagi hilibka way karisay. 6 Cadowgu beerta waa bi'iyay.

11

1 Waad keentay. 2 Mindidu waa jabtay. 3 Maanta inammadu magaalada way tegeen. 4 Maxamed awrta wuu daajiyay. 5 Nimanku way ka bexeen.

12

1 They grazed the camels on Saturday. 2 I left the house on Thursday. 3 He was ill on Wednesday. 4 She mended it on Monday. 5 I will read it on Tuesday. (Note: the use of the present

progressive in this sentence implies the future, but it is assumed that the particular Tuesday is close, otherwise the future tense is needed, which we shall look at later.)

4 Bill waa tegayaa geeska Afrika

1

1 sheeko, 2 dawooyin, 3 magaalo, 4 shaneemooyin, 5 kiilo, 6 ayeeyooyin

2

1 furayaal, 2 danjire, 3 xoghayaal, 4 gole, 5 waraabe, 6 madax-weynayaal

3

1 maleeyay, maleysay, maleeyay, maleysay, maleynay, maleyseen, maleeyeen; maleynayaa, maleynaysaa, maleynayaa, maleynaysaa, maleynaynaa, maleynaysaan, maleynayaan 2 caddeeyay, caddeysay, caddeeyay, caddeysay, caddeynay, caddeyseen, caddeeyeen; caddeynayaa, caddeynaysaa, caddeynayaa, caddeynaysaa, caddeynaynaa, caddeynaysaan, caddeynayaan 3 caweeyay, caweysay, caweeyay, caweysay, caweynay, caweyseen, caweeyeen; caweynayaa, caweynaysaa, caweynayaa, caweynaysaa, caweynaynaa, caweynaysaan, caweynayaan

4

1 Awrta wuu kexeynayaa. 2 Carruurtu miisaska way safeynayaan. 3 Buugga way caddeynaysaa. 4 Shaleyto guriga way dhammeeyeen. 5 Maanta ma qadeynaysaa?

5

1 Ninka dheeri hilibka wuu cunay. 2 Gabadha quruxsani caanaha way dhantay. 3 Buugga fudud way akhriyayaan. 4 Shandadda culus waad qaadaysaa. 5 Albaabka cusub way jabiyeen. 6 Buugga wanaagsan way qortay.

6

1 Nimanka dhaadheeri magaalada way tegeen. 2 Shimbirraha waaweyn eeg. 3 Magaalooyinka fogfog miyaydin tagaysaan? 4 Koobabka jajaban wuu helay. 5 Shandadaha culculus waan keenayaa. 6 Gabdhuhu buugag wanaagsan way akhriyayaan.

7

1 albaab dugsiga 2 xeebta geeska Afrika 3 maalinta toddobaadka 4 qalin Cali 5 hilib lo'aad 6 af Carabeed

8

1 Cali qalinka Jawaahir wuu jabiyay. 2 Buugga wanaagsan ee Samatar way caddeysay. 3 Kabaha odayga way safeeyeen. 4 Xoghayaha cusub ee danjiruhu magaalomadaxda dalka waa tagayaa. 5 Bartamaha magaalada waydin tagteen.

9

1 hal guri 2 sagaal bilood 3 shan baabuur 4 saddex koob 5 toban kabood

10

1 Laba kabood qaad! 2 Saddexda dugsi ka warran. 3 Toddoba guri way dhiseen. 4 Macallinku siddeed ardey wuu baraa. 5 Shan dameeraad wuu keenay. 6 Cali sagaal awr wuu daajinayaa.

5 Garoonka dayuuradaha

1

1 Gabadhu gaadhiga way aragtay. 2 Cali waa hadlayaa. 3 Inammadu awrta way maqleen. 4 Canab, Maxamed iyo baruhu way qoslayaan. 5 Nimanku way ordayaan. 6 Qoysku waa hurday.

2

1 Ugxan waan helay. 2 Dhagxanta way qaadeen. 3 Saddex kursi wuu sameeyey. 4 Casharrada fudfudud wuu baray. 5 Maanta dad badani jaraa'idka way akhriyayaan. 6 Maraakiibtu way ka bexeen.

3

1 tagaa, tagtaa, tagaa, tagtaa, tagnaa, tagtaan, tagaan 2 caseeyaa, caseysaa, caseeyaa, caseysaa, caseynaa, caseysaan, caseeyaan 3 bixiyaa, bixisaa, bixiyaa, bixisaa, bixinnaa, bixisaan, bixiyaan

4

1 Cali way la hadashay. 2 Hilib dukaanka ka keen! 3 Carruurtu qolka way ku ciyaarayaan. 4 Gaadhi buu ku qaadayaa. 5 Rooble kibista mindi wuu ku jadhay. 6 Shaleyto guriga waad ku sugtay.

5

1 Waan ku maqlay. 2 Canabi magaaladaway i tustay. 3 Way cunaan. (Remember there are no words for the third person pronouns.) 4 Maanta baraha cusubi waa idin barayaa. 5 Way na salaamaan. 6 Shaleyto wuu la kulmay.

6

1 baxsadaa, baxsataa, baxsadaa, baxsataa, baxsannaa, baxsataan, baxsadaan; baxsanayaa, baxsanaysaa, baxsanayaa, baxsanaysaa, baxsanaynaa, baxsanaysaan, baxsanayaan 2 iibsadaa, iibsataa, iibsadaa, iibsataa, iibsannaa, iibsataan, iibsadaan; iibsanayaa, iibsanaysaa, iibsanayaa, iibsanaysaa, iibsanaynaa, iibsanaysaan, iibsanayaan 3 guursadaa, guursataa, guursadaa, guursataa, guursannaa, guursataan, guursadaan; guursanayaa, guursanaysaa, guursanayaa, guursanaysaa, guursanaynaa, guursanaysaan, guursanayaan

6 Tagsiga

1

1 Maxaydin maqasheen?; What did you (pl.) hear? 2 Maxaynu sameynaynaa?; What are we (incl.) making? or: Maxaannu sameynaynaa?; What are we (excl.) making? 3 Maxay jabisay?; What did she break? or: Maxaad jabisay?; What did you break? 4 Cali muxuu u sheegay?; What did Cali tell him? 5 Dukaanka maxaad ka keentay?; What did you bring from the shop? or: Dukaanka maxay ka keentay?; What did she bring from the shop? 6 Makhaayadda maxay ku cuneen?; What did they eat in the restaurant?

2

1 Shimbirtu geedka bay ka duushay. 2 Ninka weyni bariis badan buu cunaa. 3 Koobabka cuscusub bay qaadeen. 4 Suuqa Canab bay la tegaysaa. 5 Suuqa bay Canab la tegaysaa. 6 Shaleyto bay Maxamed arkeen.

3

1 Haa, guriga waannu tagaynaa; or: Haa, guriga baannu tagaynaa.[2]
2 Shaah baan cabbayaa. 3 Habeenka cuntada bay keenaysaa.
4 Harar baannu tagnay. 5 Kabo badan bay dukaanka ku aragtay.
6 Haa, guri way sameeyeen; or: Haa, guri bay sameeyeen.[2]

4

1 Maxaad jabisay? Laabbisyada baan jabiyay. 2 Shalayto maxay cuneen? Shalayto kibis bay cuneen. 3 Maxay arkeen? Awr badan bay arkeen. 4 Magaalada maxay ku dhiseen? Masaajid weyn bay magaalada ku dhiseen. 5 Carruurtu maxay ka heleen? Barnaamijyada cuscusub bay ka heleen. 6 Canabi maxay doondoonaysaa? Tagsi bay doondoonaysaa.

5

1 dhegeystaa, dhegeysataa, dhegeystaa, dhegeysataa, dhegeysannaa, dhegeysataan, dhegeystaan; dhegeysanayaa, dhegeysanaysaa, dhegeysanayaa, dhegeysanaysaa, dhegeysanaynaa, dhegeysan-

aysaan, dhegeysanayaan 2 bartaa, barataa, bartaa, barataa, barannaa, barataan, bartaan; baranayaa, baranaysaa, baranayaa, baranaysaa, baranaynaa, baranaysaan, baranayaan 3 qaataa, qaadataa, qaataa, qaadataa, qaadannaa, qaadataan, qaataan; qaadanayaa, qaadanaysaa, qaadanayaa, qaadanaysaa, qaadanaynaa, qaadanaysaan, qaadanayaan

6

afar iyo toddobaatan; sagaal iyo labaatan; laba iyo konton; lix boqol iyo siddeed iyo labaatan; siddeed boqol iyo saddex iyo sagaashan; kun iyo sagaal boqol iyo labaatan; afar kun iyo siddeed boqol iyo afar iyo lixdan

7

1 laba iyo tobankii Maarso kun iyo sagaal boqol iyo laba iyo afartankii 2 shan iyo labaatankii Agoosto kun iyo sagaal boqol iyo afar iyo siddeetankii 3 lix iyo tobankii Abriil kun iyo sagaal boqol iyo saddex iyo sagaashankii 4 labaatankii Disembar kun iyo sagaal boqol iyo afar iyo kontonkii 5 sagaal iyo tobanka Septembar kun iyo sagaal boqol iyo sagaal iyo sagaashanka (a future date)

8

1 toddobada 2 laba iyo tobankii 3 shanta iyo rubuc rubuca 4 siddeeddii oo rubuc la' 5 sagaalka iyo badhka 6 toddobada iyo badhka

7 Hudheelka

1

1 safeyn, 2 xidhi, 3 qaban, 4 hadli, 5 siin, 6 qosli

2

1 Berrito wuu qadeyn doonaa. 2 Maarso casharka baan baran doonaa. 3 Warqado badan ayay danjiraha u diri doonaan. 4 Berrito buuggan miyaad ardeyda u akhrin doontaa? 5 Guriga cusub way ka bixi doontaa. 6 Bilo badan ka dib buu walaalka booqan doonaa.

3

1 Halkan awrta way daajin jireen. 2 Shaah badan baan cabbi jiray. 3 Afaf fudfudud miyaad baran jirtay? 4 Cabdullaahi buugag fiican wuu akhriyi jiray. 5 Bariis iyo hilib way keeni jirtay. 6 Maaxaad sameyn jirtay?

4

1 Ha keenin!; Do not bring it! 2 Ha sugina!; Do not wait (pl.)! 3 Ha caddeyn!; Do not explain it! 4 Inammada ha toosin!; Do not wake the boys! 5 Baraha ha dhegaysan!; Do not listen to the teacher! 6 Warqadda ha i tusina!; Do not show (pl.) me the letter!

5

1 Dugsiga maan tegin; I didn't go to the school. 2 Bill basaboorkii ma helin; Bill did not find the passport. 3 Caano ma dhami jirin; They did not [used to] drink milk. 4 Hudheelka maannu gelin; We did not enter the hotel. 5 Shaleyto barnaamijka ma dhegaysan; Yesterday I did not listen to the programme. 6 Waxba maan arkin; I didn't see anything.

Remember that **ma** on its own is possible in any of these sentences.

8 *Bill telefoon buu diraa*

1

1 Kabaha way qaadayeen. 2 Cali baad u akhriyaysay. 3 Miyuu casheynayay? 4 Shaleyto jidka baad maraysay. 5 Roobku waa da'ayay. 6 Miyaad u keenaysay?

2

1 Afaf badan ma dhigaan. 2 Cadowgu waxyaabo badan ma bi'iyo. 3 Waqooyiga dalka ma tago. 4 Albaabbada ma furaan. 5 Shimbiraha quruxsan ma aragto (or aragtid). 6 Koobab badan maan jebiyo.

3

1 Ninkaas miyaad maqashay? 2 Albaabkaas ha furan! 3 Dalkoo ma tegin. 4 Gurigaas ma arkin. 5 Cuntadaas bay dukaanka ka keentay, wayna karisay. 6 Caanahan koobkaas buu ku shubay.

4

1 This man used to teach. (Note the lack of subject marking on the subject because it is focused.) 2 I brought forty eight books from the library. 3 Will you (pl.) go to the south of the Horn of Africa? 4 Today I will not write in the library. 5 Don't break Canab's new pen! 6 She left the house and visited a friend.

5

1 Nimanka buu arki waayay. 2 Cuntada baan keeni karaa laakin maan karin karo. 3 Jidka miyaad gudbi kartaa? 4 Inammada u ma yeedhin. 5 Qoyska miyay telefoon u diri rabtaa? 6 Casharrada baydin baran rabtaan.

6

1 Kibista baa la cunay. 2 Masaajidka baa la dhisay. 3 Shaleyto caanaha baa la keenay. 4 Nambarka baa la garaacay. 5 Kabaha baa la sameeyey. 6 Awrta baa la daajiyay.

9 *Bill lacag buu sariftaa*

1

1 Koobkayga waan buuxsaday; I filled my cup. 2 Bariiskooda ma karin; They[3] did not cook their rice. 3 Baabuurkaaga cusub buu wadanayaa; He is driving your new car. 4 Shandadihiisa baan qaaday; I took his suitcases. 5 Dameerkeedu ma ordo; Her donkey does not run. 6 Cuntadeennu waa cunto wanaagsan; Our food is good food.

2

1 Danjirohooda cusubi madaxweynaha dalka wuu booqday. 2 Shaleyto jariidaddeeda way akhriday. 3 Maxaabiistoodu ma baxsan. 4 Berrito walaalkaa baan la kulmi doonaa. 5 Inankaa baa lugtay jabiyay. 6 Tagsigiisa buu hagaajiyay.

3

1 Qalinkaaga miiska dushiisa baan ka qaaday. 2 Gurigoodu magaalada dhexdeeda baa jiraa. 3 Beertaydu magaalada debedeeda baa jiraa. 4 Roobka dartiisa guriga way galeen. 5 Lacag miiska hoostiisa bay ka heshay. 6 Boostadu masaajidka geestiisa baa jiraa.

4

1 Hooyada ninku waa tagtay; The man's mother went. 2 Maxamed qalinkiisa ha jebin!; Do not break Maxamed's pen! 3 Ardeyga buuggiisu waa buug fiican; The student's book is a good book. 4 Shaleyto gaadhiga aabbahay ayaan watay; Yesterday I drove my father's car. 5 Daarta albaabkeeda ayay furayeen; They were opening the door of the house. 6 Magaca inanta waa Shamis; The girl's name is Shamis.

5

1 Shan shandadood ma keenayo (keeni maayo); He is not bringing five suitcases. 2 Warqad may qoraynin; She was not writing a letter. 3 Suuqa may tagayaan (tegi maayaan); They are not going to the market. 4 Barnaamijka cusub maan dhegaysanayn; I was not listening to the new programme. 5 Caano ma dhamaysaan (dhami maysaan); You (pl.) are not drinking milk. 6 Casharkii muu caddeynaynin; He was not explaining the lesson.

10 Safarka baa la bilaabayaa

1

1 Berrito way iman doonaan. 2 Halkan kaalaya! 3 Shaleyto ardeydu dugsiga bay ka yimaaddeen. 4 Shaleyto ardeyda baa dugsiga

ka yimi. 5 Berrito ma iman doono. Walaakay gurigiisa baan tegi doonaa. 6 Janaayo halkan bay yimaaddeen.

2

1 Waxay yidhaahdeen, 'Berrito ma iman doonno, saacad ka dib baynu iman doonnaa.' 2 Muxuu yidhi? Wuxuu yidhi, 'Cuntada Canab u qaad.' 3 'Haa' miyaad tidhi? 4 Odhan maayo, 'Hilibka ma soo iibsan karaan.' 5 'Is ka warran' dheh. 6 Waxay tagayaan guriga baraha waxayna odhan doonaan, 'Subax wanaagsan'.

3

1 Waxaan ku siiyay kubbad; I gave you a ball. 2 Waxa masaajidka ka yimi baraha cusub ee dugsiga; The school's new teacher came from the mosque. 3 Waxay shaaha ku shubtay sonkor; She poured sugar into the tea. 4 Warqad dheer waxay u dirtay saaxiibaddeeda; She sent a long letter to her friend. 5 Waxa danjirayaasha la kulmay odayaasha; The elders met with the ambassadors. 6 Wuxuu furay albaabka kale; He opened the other door.

4

1 Basaboorkiisa buu tusay; He showed his passport. 2 Odayaasha baa ka yimi; The elders came from there. 3 Berrito gaadhiga cusub baan wadan doonaa; Tomorrow I will drive the new car. 4 Buugga cusub ee madaxweynaha bay caddeynayaan; They are explaining the president's new book. 5 Maanta bariis, hilib iyo khudrad badan baan karin doonaa; Today I will cook rice, meat and many vegetables. 6 Inammada baa awrta daajin doona; The boys will graze the burden camels.

11 *Tuulo baa la joogaa*

1

1 Waan aqaan. 2 I ma oqoonin. 3 Berrito danjiraha cusub baydin oqoon doontaan. Madaxweynaha wuu la iman doonaa. 4 Odayga miyaad tiqiin? 5 Maan oqoonayn laakin walaalkiis baan aqoonayay. 6 Sheekadaas ma aqaan.

2

1 Ma taqaan in nacasku kabaha keenay? 2 Inammadu waxay u sheegeen inay dugsiga tegi doonaan. 3 Gabadhu waxay maqashay in maxaabiistu baxsadeen. 4 Waxaan maqlay in madaxweynuhu halkan iman doono saddex saacadood ka dib. 5 Waxay u maleynayaan inay shaah cabbi doonaan.

3

1 U sheeg inay shandadaha berrito keeni karaan. 2 Waxaan makhaayadda u tagayaa inaan qadeeyo. 3 Waxaad dugsiga u tegi doontaa inaad wax barato. 4 Baraha gurigiisa waxaan u tagay inaan u sheego in walaalkay dugsiga tegi doono berrito. 5 Waxay dukaanka u tegeen inay laabbisyo cuscusub soo iibsadaan. 6 Waa inaad makhaayadda tagto. 7 Waa inaan baasaboorkayga helo.

4

1 Wuu ii sheegay. 2 Maxamed baa dukaanka iiga keenay. 3 Lacagta buu naga qaadey. 4 Koobka iigu shub. 5 Way kaa qaadeen. 6 Way iiga warrantay.

12 Ma xanuunsantahay

1

1 Ninka aan makhaayadda ku arkay baan la hadlay. 2 Awrta inanku daajinayo way keeneen. 3 Waxay dhegeystaan barnaamijka BBCdu wartebiso. 4 Waranka aan sameeyay wuu tuuray. 5 Cuntada aan kariyay miyaad cunaysaa? 6 Buugagga baruhu soo iibsaday miyuu keeni doonaa? 7 Waxay tagaan dugsiga Burco lagu dhisay. 8 Awrka aan soo iibsaday maanta waa daaqayaa. 9 Canab oo ay makhaayadda kula kulmeen dugsiga cusub bay tagtaa. 10 Guriga uu dhisayaa bartamaha magaalada baa ku yaal.

2

1 Gabadha cuntada karisay waa walaashay. 2 Axmed oo awrta daajinaya miyaad maqashaa? 3 Inammada jebiyay i tus. 4 Libaaxyada shaleyto ciyay baa awr dilay. 5 Kursiga uu samaynayo baan

soo iibsan doonaa. 6 Naagaha danjirayaasha la kulmay magaalada way ku noqdeen. 7 Inanka raydiyowga jebiyay gurigiisa wuu u orday. 8 Labada nin oo shaleyto halkan yimi waa odayaal. 9 Naagta cuntada karisay baan arkay. 10 Waxaan helay baasaboorka kaa lumay.

3

1 When did they come from there? 2 Why did you (pl.) return? 3 Who visited you yesterday? 4 Whom do you want to speak with? 5 When will they return? 6 Why did you make it? 7 How did they come?

4

1 Aniga baa buugagga keenay. 2 Idinka baa warqado u diray. 3 Saddexda siraad iyaga baan u qaadey. 4 Iyagoo hees qaadayeen bay qoslayeen. 5 Anigoo hudheelka joogay baan Maxamed la kulmay. 6 Iyadoo karinaysay inanku kibista wuu cunay.

Jariidadda

1

1 Dhakhtarad bay tahay. Dhakhtarad bay ahayd. 2 Inammadu ardey wanaagsan bay yihiin. Inammadu ardey wanaagsan bay ahaayeen. 3 Ninka dhakhtar ah bay aragtaa. Ninka dhakhtar ahaa bay aragtay. 4 Ninka bare ihi wuu i booqdaa. Ninka bare ahaa wuu i booqday. 5 Awr daajinaya bay yihiin. Awr daajinayay bay ahaayeen. 6 Naagaha danjirayaal ihi wasiirka way la kulmaan. Naagaha danjirayaal ahaa wasiirka way la kulmeen.

2

1 Gurigu waa cusubyahay. 2 Axmed oo ardey ihi waa dheeryahay. 3 Way fiicanyihiin. 4 Waan gaajeysanaa laakiin waan cunay imminkana waan dheregsanahay. 5 Wuxuu ka tirsanyahay dugsiga. 6 Garoonka dayuuraduhu waa ballaadhanyahay.

3

1 Baraha cusubi waa wanaagsanyahay. 2 Waxaan tusay gurigayga weyn. 3 Waxaannu tagnay magaalada oo fog. 4 Ninka dheeri albaabka xidhan ma furi karin. 5 Inanka oo dugsiga ka tirsanaa wuxuu cuntay cuntada aan sameeyay. 6 Waxaan ku daray biyaha kulula.

4

1 Kabahani way qoyanyihiin. 2 Imminka way ladantahay shaleytose aad bay u jirranayd. 3 Ninkaasu waa iga dheeryahay. 4 Waxaan u maleynayaa inaan qaadayo shandadda ugu culus. 5 Sonkori aad bay u macaantahay. 6 Koofiyaddaasu waa ka jaban yahay kii aan soo iibsaday shaleyto.

5

1 Xaggee baad ka timi? 2 Immisa bay ka keentay? 3 Intee baad joogaysaa? 4 Kee baad ii qaadi doontaa? 5 Halkee buu joogaa? 6 Immisa koob buu jabiyay?

6

1 Afar koob oo shaah ah baan cabbay maanta. 2 Hal kiilo oo sonkor ah suuqa iiga keen. 3 Koob biyo ah ii keen! 4 Dadka halkan yimi Carab bay yihiin. 5 Saddex carruur ah dugsiga bay tegeen shaleyto. 6 Adhiga waxaan u qaadi doonaa si aan u daajiyo.

14 Raydiyowga

1

1 Haddii aad makhaayadda tagto waxaad la kulmi doontaa walaalkay. 2 Markii wasiirku danjiraha la kulmay bay faraxsanaayeen. 3 Kaddib markay ka baxday bay u sheegeen. 4 Intii aan u warramayay buu iga cararay. 5 Isla markaasay aragtaa bay lacagta siin doontaa. 6 Markuu dabka shiday bay soo fadhiisteen.

2

1 Waxaan sameeyay shaaha aanu cabbin. 2 Gaadhiga aanay hagaajin wuu cusbaa. 3 Waxay qortay warqadda aanay dirin. 4 Waxaan u maleynayaa in aan booqan doono inanka aan dugsiga yimaaddo. 5 Kii aan casa ii keen. 6 Markaanu iman baan tagay.

3

1 Ma isaga baad aragtay? 2 Ma tuulada yar baydin gaadheen? 3 Ma adhiga buu daajiyay. 4 Danjirayaasha miyaa madaxweynaha la kulmay? 5 Ma gacanta baa ku xanuunaysa? 6 Ma Muqdisho bay tagaysaa?

4

1 Sow hilib muu cunin? 2 Ma Cali baan ka iman? 3 Berrito dugsiga sow maad tegi doonto? 4 Miyaanad tagaysaa? 5 Farasmagaalada sow muu deggana? 6 Maxaabiixstu sow ma ka baxsan?

5

1 Makhaayadda aynu tagno. 2 Waan keeni lahaa wuuse iga qaaday. 3 Berrito show ku arkee; or Waa laga yaabaa inaan ku arki doono berrito. 4 Haddii ay arkeen ii may sheegeen. 5 Aan eego. 6 Waan kuu sameyn lahaa halkaasse maad joogin.

Notes

1 Note the geminate **bb** in this verb. This is an irregular characteristic of the verb **cab**: the **b** is geminated when an ending beginning with a vowel follows it.
2 These two answers are possible here because the **miyáa** construction is a possible way of focusing a noun phrase in a question as well as being a general interrogative marker. See Lesson 14.
3 Any other pronoun is, of course, possible here.

English–Somali glossary

able, to be	**kar** (1)	answer	**jawaab** (1)
abroad	**dibad** (f.)	approve	**oggolow** (3B,
accompany	**raac** (1)		**oggolaaday,**
activity	**hawl** (f. d1)		**oggolaatay)**
add to	**ku dar** (1)	April	**Abriil** (f.)
advice	**talo** (f. d6)	Arab	**Carab** (m. d5)
aeroplane	**dayuurad** (f. d1)	area	**gobol** (m. d2)
after	**ka dib**	army	**xoog** (m. d4)
afternoon	**galab** (f. d3)	arrive	**gaadh** (1)
afterwards	**ka dib**	ask	**weydii** (2A)
air	**hawo** (f. d6)	assembly	**gole** (m. d7)
airport	**garoon dayuuradaha**	astonished, be astonished	**yaab** (1)
alliance	**isbahaysi** (m. d2)	attack	**weerar** (m. d2)
allies	**xulufo** (f.)	attack	**weerar qaad** (1)
allow	**oggolow** (3B, **oggolaaday, oggolaatay)**	August aunt (maternal)	**Agoosto** (f.) **habaryar** (f. d1)
ally together	**isbahayso** (3B)	back part	**dabo** (f.)
ambassador	**danjire** (m. d7)	bad	**xun** (adj.)
amount	**in** (f.)	ball	**kubbad** (f. d1)
and	**-na, iyo**	banana	**muus** (m. d4)
anger	**cadho** (f. d6)	bank	**bangi** (m. d2)
angry	**cadhosan** (adj.)	bathroom	**musqul** (f. d1)
angry, get angry	**(u: with) cadhow** (3B, **cahdaaday, cadhaatay)**	beans beautiful beauty	**digir** (f. collec.) **quruxsan** (adj.) **qurux** (f.)
animals (wild)	**habardugaag** (m. collec.)	because of that because	**sidaas darteed waayo**
announce	**baaq** (1), **ku dhawaaqay**	begin behind	**bilaab** (1) **dabo** (f.)

behind	**dambe** (adj. attrib.)	but	**-se, laakiin**
belonging to, member of	**ka tirsan** (adj.)	butter (especially clarified butter)	**subag** (m.)
bent	**qalloocan** (adj.)	buy	**gado** (3B), **iibso** (3B) (used often with **soo**), **soo gado** (3B)
between	**dhexe** (adj. attrib.)		
between, be in	**dhexee** (2B)	calamity	**masiibo** (f. d6)
big	**weyn** (adj.)	call someone	**u yeedh** (1)
bird (large, esp. bird of prey)	**haad** (m. d5)	camel (burden)	**awr** (m. d5)
		camel (female)	**hal** (f. d1)
bird (not a bird of prey)	**shimbir** (f. d1)	camels	**geel** (m. collec)
		can	**qasacad** (f. d1)
bite	**qaniin** (1)	capital	**xarun** (f. d1, xarumo)
bitter	**qadhaadh** (adj.)		
black	**madow** (adj.)	car	**baabuur** (m. d2), **gaadhi** (m. d2)
blanket	**buste** (m. d7)		
block	**xayir** (1)	cardamom	**heyl** (m. d4)
blue	**buluug** (m. d2)	cassava	**moxoggo** (f. d6)
body	**jidh** (m. d1/d4)	catch	**qabo** (3B)
boil (intr.)	**kar** (1)	cattle	**lo'** (f. collec.)
boil (tr.)	**kari** (2A)	cause to leave	**bixi** (2A)
book	**buug** (m. d4)	ceasefire	**rasaas joojin** (f.)
bottom	**hoos** (f. d1)	centre	**bartame** (m. d7)
boy	**inan** (m. d2 **-m**)	chair	**kursi** (m. d2 / **karaasi** (f.))
bread	**kibis** (f. d3)		
break (intr.)	**jab** (1)	change something for	**u beddel** (1)
break (tr.)	**jabi** (2A)		
breakfast	**quraac** (f. d2)	charcoal	**dhuxul** (f.)
breakfast, have breakfast	**quraaco** (3B)	cheap	**jaban** (adj.)
		check	**jeeg garee** (2B)
bring	**keen** (1)	children	**carruur** (f. collec.)
broad	**ballaadhan** (adj.)		
broadness	**ballaadh** (m. d2)	chilli pepper	**basbaas** (m. d2)
broken	**jaban** (adj.)	chop up	**jarjar** (1)
brother	**walaal** (m. d1)	cinnamon	**qorfe** (m. d7)
build	**dhis** (1)	city centre	**farasmagaalo** (m.)
building	**dhismo** (f. or m. d6)	civil war	**dagaal sokeeye**
		clean	**nadiifi** (2A), **safee** (2B)
burn (intr.)	**gubo** (3B)		
burn (tr.)	**gub** (1)	clear, make clear	**caddee** (2B)
burnt	**guban** (adj.)	clock	**saacad** (f. d1)

close	**xidh** (1)				**gudbaa**)
closed	**xidhan** (adj.)	cultivate			**beer** (1)
closed, become closed	**xidhan** (1, **xidhmaa**)	cup cupboard			**koob** (m. d4) **kabadh** (m. d2)
clothes	**dhar** (m. d4)	curved			**qalloocan** (adj.)
clove	**dhegayare** (m. d7)	cut (intr.) cut (tr.)			**go'** (1) **goy** (2A)
coast	**xeeb** (f. d1)	dates			**timir** (f. collec.)
coconut	**qumbe** (m. d7)	day			**casho** (f. d6),
coldness	**dhaxan** (f.)				**maalin** (f. d3
colour	**midab** (m. d2)				**-m**), **beri** (m. d1)
come after	**dambee** (2B)	December			**Disembar** (f.)
committee	**gole** (m. d7)	decision			**go'aan** (m. d2,
community	**degmo** (f. d6)				**go'aammo**),
comprised of	**ka kooban** (adj.)				**talo** (f. d6)
concerning	**ku saabsan** (adj.)	delay			**u kaadi** (2A)
confirm	**xaqiiji** (2A)	describe as			**ku tilmaan** (1,
conflict, be in conflict with	**ka soo horjeed** (1)	desert			**tilmaamaa**) **lamaddegaan**
confrontation	**iska horimaad** (m. d2)	desire			(m.) **rab** (1)
consider	**tasho** (3A)	destroy			**baabbi'i** (2A),
continue on	**u soco** (3B)				**bi'i** (2A)
continue	**soco** (3B), **sii wad** (1)	destroyed, be dial (on a			**ba'** (1) **garaac** (1)
cook (tr.)	**kari** (1)	number-pad			
cooked, be	**bislow** (3B, **bislaaday**, **bislaatay**, **bislaanayaa**)	telephone) die difficult			**dhimo** (3B, **dhintaa**) **adag** (adj.)
cooked together (i.e. lots of things)	**isku karis ah**	difficulty dine (evening meal)			**dhib** (m. d4) **cashee** (2B)
cooking	**bisleyn** (f.)	direction			**xag** (m. d4)
count	**tiri** (2A)	directness			**toos** (m. d4)
counted	**tirsan** (adj.)	disturbance			**qalalaase** (m. d7)
country	**dal** (m. d4), **waddan** (m. d2, **waddamo**)	divided into do			**u qaybsan** (1, **qaybsamaa**) **samee** (2B)
cover	**dabool** (1)	doctor (female)			**dhakhtarad**
cow	**sac** (m. d2)				(f. d1)
cross	**gudub** (1,	doctor (male)			**dhakhtar** (m. d2)

dog	**ey** (m. d5)			attrib.), **walba**	
dollar	**doollar** (m. d2)			(adj. attrib.)	
donkey (female)	**dameer** (f. d1)	examine		**day** (2A)	
donkey (male)	**dameer** (m. d2/ d5)	exchange money		**sarifo** (3B)	
		excuse me		**raalli ahow**	
door	**albaab** (m. d2)	expand		**fidi** (2A)	
dressed	**xidhan** (adj.)	expensive thing		**qaali** (m.)	
drink (general)	**cab** (1)	explain		**caddee** (2B)	
drink (used only with milk)	**dhan** (1, **dhamaa**)	export		**dhoofi** (2A)	
		exterior		**debed** (f. d1)	
drive (car)	**wado** (3B **watay**)	extra		**dheeraad** (m. d2)	
drive	**kexee** (2B), **wad** (1)	extract		**bixi** (2A)	
drought	**abaar** (f. d1)	eye		**il** (f. **indho** (m.))	
dry	**engegan** (adj.)	fabric		**dhar** (m. d4)	
dry valley	**tog** (m. d4)	facing		**ka taagan** (adj.)	
each	**kasta** (adj. attrib.), **walba** (adj. attrib.)	fail		**waa** (1)	
		fall (of rain), rain		**da'** (1)	
		fall		**dhac** (1)	
earth	**dhul** (m. d4)	fame		**caan** (m. d4)	
east	**bari** (m.)	family (extended)		**reer** (m. d1)	
easy	**fudud** (adj.)	family		**qoys** (m. d4)	
eat	**cun** (1)	far		**fog** (adj.) **ka**: from; **shishe** (adj. attrib.)	
egg (of birds other than chickens)	**ugax** (m. d5/ **ugxan** (f.)), (of chickens: **ukun** (f. collec.)				
		farm		**beer** (f. d1)	
		farmers		**beeraley** (f. collec.)	
eight	**siddeed** (f.)				
eighty	**siddeetan** (m.)	fascinating		**xiiso leh** (adj.)	
elder	**oday** (m. d7)	fascination		**xiiso** (f. d6)	
endurance	**adkaysi** (m. d7)	fat		**buuran** (adj.)	
enemy	**cadow** (m. d2)	father		**aabbe** (m. d7)	
enjoy	**ka hel** (1)	February		**Febraayo** (f.)	
enter	**gal** (1)	few		**dhowr**	
entertain (guests)	**martiqaad** (1)	field		**garoon** (m. d2)	
escape	**baxso** (3A)	fifty		**konton** (m.)	
especially	**khaas ahaan**	fighting		**dagaal** (m. d2)	
even	**xataa**	fill for oneself		**buuxso** (3A)	
evening	**habeen** (m. d2); this evening **caawa** (adverb)	film		**shaneemo** (f. d6)	
		find from		**ka hel** (1)	
		find		**hel** (1)	
every	**kasta** (adj.	finish		**dhammee** (2B)	

fire	**dab** (m. d4)	girl	**gabadh** (f. d3)
first-born child	**curad** (m. d2 or f. d1)	give news	**warran** (1 **warramaa**) ka: about
first	**hore** (adj. attrib.)	give	**sii** (2A)
firstly	**marka hore**	go around	**wareeg** (1)
fish	**kalluun** (m. d2, also collec., **kalluumo**)	go by car	**gaadhi raac** (1)
		go mad (intr.)	**waalo** (3B)
		go	**tag** (1)
five	**shan** (f.)	go with	**raac** (1)
flour	**budo** (f. d6)	goats (in general)	**riyo** (plural of **ri**)
fly	**duul** (1)		
folded	**laaban** (adj.)	God	**Eebbe** (m.), **Allaah** (m.)
food	**cunto** (f. d6 mass)	goodbye	**nabad gelyo**
fool	**nacas** (m. d2)	goodbye, say goodbye to	**soo nabadgelyee** (2B)
foot	**lug** (f. d1)	good	**wanaagsan** (adj.)
force	**xoog** (m. d4)	government	**dawlad** (f. d1), **xukumad** (f. d1)
forces	**ciidammo** (f. pl.)		
foreign minister	**wasiirka arrimaha dibadda**		
		grandmother	**ayeeyo** (f. d6)
fork	**mudac** (m. d2)	grapes	**canab** (m. d2 collec.)
forty	**afartan** (m.)		
four	**afar** (f.)	grave	**xabaal** (f. d1)
Friday	**jimce** (m.)	gravy	**sanuunad** (f. d1)
fried	**shiilan** (adj.)	graze (intr.)	**daaq** (1)
friend (female)	**saaxiibad** (f. d1)	graze (tr.)	**daaji** (2A)
friend (male)	**saaxiib** (m. d2)	grease	**dufan** (m. d2)
frog	**rah** (m. d4)	green	**cagaaran** (adj.)
front part	**hor** (f. d4)	greet	**salaan** (1 **salaamaa**)
fruit	**midho** (m. collec.)		
		grind	**tun** (1)
full	**dheregsan** (adj.)	ground	**garoon** (m. d2)
full, be full (of eating and drinking)	**dhereg** (1)	ground	**tuman** (adj.)
		group	**koox** (f. d1)
		group of related people	**reer** (m. d1)
garden	**beer** (f. d1)		
garlic	**toon** (f.)	grow	**beer** (1)
get	**ka qaado** (3B)	half	**badh** (m. d4)
get married	**guurso** (3A)	hand	**gacan** (f. d3 -m)
get up (intr.)	**toos** (1)	happen	**dhac** (1)

happy	**faraxsan** (adj.)	hurry	**degdeg** (1)
happy, be happy	**farax** (1)	husband	**nin** (m. d4
hard	**adag** (adj.)		**niman**)
hat	**koofiyad** (f. d1)	hyena	**waraabe** (m. d7)
have	**hay** (2A), **hayso** (3B)	ill	**jirran** (adj.)
		increase (intr.)	**korodh** (1)
head	**madax** (m. d2/ d5)	increase (tr.)	**kordhi** (2A)
		independent	**madaxbannaan** (adj.)
healthy	**ladan** (adj.)		
hear	**maqal** (1 **maqlaa**)	inside	**gudo** (m. d6)
		interest	**xiiso** (f. d6)
heat (tr.)	**diiri** (2A)	interesting	**xiiso leh** (adj.)
heat	**kulayl** (m.)	interior	**gudo** (m. d6)
heated	**diiran** (adj.)	international community	**adduunweyne** (m. d7)
heavy	**culus** (adj.)		
hide	**saan** (f. d1, **saamo**)	intervene	**faraggeli** (2A)
		interview	**wareysi** (m.)
hit	**dil** (1)	investigation	**baadhis** (f. d1)
hit with	**ku dhufo** (3B)	January	**Janaayo** (f.)
hold	**qabo** (3B), **yeelo** (3B)	journey	**safar** (m. d2)
		July	**Luulyo** (f.)
hole (especially in the ground)	**god** (m. d4)	June	**Juun** (f.)
		kettle	**kildhi** (m. d2)
hope	**rajee** (2B)	key	**fure** (m. d7)
horn	**gees** (m. d1)	kill	**dil** (1)
hot (of food)	**basbaas leh** (adj.)	kilogram	**kiilo** (f. d6)
		kitchen	**madbakh** (m. d2)
hot	**kulul** (adj.)		
hotel	**hudheel** (m. d2)	knee	**jilib** (m. d3)
hour	**saacad** (f. d1)	knife	**mindi** (f. d1)
house (of stone)	**daar** (f. d1)	knock	**garaac** (1)
house	**guri** (m. d1)	lamp	**siraad** (m. d2)
how (lit.: which way)	**sidee**	land (of an aeroplane)	**soo deg**
humanitarianism	**bani aadnimo** (f.)	land	**dhul** (m. d4)
		language	**af** (m. d4)
humanity	**bani aadnimo** (f.)	last	**ugu dambe** (adj. attrib.)
hundred	**boqol** (m. **boqolaal**)	laugh	**qosol** (1 **qoslaa**)
		law	**sharci** (m. d2)
hunger	**gaajo** (f.)	lead (animals)	**kexee** (2B)
hungry	**gaajeysan** (adj.)		

leader	**hoggaamiye** (m. d7)	matter	**arrin** (f. d1, **arrimo**)
learn	**baro** (3B)	May	**Maajo** (f.)
leave	**bax** (1)	meat	**hilib** (m. d3)
leaves	**caleen** (f. d1 collec.)	meet	**kulan** (1, **kulmaa**)
left	**bidix** (f.)	meeting	**shir** (m. d4)
leg	**lug** (f. d1)	member	**xubin** (f. d3)
lesson	**cashar** (m. d2)	men	**rag** (m. collec.)
letter	**warqad** (f. d1)	mend	**hagaaji** (2A)
library	**laybreeri** (m. d2)	middle	**dhexe** (adj. attrib.)
light	**fudud** (adj.)		
like	**jeclayso** (3B), **ka hel** (1)	milk (tr.)	**lis** (1)
		milk	**caano** (m. mass)
listen	**dhegeyso** (3B)	million	**malyuun** (m. **malaayiin** (f.))
literature	**suugaan** (f.)		
live (in a place)	**deg** (1)	minister	**wasiir** (m. d2)
livestock keepers	**xoolaley** (f. collec.)	minute	**daqiiqad** (f. d1)
		miss	**waa** (1)
living (in a place)	**nool** (adj.)	Monday	**isniin** (f.)
living in (a place)	**deggan** (adj.)	money	**lacag** (f. mass)
long	**dheer** (adj.)	month	**bil** (f. d1)
look around	**ka eegeeg** (1)	morning	**subax** (f. d2)
look at	**day** (2A)	mortar	**mooye** (m. d7)
look	**eeg** (1)	mosque	**masaajid** (m. d2)
look for	**doondoon** (1)	mother	**hooyo** (f. d6)
lorry	**baabuur** (m. d2)	mountain	**buur** (m. d1)
lower	**hoose** (adj. attrib.)	mouth	**af** (m. d4)
		move nearer	**dhowow** (3, **dhowaaday**, **dhowaatay**); **soo dhowow**: come in
lower part	**hoos** (f. d1)		
lunch, have lunch	**qadee** (2B)		
mad, make mad	**waal** (1)		
maize	**gallay** (f.)		
make	**samee** (2B); **ka**: from	movement	**dhaqdhaqaaq** (m. d2)
man	**nin** (m. d4 -m)	name	**magac** (m. d2)
manage without something	**ka maaran** (1, **maarmaa**)	nanny goat	**ri** (f. d1)
		nation	**waddan** (m. d2, **waddamo**)
mango	**cambe** (m. d7)		
many	**badan** (adj.)	near	**dhow** (adj.) to: **u**, **soke** (adj. attrib.)
March	**Maarso** (f.)		
market	**suuq** (m. d2)		

nearness	**ag** (f. d1)	onion	**basal** (f. collec.)
neck	**qoor** (f. d4)	open for oneself	**furo** (3B)
needing	**u baahan** (adj.)	open	**fur** (1)
neighbourhood	**agagaar** (m.)	open	**furan** (adj.)
new	**cusub** (adj.)	oppose	**hortag** (1), **ka soo horjeed** (1)
news	**war** (m. d4)		
newspaper	**jariidad** (f.; **jaraa'id** (m.))	opposition (political)	**mucaarad** (m. d2)
next	**dambe** (adj. attrib.)	oppressor	**daallin** (m., **daallimiin** (f.))
nine	**sagaal** (m.)	or	**amba** (in statements), **mise** (in questions)
ninety	**sagaashan** (m.)		
no	**maya**, **may**		
normal	**caadi** (m. d2)		
north	**waqooyi** (m.)	ordinary	**caadi** (m. d2)
nose	**san** (m. d4)	other	**kale** (adj. attrib.)
nothing	**waxba** (used with a negative verb)	outside	**debed** (f. d1), **dibad** (f.)
		owning	**-leh**
nourishing	**nuxurleh** (adj.)	pact, make a pact	**wacatan** (1, **wacatamaa**)
nourishment	**nuxur** (m. collec.)	pain	**xanuun** (m. d2)
November	**Noofembar** (f.)	papaya	**babbay** (m. d2)
now	**imminka**	paper	**waraaq** (f. d1)
number	**nambar** (m. d2)	parents	**waalid** (m. collec.)
occasion	**mar** (m. d4)		
October	**Oktoobar** (f.)	part	**in** (f.), **qayb** (f. d1)
oil	**saliid** (f. mass)		
OK	**waa hagaag**	party (political)	**xisbi** (m. d2)
on top of	**saaran** (adj.)	pass along	**soo mar** (1)
one (pronoun)	**la**	pass by	**dhaaf** (1)
one (used on its own when 'one' particular thing is referred to)	**mid** (m. /f.)	pass	**mar** (1)
		passport	**baasaboor** (m. d2)
		pasta	**baasto** (f. d6, mass)
one (used only in counting)	**kow** (f.)	pay	**bixi** (2A)
one (used with a noun when one object is counted)	**hal** (m.)	peace-keeping	**nabad ilaalin** (f.)
		peace	**nabad** (f. d1)
		peas	**digir** (f. collec.)
		peel	**diir** (1)
oneself	**is**	pen	**qalin** (m. d3 **-m**)

pencil	**laabbis** (m. d2)	pumpkin	**bocor** (f.)
people	**dad** (m. coll.)	put down	**dhig** (1)
pepper (black)	**filfil** (f. mass)	put in together	**isku dar** (1)
pestle	**kal** (f. d1)	put on top of something	**saar** (1)
petrol	**baansiin** (m. d2 mass)	quarter	**rubuc** (m. d2)
piece	**xabbad** (f.)	question	**su'aal** (f. d1)
place	**meel** (f. d1)	quiet, be quiet	**aammus** (1)
plate	**saxan** (m., **suxuun** (f.))	rain	**roob** (m. d4)
pocket	**jeeb** (m. d4)	ratify	**oggolow** (3B, **oggolaaday**,
porridge-type food made from different grains	**soor** (f. mass)	ravine reach read	**oggolaatay**) **tog** (m. d4) **gaadh** (1) **akhri** (1)
position	**goob** (f. d4)	rear	**dib** (f.)
post office	**boosto** (f. d6)	reason	**dar** (f.), **sabab**
postpone	**baaji** (2A)		(f. d1)
pour	**shub** (1) **ku shub**: pour into	red reddish brown,	**cas** (adj.) **guduudo** (3B)
pray	**tuko** (3A)	become	
prayer mat	**masalle** (m. d7)	refuse	**diid** (1)
prepare for	**u diyaargarow** (1, **diyaarga-roobaa**, **diyaar-garowdaa**)	restaurant return return to	**makhaayad** (f. d1) **celi** (2A); **ku celi**: repeat **ku soo noqo**
prepared	**diyaar** (adj.) **u**: for	revolve	(3B) **wareeg** (1)
president	**madaxweyne** (m. d7)	rice	**bariis** (m. d2 mass)
prevent	**baaji** (2A)	right	**midig** (f.)
previous	**hore** (adj. attrib.)	rise river	**kac** (1) **webi** (m. d2)
prisoner	**maxbuus** (m. **maxaabiis** (f.))	road	**dariiq** (m. d2), **jid** (m. d4),
problem	**dhib** (m. d4)		**waddo** (f. d6)
proceed	**soco** (3B)	room	**qol** (m. d4)
programme	**barnaamij** (m. d2)	rope	**xadhig** (m. d3 **-k**)
provisions	**raashin** (m. d2 collec.)	run away run	**carar** (1) **orod** (1 **ordaa**)

salt	**cusbo** (f. mass)	side	**dhinac** (m. d2); with, **ka**: from the direction of, **gees** (f. d4), **xag** (m. d4)
sari-like women's garment	**guntiino** (f. d6)		
satisfied	**dheregsan** (adj.)		
satisfied, be satisfied	**dhereg** (1)	sing a song	**hees qaad**
		sister	**walaal** (f. d1)
Saturday	**sabti** (f.)	sit down	**fadhiiso** (3B)
school	**dugsi** (m. d2)	site	**goob** (f. d4)
sea	**bad** (f. d1)	six	**lix** (f.)
season	**xilli** (m. d2)	sixty	**lixdan** (m.)
secretary	**xoghaye** (m. d7)	sleep	**hurdo** (f.)
see	**arag** (1 **arkaa**)	sleep	**hurud** (1 **hurdaa**), **seexo** (3B)
seek advice	**talo geli** (2A); **ka**: from		
seeking advice	**talogelyo** (f.)	small	**yar** (adj.)
segment	**xubin** (f. d3)	snake	**mas** (m. d4)
send	**dir** (1)	soft	**jilicsan** (adj.)
separately	**kala**	soldier	**askari** (m. **askar** (f.))
September	**Sebtember** (f.)		
sesame	**sisin** (f.)	Somali	**Soomaali** (m. d5)
set down to stay	**deg** (1)		
settlement	**degmo** (f. d6)	someone	**cid** (f.)
seven	**toddoba** (f.)	song	**hees** (f. d1)
seventy	**toddobaatan** (m.)	sorghum	**hadhuudh** (m.)
		soup	**maraq** (m. mass)
shade	**hadh** (m. d4)	south	**koonfur** (f.)
share	**qayb** (f. d1)	speak	**hadal** (1 **hadlaa**) with: **la**
sheep and goats	**adhi** (m. collec.)		
sheep	**ido** (m. collec.)	spear	**waran** (m. d3 **warmo**)
ship	**markab** (m. **maraakiib** (f.))		
		spend the evening	**cawee** (2B)
shirt	**shaadhi** (m. d2)	spend the night in/at	**ku bari** (1)
shoe	**kab** (f. d1)		
shop	**dukaan** (m. d2 **dukaammo**)	spices	**xawaash** (m. collec.)
shopkeeper	**dukaanle** (m. d7)	spicy	**basbaas leh** (adj.)
short	**gaaban** (adj.)		
shortness	**gaab** (m. d4)	spoon (metal)	**macalgad** (f. d1)
shoulder	**garab** (m. d3)	spoon (wooden Somali spoon)	**fandhaal** (m. d2)
show	**tus** (1)		
sick	**jirran** (adj.)	spoon	**qaaddo** (f. d6)

English	Somali
stand up	toos (1)
sting	qaniin (1)
stir together	isku walaaq (1)
stone	dhagax (m., dhagxan (f.))
stop (intr.)	joogso (3A)
stop (trans.)	jooji (2A)
story	sheeko (f. d6)
straight	toosan (adj.)
straight, be straight	hagaag (1)
straighten (tr.)	hagaaji (2A)
straightness	hagaag (m. d2), toos (m. d4)
student	ardey (m. d5)
succeed in	ku guuleyso (3B)
sugar cane	qasab (m.)
sugar	sonkor (f. mass)
suitcase	shandad (f. d1)
Sunday	axad (f.)
suppose	malee (2B) (used often with u)
surface	dul (f. d4)
surrounded by	ku wareegsan (adj.)
surroundings	agagaar (m.)
sweet	macaan (adj.)
sword	seef (f. d4)
table	miis (m. d4)
take for oneself	qaado (3B qaatay)
take from	ka qaado (3B)
take hold	qabso (3A)
take	qaad (1)
talks	wadahadal (m. d2)
tall	dheer (adj.)
taxi owner	tagsile (m. d7)
taxi	tagsi (m. d2)
tea	shaah (m. d2 mass)
teach	bar (1), dhig (1)
teacher (female)	macallimad (f. d1)
teacher (male)	macallin (m. d2)
teacher	bare (m. d7)
teashop	makhaayad (f. d1)
telephone	telefoon (m. d2)
telephone	telefoon dir (1) u: to someone
television	telefishan (m.)
tell	sheeg (1); u: to
ten	toban (m.)
tend towards	u xagli (2A)
thank you	mahadsanid
thanked	mahadsan (adj.)
there	halkaas
therefore	sidaas darteed
thermos flask	termuus (m. d2)
thin	dhuuban (adj.)
thing	wax (m., waxyaabo (m.))
think	feker (1)
thirst	harraad (m.)
thirsty	harraadsan (adj.)
thirty	soddon (m.)
thousand	kun (m., kumanyaal (m.))
three	saddex (f.)
Thursday	khamiis (f.)
tied	xidhan (1, xidhmaa)
time	mar (m. d4), waqti (m.)
tin	qasacad (f. d1)
today	maanta
together (pre-verbal word)	wada
tomato	yaanyo (f. d6)
tooth-brushing stick	caday (m. d5 / d2)

tooth	**ilig** (m. d3 **-k**)	very	**aad** with **u**
top	**dul** (f. d4)	village	**tuulo** (f. d6)
top	**sare** (adj. attrib.)	visa	**fiise** (m. d7)
tour around	**wareeg** (1)	visit	**booqo** (3B)
town centre	**farasmagaalo** (m.)	vulture	**geeltoosiye** (m. d7)
town	**magaalo** (f. d6)	wait	**sug** (1), **u kaadi** (2A)
townspeople	**reer magaal**		
trade	**iibis** (m. d2)	wake up (tr.)	**toosi** (2)
training	**tababbar** (m.)	wall	**gidaar** (m. d2)
travel	**safar** (1, **safraa**)	want	**doon** (1), **rab** (1)
travellers	**socoto** (f. d6 collec.)	war	**dagaal** (m. d2)
		watching over	**ilaalin** (f.)
tree	**geed** (m. d1)	water	**biyo** (m. d7)
tree trunk	**jirrid** (f. d1)	way	**si** (f., **siyaabo** (m.))
trousers	**surwaal** (m. d2, saraawiil** (m.))	weather	**hawo** (f. d6)
truck	**baabuur** (m. d2)	Wednesday	**arbaca** (f.)
truth	**run** (f.)	week	**toddobaad** (m. d2)
try	**isku day** (2A)		
Tuesday	**salaasa** (f.)	well	**fiican** (adj.), **ladan** (adj.)
turn to	**u leexo** (3B)		
twenty	**labaatan** (m.)	west	**galbeed** (m.)
two	**laba** (f.)	wet	**qoyan** (adj.)
tyre	**shaag** (m. d4)	wheat	**sarreen** (m. mass)
ugly	**foolxun** (adj.)	where?	**mee**
uncle paternal	**adeer** (m. d2)	whiten	**caddee** (2B)
unit (of something)	**xabbad** (f.)	why?	**waayo**
		wide	**ballaadhan** (adj.)
university	**jaamacad** (f. d1)	width	**ballaadh** (m. d2)
until	**ilaa**	wife	**afo** (f. d6), **xaas** (m. d4)
up to (in time and also in space)	**ilaa**		
		wife and children	**xaas** (m. d4)
upper	**kore** (adj. attrib.), **sare** (adj. attrib.)	wind	**dabayl** (f. d1)
		wish	**doon** (1), **rab** (1)
		with	**-leh**, **la** (preverbal preposition)
upright	**toosan** (adj.)		
useful	**waxtar leh** (adj.)	without	**-la'**
usefulness	**waxtar** (m.)	woman	**naag** (f. d1)
vegetables	**khudrad** (f. d1 collec.)	women	**dumar** (m. collec.)

work	**hawl** (f. d1),	write	**qor** (1)
	shaqo (f. d6)	year	**sanad** (m. d1)
work	**shaqee** (2A)	yes	**haa**
	ka: for	yesterday	**shaleyto** (**shaley**)

Somali–English glossary

-ay	feminine vocative suffix		someone either much older or younger than the speaker
-ba	emphasizing suffix, as well as	**adhi** (m. collec.)	caprines (sheep and goats)
-la'	without		
-leh	owning, with	**adiga**	you (independent pronoun)
-na	and (joining two declarative clauses)	**adkaysi** (m. d7)	endurance
		af (m. d4)	mouth, language
-ow	masculine vocative suffix	**afar** (f.)	four
-se	but	**afartan** (m.)	forty
-ye	a word linking an imperative with a declarative	**afo** (f. d6)	wife
		ag (f. d1)	nearness
		agagaar (m.)	surroundings, neighbourhood
		Agoosto (f.)	August
aabbe (m. d7)	father	**agteeda**	by, at the side of
aad	with **u**: very	**akhri** (1 or 2A)	read
aammus (1)	be quiet	**albaab** (m. d2)	door
abaar (f. d1)	drought	**ama/amba**	or; this word is used in statements
Abriil (f.)	April		
adaa mudan	you're welcome		
adag (adj.)	hard, difficult	**arag** (1 **arkaa**)	see
adduunweyne (m. d7)	international community	**arbaca** (f.)	Wednesday
		ardey (m. d5)	student
adeer (m. d2)	paternal uncle, can also be used as a term of address to	**arrin** (f. d1, **arrimo**)	matter
		askari (m., **askar** (f.))	soldier

assalaamu calaykum	an Islamic greeting which is used by Somalis; the words are Arabic, meaning 'Peace be with you'	bari (1)	break the day
		bari (1) ku:	spend the night in/at (infinitive: baryi)
		bari (m.)	east
		bariis (m. d2 mass)	rice
		barnaamij (m. d2)	programme
awr (m. d5)	burden camel	baro (3B)	learn
axad (f.)	Sunday	bartame (m. d7)	centre
ayaa	focus marker	barwaaqo (f. d6)	verdant land, and the accompanying plentiful milk and food etc.
ayeeyo (f. d6)	grandmother		
ba' (1)	be destroyed		
baa	a focus marker		
baabbi'i (2A)	destroy		
baabuur (m. d2)	car, truck, lorry	basal (f. collec.)	onion
baadhis (f. d1)	investigation	basbaas (m. d2)	chilli pepper
baahan (adj.)	u: needing	basbaas leh (adj.)	hot, spicy
baaji (2A)	prevent, postpone	bax (1)	leave
		baxso (3A)	escape
baansiin (m. d2 mass)	petrol	beddel (1)	u: change something for
baaq (1)	announce	beer (1)	cultivate, grow
Baariis	Paris	beer (f. d1)	garden, farm
baasaboor (m. d2)	passport	beeraley (f. collec.)	farmers
baasto (f. d6 mass)	pasta	beri (m. d1)	day, time
		bidix (f.)	left
babbay (m. d2)	papaya	bi'i (2A)	destroy
bad (f. d1)	sea	bil (f. d1)	month
badan (adj.)	many	bilaab (1)	begin
badh (m. d4)	half	bisleyn (f.)	cooking
bal	an interjection, so	bislow (3B, bislaaday, bislaatay, bislaanayaa)	be cooked
ballaadh (m. d2)	width, broadness		
ballaadhan (adj.)	broad, wide		
bangi (m. d2)	bank	bismillaah	in the name of God (Arabic), said before eating or drinking
bani aadnimo (f.)	humanitarianism, humanity		
bar (1)	teach		
bare (m. d7)	teacher		

bixi (2A)	cause to leave, extract; pay	carar (1)	run away
biyo (m. d7)	water	carruur (f. coll.)	children
bocor (f.)	pumpkin	cas (adj.)	red
booqo (3B)	visit	cashar (m. d2)	lesson
boosto (f. d6)	post office	cashee (2B)	have dinner (evening meal)
boqol (m. boqolaal)	hundred	casho (f. d6)	day
budo (f. d6)	flour	cawee (2B)	spend the evening
buluug (m. d2)	blue	celi (2A)	return; ku celi: repeat
buste (m. d7)	blanket		
buug (m. d4)	book	cid (f.)	someone
buur (m. d1)	mountain	cidna	no-one (when used with a negative verb, cidina no-one, marked as subject)
buuran (adj.)	fat		
buuxso (3A)	fill for oneself		
caadi (m. d2)	ordinary, normal		
caan (m. d4)	fame		
caano (m. mass)	milk		
caawa (adverb)	this evening	ciidammo (f. pl.)	forces
cab (1)	drink	culus (adj.)	heavy
caday (m. d5/d2)	tooth-brushing stick	cun (1)	eat
		cunto (f. d6 mass)	food
caddee (2B)	whiten, make clear, explain	curad (m. d2 or f. d1)	first-born child
cadho (f. d6)	anger	cusbo (f. mass)	salt
cadhosan (adj.)	angry	cusub (adj.)	new
cadhow (3B, cahdaaday, cadhaatay)	get angry (u: with)	da' (1)	fall (of rain), rain
		daadguree (2B)	ka soo: evacuate
cadow (m. d2)	enemy	daaji (2A)	graze (tr.)
cagaaran (adj.)	green	daalin (m., daalimiin (f.))	oppressor
calaykum assalaam	reply to assalaamu calaykum, again Arabic, meaning 'With you peace'		
		daaq (1)	graze (intr.)
		daar (f. d1)	house (of stone)
		dab (m. d4)	fire
		dabadeedna	and then
caleen (f. d1 collec.)	leaves	dabayl (f. d1)	wind
		dabo (f.)	back part, behind
cambe (m. d7)	mango		
canab (m. d2 collec.)	grapes	dabool (1)	cover
		dad (m. collec.)	people
Carab (m. d5)	an Arab	dagaal (m. d2)	fighting, war

dagaal sokeeye	civil war
dal (m. d4)	country
dambe (adj. attrib.)	next, last, behind
dambee (2B)	come after
dameer (f. d1)	female donkey
dameer (m. d2/d5)	male donkey
danjire (m. d7)	ambassador
daqiiqad (f. d1)	minute
dar (1) **isku**	put in together
dar (1) **ku**	add to
dar (f.)	reason
dariiq (m. d2)	road
dawlad (f. d1)	government
day (2A) **isku**	try
day (2A)	look at, examine
Dayr (f.)	September to November (a lesser wet season)
dayuurad (f. d1)	aeroplane
debed (f. d1)	outside, exterior
deg (1)	live (in a place), set down to stay; **soo deg**: land (of an aeroplane)
degdeg (1)	hurry
deggan (adj.)	living in (a place)
degmo (f. d6)	settlement, community
dhaaf (1)	pass by
dhac (1)	happen; fall
dhagax (m. **dhagxan** (f.))	stone
dhakhtar (m. d2)	male doctor
dhakhtarad (f. d1)	female doctor
dhammee (2B)	finish
dhan (1, **dhamaa**)	drink (used only with milk)
dhaqdhaqaaq (m. d2)	movement
dhar (m. d4)	clothes, fabric
dhawaaq ku	announce
dhaxan (f.)	coldness
dheer (adj.)	long, tall
dheeraad (m. d2)	extra
dhegayare (m. d7)	clove
dhegeyso (3B)	listen
dhereg (1)	be satisfied, full (of eating and drinking)
dheregsan (adj.)	satisfied, full
dhexe (adj. attrib.)	middle, between
dhexee (2B)	be in between
dhib (m. d4)	problem, difficulty
dhig (1)	put down; teach
dhimo (3B, **dhintaa**)	die
dhinac (m. d2)	side; with **ka**: from the direction of
dhis (1)	build
dhismo (f. or m. d6)	building
dhoofi (2A)	export
dhow (adj.)	near
dhow u	near to
dhowow (3, **dhowaaday, dhowaatay**)	move nearer; **soo dhowow**: come in
dhowr	few
dhufo (3B) **ku**	hit with
dhul (m. d4)	earth, land
dhuuban (adj.)	thin
dhuxul (f.)	charcoal
dib (f.)	rear; **ka dib**: after
dibad (f.)	outside, abroad

digir (f. collec.)	beans, peas	fadhiiso	sit down
diid (1)	refuse		
diir (1)	peel	fandhaal (m. d2)	spoon (wooden Somali spoon)
diiran (adj.)	heated		
diiri (2A)	heat (tr.)	faraggeli (2A)	intervene
dil (1)	kill, hit	farasmagaalo (m.)	city centre, town centre
dir (1)	send		
Disembar (f.)	December	farax (1)	be happy
diyaar (adj.)	prepared, u: for	faraxsan (adj.)	happy
diyaargarow (1, diyaargaroobaa, diyaargarowdaa)	prepare, u: for	Febraayo (f.)	February
		feker (1)	think
		fidi (2A)	expand
doollar (m. d2)	dollar	fiican (adj.)	well
doon (1)	want, wish (used in the general present with the infinitive to form the future)	fiise (m. d7)	visa
		filfil (f. mass)	black pepper
		fog (adj.)	far; ka: from
		foolxun (adj.)	ugly
		fudud (adj.)	light, easy
doondoon (1)	look for	fur (1)	open, divorce
dufan (m. d2)	grease	furan (adj.)	open
dugsi (m. d2)	school	fure (m. d7)	key
dukaan (m. d2 dukaammo)	shop	furo (3B)	open for oneself
		gaab (m. d4)	shortness
dukaanle (m. d7)	shopkeeper	gaaban (adj.)	short
dul (f. d4)	top, surface	gaadh (1)	arrive, reach
dumar (m. collec.)	women	gaadhi (m. d2)	car
duul (1)	fly	gaadhi raac (1)	go by car
ee	and (used to join declaratives with imperatives, also used to join a negative declarative with a positive declarative)	gaajeysan (adj.)	hungry
		gaajo (f.)	hunger
		gabadh (f. d3)	girl, may also be used for young woman
		gacan (f. d3 -m)	hand
		gacanta ugu jir (1)	be in the hands of
		gado (3B)	buy
Eebbe (m.)	God	gal (1)	enter
eeg (1)	look	galab (f. d3)	afternoon
eegeeg (1) ka	look around	galbeed (m.)	west
engegan (adj.)	dry	gallay (f.)	maize
ey (m. d5)	dog	garaac (1)	knock, dial (on a number-pad
fadhiiso (3B)	sit down; soo		

garab (m. d3) shoulder
garee (2B) this is a verb that is used with words from other languages (such as **jeeg**, 'to check') to form a verb which is not otherwise found in Somali. Another example is **telefoongaree**, 'to make a telephone call'
garoon (m. d2) ground, field
garoon dayuuradaha airport
gee (2B) take someone/something (in the sense of, for example, in a taxi)
geed (m. d1) tree
geel (m. collec.) camels (the form **geela** means 'the camels'; it is an irregular definite article)
geeltoosiye (m. d7) a type of vulture
gees (f. d4) side
gees (m. d1) horn
gidaar (m. d2) wall
go' (1) cut (intr.)
go'aan (m. d2, **go'aammo**) decision

gobol (m. d2) area
god (m. d4) hole (especially in the ground)
gole (m. d7) assembly, committee
goob (f. d4) site, position
goy (2A) cut (tr.)
Gu' (f.) April to June (main wet season)
gub (1) burn (tr.)
guban (adj.) burnt
gubo (3B) burn (intr.)
gudo (m. d6) inside, interior
gudub (1, **gudbaa**) cross
guduudo (3B) become reddish brown
guntiino (f. d6) woman's dress-like garment made of a cloth wrapped around the body; similar to a sari
guri (m. d1) house
guuleyso (3B) **ku** succeed in
guurso (3A) get married
haa yes
haad (m. d5) large bird (esp. bird of prey)
habardugaag (m. collec.) wild animals
habaryar (f. d1) maternal aunt
habeen (m. d2) evening
hadal (1 **hadlaa**) speak; **la**: with
haddii Eebbe yidhaahdo God willing (lit.: if God says it)
hadh (m. d4) shade
hadhuudh (m.) sorghum
hagaag (1) be straight; **waa hagaag**: right, OK

hagaag (m. d2)	straightness	hudheel (m. d2)	hotel
hagaaji (2A)	straighten (tr.), mend	hurdo (f.)	sleep
		hurud (1 hurdaa)	sleep
hal (f. d1)	female camel	ido (m. collec.)	sheep
hal (m.)	one (used with a noun when one object is counted)	iibis (m. d2)	trade
		iibso (3B)	buy (used often with soo); sii iibso: sell
halkaas	there	il (f., indho (m.))	eye
harraad (m.)	thirst	ilaa	until, up to (in time and also in space)
harraadsan (adj.)	thirsty		
hawl (f. d1)	work, activity		
hawo (f. d6)	air, weather	ilaalin (f.)	watching over
hay (2A)	have	ilig (m. d3 -k)	tooth
hayso (3B)	have	Illaah mahaddi	Thanks be to God (Illaah: God; Illaah mahadi: Thanks be to God)
hayye	an interjection; this word is used a lot in Somali		
heedheh	this is an interjection which is often used to call somebody		
		imminka	now
		in (f.)	part, amount
		inan (m. d2 -m)	boy
		is	oneself
hees (f. d1)	song	isbahaysi (m. d2)	alliance
hel (1)	find	isbahayso (3B)	to make an alliance
hel (1) ka	like, enjoy; find from		
		iska horimaad (m. d2)	confrontation
heyl (m. d4)	cardamom		
hilib (m. d3)	meat	isla markaasi (adverb)	at the same time
hoggaamiye (m. d7)	leader		
		isniin (f.)	Monday
hoos (f. d1)	bottom, lower part	iyo	and (used only between noun phrases)
hoose (adj. attrib.)	lower		
		jaamacad (f. d1)	university
hooyo (f. d6)	mother	jab (1)	break (intr.)
hor (f. d4)	front part	jaban (adj.)	broken, cheap
hore (adj. attrib.)	first, previous	jabi (2A)	break (tr.)
horjeed (1) ka soo	oppose, be in conflict with oppose	Janaayo (f.)	January
		jariidad (f., jaraa'id (m.))	newspaper
hortag (1)			

jarjar (1)	chop up		is...
jawaab (1)	answer	kar (1)	be able to
jeclayso (3B)	like	kar (1)	boil (intr.)
jeeb (m. d4)	pocket	kari (1)	boil (tr.), cook
jeeg garee (2B)	check	karis ah, isku	cooked together (i.e. lots of things)
jid (m. d4)	road		
jidh (m. d1/d4)	body		
Jiilaal (m.)	December to March (hot, dry season)	kasta (adj. attrib.)	each, every
		keen (1)	bring
		kexee (2B)	drive, lead (animals)
jilib (m. d3)	knee		
jilicsan (adj.)	soft	khaas ahaan	especially
jimce (m.)	Friday	khamiis (f.)	Thursday
jir (1)	be in a place (animate and inanimate subjects; used with the infinitive in the general past to form the past habitual)	khudrad (f. d1 coll.)	vegetables
		kibis (f. d3)	bread
		kici (2A)	cause to rise, start up (tr.)
		kiilo (f. d6)	kilogram
		kildhi (m. d2)	kettle
		konton (m.)	fifty
		koob (m. d4)	cup
jirran (adj.)	sick, ill	kooban (adj.) ka	comprised of
jirrid (f. d1)	tree trunk	koofiyad (f. d1)	hat
joogso (3A)	stop (intr.)	koonfur (f.)	south
jooji (2A)	stop (trans.)	koox (f. d1)	group
Juun (f.)	June	kordhi (2A)	increase (tr.)
ka dib	afterwards, after	kore (adj. attrib.)	upper
ka mid ah	one of	korodh (1)	increase (intr.)
kaadi (2A) u	wait, delay	kow (f.)	one (used only in counting)
kab (f. d1)	shoe		
kabadh (m. d2)	cupboard	kubbad (f. d1)	ball
kac (1)	rise	kulan (1, kulmaa)	meet
kal (f. d1)	pestle	kulayl (m.)	heat, hot
kala	separately	kulul (adj.)	hot
kale (adj. attrib.)	other	kun (m., kumanyaal (m.))	thousand
kalluun (m. d2, also collec., kalluumo)	fish		
		kursi (m. d2/ karaasi (f.)	chair
kan	this; waa kan: here it is; waa kan...: here	la	one (pronoun)
		laaban (adj.)	folded
		laabbis (m. d2)	pencil

laakiin	but	**malaayiin** (f.))	
laba (f.)	two	**maqal** (1 **maqlaa**)	hear
labaatan (m.)	twenty	**mar** (1)	pass; **soo mar**: pass along
lacag (f. mass)	money		
ladan (adj.)	well, healthy	**mar** (f. d1)	women's clothing (in plural, it may mean material)
lamaddegaan (m.)	desert		
laybreeri (m. d2)	library		
leexo (3B) **u**	turn to	**mar** (m. d4)	time, occasion
lis (1)	milk (tr.)	**maraq** (m. mass)	soup
lix (f.)	six	**marka hore**	firstly
lixdan (m.)	sixty	**markaas**	at that time
lo' (f. collec.)	cattle	**markab** (m., **maraakiib** (f.))	ship
lug (f. d1)	leg, foot		
Luulyo (f.)	July	**martiqaad** (1)	entertain (guests)
Maajo (f.)	May	**mas** (m. d4)	snake
maalin (f. d3 **-m**)	day	**masalle** (m. d7)	prayer mat
maanta	today	**masiibo** (f. d6)	calamity
maaran (1, **maarmaa**) **ka**	manage without something	**masaajid** (m. d2)	mosque
		maxbuus (m., **maxaabiis** (f.))	prisoner
Maarso (f.)	March		
macaan (adj.)	sweet	**may**	no
macalgad (f. d1)	metal spoon	**maya**	no
macallimad (f. d1)	female teacher	**meeday**	where? (f.)
		meel (f. d1)	place
macallin (m. d2)	male teacher	**mid** (m. /f.)	one (used on its own when 'one' particular thing is referred to
madax (m. d2/d5)	head		
madaxbannaan (adj.)	independent		
madaxweyne (m. d7)	president		
		midab (m. d2)	colour
madbakh (m. d2)	kitchen	**midho** (m. collec.)	fruit
madow (adj.)	black	**midig** (f.)	right
magaalo (f. d6)	town	**miis** (m. d4)	table
magac (m. d2)	name	**mindi** (f. d1)	knife
mahadsan (adj.)	thanked	**mise**	or; this word for 'or' is only used in questions
mahadsanid	thank you		
makhaayad (f. d1)	teashop, restaurant		
malee (2B)	suppose (used often with **u**)	**miyaa**	question word, 'Is it . . .?'
malyuun (m.,	million	**mooye** (m. d7)	mortar

moxoggo (f. d6)	cassava
mucaarad (m. d2)	opposition (political)
mudac (m. d2)	fork
musqul (f. d1)	bathroom
muus (m. d4)	banana
naag (f. d1)	woman
nabad (f. d1)	peace; **nabad gelyo** goodbye
nabad ilaalin (f.)	peace-keeping
nacas (m. d2)	fool
nadiifi (2A)	clean
nambar (m. d2)	number
nin (m. d4 -m)	man
Noofembar (f.)	November
nool (adj.)	living
noqo (3B) ku soo	return to
nuxur (m. collec.)	nourishment
nuxurleh (adj.)	nourishing (lit.: possessing nourishment)
oday (m. d7)	old man, elder
oggolow (3B, oggolaaday, oggolaatay)	allow, approve, ratify
Oktoobar (f.)	October
oo	and (this word is used to join two clauses of equal status)
orod (1 ordaa)	run
qaad (1)	take; **hees qaad**: sing a song
qaaddo (f. d6)	spoon
qaado (3B qaatay)	take for oneself
qaado (3B)	get, take; **ka**: from
qaali (m.)	expensive thing
qabo (3B)	catch, hold
qabso (3A)	take hold
qadee (2B)	have lunch
qadhaadh (adj.)	bitter
qalalaase (m. d7)	disturbance
qalin (m. d3 -m)	pen
qalloocan (adj.)	curved, bent
qaniin (1)	bite, sting
qasab (m.)	sugar cane
qasacad (f. d1)	tin, can
qayb (f. d1)	part, share
qaybsan (1, qaybsamaa)	divided; **u**: into
qol (m. d4)	room
qoor (f. d4)	neck
qor (1)	write
qorfe (m. d7)	cinnamon
qosol (1 qoslaa)	laugh
qoyan (adj.)	wet
qoys (m. d4)	family
qumbe (m. d7)	coconut
quraac (f. d2)	breakfast
quraaco (3B)	have breakfast
qurux (f.)	beauty
quruxsan (adj.)	beautiful
raac (1)	accompany, go with
raalli ahow	excuse me (lit.: be tolerant, agreeable)
raashin (m. d2 collec.)	provisions
rab (1)	want, desire (used as an auxiliary verb with the infinitive to express a desire to do something)
rag (m. collec.)	men
rah (m. d4)	frog
rajee (2B)	hope
rasaas joojin (f.)	ceasefire
reer (m. d1)	family, group of

	people
reer magaal	townspeople
ri (f. d1)	nanny goat
riyo (plural or **ri**)	goats in general
roob (m. d4)	rain
rubuc (m. d2)	quarter
run (f.)	truth
runtii	lit.: the truth; of course
saabsan (adj.) **ku**	concerning
saacad (f. d1)	hour, clock
saan (f. d1, **saamo**)	hide
saar (1)	put on top of something
saaran (adj.)	on top of
saaxiib (m. d2)	male friend
saaxiibad (f. d1)	female friend
sabab (f. d1)	reason
sabti (f.)	Saturday
sac (m. d2)	cow
saddex (f.)	three
safar (1, **safraa**)	travel
safar (m. d2)	journey
safee (2B)	clean
sagaal (m.)	nine
sagaashan (m.)	ninety
salaan (1 **salaamaa**)	greet
salaasa (f.)	Tuesday
saliid (f. mass)	oil
samee (2B)	do, make **ka**: from
san (m. d4)	nose
sanad (m. d1)	year
sanuunad (f. d1)	gravy
sare (adj. attrib.)	upper, top
sarifo (3B)	exchange money
sarreen (m. mass)	wheat
saxan (m., **suxuun** (f.))	plate
Sebtember (f.)	September
seef (f. d4)	sword
seexo (3B)	sleep
seexseexo (3B)	sleep (of a number of people)
shaadh (m. d4)	shirt
shaag (m. d4)	tyre
shaah (m. d2 mass)	tea
shaleyto (**shaley**)	yesterday
shan (f.)	five
shandad (f. d1)	suitcase
shaneemo (f. d6)	film
shaqee (2A)	work **ka**: for
shaqo (f. d6)	work
sharci (m. d2)	law
sheeg (1)	tell; **u**: to
sheeko (f. d6)	story
shiilan (adj.)	fried
shimbir (f. d1)	bird (not a bird of prey)
shir (m. d4)	meeting
shishe (adj. attrib.)	far
shub (1)	pour; **ku shub**: pour into
si (f., **siyaabo** (m.))	way
sidaas darteed	because of that, therefore
siddeed (f.)	eight
siddeetan (m.)	eighty
sidee	how (lit.: which way)
sii (2A)	give
sii	directional word, away from the speaker
sii wad (1)	continue
siraad (m. d2)	lamp
sisin (f.)	sesame

soco (3B)	proceed, continue; **u**: on travellers	**telefishan** (m.)	television
socoto (f. d6 collec.)		**termuus** (m. d2)	thermos flask
		tilmaan (1, **tilmaamaa**)	describe; **ku**: as
soddon (m.)	thirty		
soke (adj. attrib.)	near	**timir** (f. collec.)	dates
sonkor (f. mass)	sugar	**tiri** (2A)	count
soo deg (1)	land	**tirsan** (adj.)	counted; **ka tirsan**: belonging to
soo	directional word, towards the speaker		
		toban (m.)	ten
		toddoba (f.)	seven
soo gado (3B)	buy	**toddobaad** (m. d2)	week
soo nabadgelyee (2B)	say goodbye to		
		toddobaatan (m.)	seventy
Soomaali (m. d5)	a Somali	**tog** (m. d4)	dry valley, ravine
soor (f. collec.)	porridge-type food made from different grains		
		toon (f.)	garlic
		toos (1)	get up, stand up (intr.)
su'aal (f. d1)	question	**toos** (m. d4)	directness, straightness
subag (m. d2 mass)	butter (especially clarified butter)		
		toosan (adj.)	straight, upright
		toosi (2)	wake up (tr.)
subax (f. d2)	morning	**tuko** (3A)	pray
sug (1)	wait	**tuman** (adj.)	ground
surwaal (m. d2, **saraawiil** (m.))	trousers	**tun** (1)	grind
		tus (1)	show
suugaan (f.)	literature	**tuulo** (f. d6)	village
suuq (m. d2)	market	**ugax** (m. d5, **ugxan** (f.))	egg (of birds other than chickens)
taagan (adj.) **ka**	facing		
tababbar (m.)	training		
tag (1)	go	**ukun** (f. collec.)	eggs (edible, mostly of chickens)
tagsi (m. d2)	taxi		
tagsile (m. d7)	taxi owner		
talo (f. d6)	advice, decision	**waa** (1)	fail, miss
talo geli (2A)	seek advice; **ka**: from	**waal** (1)	make mad
		waalid (m. collec.)	parents
talogelyo (f.)	seeking advice		
tasho (3A)	consider	**waalo** (3B)	go mad (intr.)
telefoon (m. d2)	telephone	**waayo**	because; why?
telefoon dir (1)	telephone; **u**: someone	**wacatan** (1, **wacatamaa**)	make a pact

wad (1)	continue, drive
wada	together (preverbal word)
wadahadal (m. d2)	talks
waddan (m. d2, waddamo)	country, nation
waddo (f. d6)	road
wado (3B watay)	drive (car)
walaal (f. d1)	sister and (m. d1) brother
walaaq (1)	isku: stir together
walba (adj. attrib.)	each, every
wallaah	an exclamation used when someone is rather surprised at something (from wa and Allaah, Arabic meaning 'and God')
wanaagsan (adj.)	good
waqooyi (m.)	north
waqti (m.)	time
war (m. d4)	news
waraabe (m. d7)	hyena
waraaq (f. d1)	paper
waran (m. d3 warmo)	spear
wareeg (1)	revolve, go around, tour around
wareegsan (adj.) ku	surrounded by
wareysi (m.)	interview
warqad (f. d1)	letter
warran (1 warramaa)	give news; ka: about
waryaa	hey!, hi!
wasiir (m. d2)	minister
wasiirka arrimaha dibadda	foreign minister
wax (m., waxyaabo (m.))	thing
waxba	with a negative verb, 'nothing'
waxtar (m.)	usefulness
waxtar leh (adj.)	useful
webi (m. d2)	river
weerar (m. d2)	attack
weerar qaad (1)	make an attack
weydii (2A)	ask someone something
weyn (adj.)	big
xaas (m. d4)	wife, wife and children
xabaal (f. d1)	grave
xabbad (f.)	unit (of something), piece
xadhig (m. d3 -k)	rope
xag (m. d4)	direction, side
Xagaa (m.)	July to August (mainly a dry season)
xagli (2A)	tend; u: towards, favour
xanuun (m. d2)	pain
xaqiiji (2A)	confirm
xarun (f. d1 xarumo)	capital
xataa	even
xawaash (m. collec.)	spices
xayir (1)	block
xeeb (f. d1)	coast
xidh (1)	close
xidhan (1, xidhmaa)	become closed, tied
xidhan (adj.)	closed, dressed
xiiso (f. d6)	interest, fascination

xiiso leh (adj.)	interesting, fascinating	xukumad (f. d1)	government
xilli (m. d2)	season	xulufo (f.)	allies
xisbi (m. d2)	party (political)	xun (adj.)	bad
xoghaye (m. d7)	secretary	yaab (1)	be astonished
xoog (m. d4)	force, army	yaanyo (f. d6)	tomato
xoolaley (f. collec.)	livestock keepers	yar (adj.)	small
xubin (f. d3)	member, segment	yeedh (1)u:	call someone
		yeelo (3B)	have, hold

Index

The numbers refer to lesson numbers.

absolutive case, 3
address form, 1
adjectives, 4, 13
adjectives used with **yahay**, 13
adverbial relative clauses, 14
after, 14
although, 14
and, 2
as soon as, 14
attributive adjectives, 13
auxiliary verbs, 8
-ay, 1
ayaa, 6

baa, 6

cardinal numbers, 4
case, 3
collective nouns, 13
comparative, 13
complement clauses, 11
conditional, 14
conjugation 1, 1
conjugation 2, 3
conjugation 2A, 3
conjugation 2B, 4
conjugation 3, 5
conjugation 3A, 5
conjugation 3B, 6
consonant doubling, Introduction

date, 6
days of the week, 3
declension 1, 2
declension 2, 2
declension 3, 2
declension 4, 3
declension 5, 3
declension 6, 4
declension 7, 4
declensions, 2
definite article, 3
deictics, 5
demonstrative suffixes, 8

focus markers, 6, 10
focusing in *yes–no* questions, 14
focusing the subject, 6, 10
future tense, 7

gemination, Introduction
gender, 2
general past, 1
general past negative, 7
general present, 5
general present negative, 8
genitive case, 4
greetings, 1, 2

habitual past tense, 7
have to, 11
how? 12

how many?, 13
how much?, 13

if, 14
imperative, 1
impersonal pronoun, 8
in clauses, 11
in order to, 11
independent pronouns, 12
infinitive, 3, 7
irregular plurals, 5
iyo, 2

jir, 9
joog, 9

kar (1), 8

la (impersonal pronoun), 8

ma (negative), 7
ma ... baa?, 1
ma? (question), 1
mass nouns, 13
max-?, 6
maybe, 14
miyaa?, 2
mood, 1
mood classifiers, 1
must, 11

-na, 2
names, 7
negative imperative, 7
negative questions, 14
negative subordinate clauses, 14
nouns, 2
number one, 4
numbers above ten, 6

object pronouns, 5
object pronouns (third person), 1

optative, 14
order form, 1
ordinal numbers, 5
-ow, 1

past progressive, 8
past progressive negative, 9
perhaps, 14
plural of adjectives, 4
positive declarative mood classifier, 1
positive interrogative classifier, 1
possessive suffixes, 9
potential, 14
prefixing verbs, 9
premodifier form, 3
preposition clusters, 11
prepositional phrases, 9
prepositions, 5
present progressive, 2
present progressive negative, 9
preverbal prepositions, 5
pronoun clusters, 11
pronunciation, Introduction

rab (1), 8
reduced verb paradigm, 6
relative clauses, 12

see-saw stress-tone, Introduction
sheeg, 11
since, 14
sound changes, Introduction, 1, 3
spelling, Introduction
stress-tone, Introduction
subject case, 3, 4
subject pronouns, 1
subordinate clauses, 11
subordinate verb forms, 11
superlative, 13

tense, 1

time, 6
to be, 13

verbal object pronouns, 5
verbal subject pronouns, 1
very, 13
vocative, 1
vowels, Introduction

waa (1), 8
waa (mood classifier) 1
waxa focus construction, 10
wh- questions, 12
what?, 6

when, 14
when?, 12
where?, 13
which?, 13
while, 12, 14
who?, 12
why?, 12
word order, 3, 10

yahay, 13
yidhi, 10
yiil, 9
yimi, 10
yiqiin, 11